The Immigration Crisis in Europe and the U.S.-Mexico Border in the New Era of Heightened Nativism

The Immigration Crisis in Europe and the U.S.-Mexico Border in the New Era of Heightened Nativism

Victoria Carty

LEXINGTON BOOKS

Lanham • Boulder • New York • London

Published by Lexington Books
An imprint of The Rowman & Littlefield Publishing Group, Inc.
4501 Forbes Boulevard, Suite 200, Lanham, Maryland 20706
www.rowman.com

6 Tinworth Street, London SE11 5AL, United Kingdom

British Library Cataloguing in Publication Information Available

Library of Congress Control Number: 2020943838
ISBN 978-1-4985-8389-3 (cloth)
ISBN 978-1-4985-8391-6 (pbk)
ISBN 978-1-4985-8390-9 (electronic)

Contents

Acknowledgments

I would like to thank the wonderful staff at Lexington for their patience and diligence working under the conditions of a global pandemic to assist me in completing this manuscript, and for the grace of God who has helped us all to perceive in these most difficult times.

Introduction

People across the globe are migrating at higher levels than at any other time. Over the past decade there has been a sharp increase of people fleeing their countries due to war, economic destabilization, gang violence, drought, and other natural disasters. In 2018, the United Nations High Commission Report (UNHCR) declared that the world has witnessed "the highest levels of displacement on record since World War II. Nearly 1 person is forcibly displaced every 2 seconds because of conflict or persecution; over half of whom are under the age of 18" (United Nations Human Rights Committee). Fueling most of the current immigration crisis on the U.S.–Mexico border and travel routes between Africa and Europe is desperate situations across the Middle East, Northern Africa, Mexico, and Central America (United Nations Human Rights Committee; Menjuar 2014).

However, neither the United States nor Europe is addressing the fundamental crisis. Rather, and especially during the 2014–2017 exodus of migrants across the Mediterranean/Africa and Central America/Mexico/U.S. regions, government officials have put forth a narrative that blames immigrants for fleeing and criticizes the governments of states from which they are fleeing for failing to impede the exodus. This has influenced public opinion and fostered support for strict measures that have been put into place and/or reinforced to try to deter immigrants from seeking refuge or asylum status (Blinder and Richards 2020).

After the collapse of the Berlin Wall in 1989, followed by the disintegration of the Soviet Union and the downfall of many dictators throughout Latin America, many citizens mobilized to bring freedom, democracy, and respect for civil liberties to their perspective regions of the world (Tilly 2007; Tilly 2006). They established a transatlantic system of liberal democracy and created international institutions to solidify capitalism and democracy as the cornerstone of the Western World. These events inspired American political scientist, Francis Fukyamana (1992), to famously claim this to be "the end of history." Other scholars agreed that ideological debates had ended as Western liberal democracy would certainly be embraced universally as the sole form of government (Berman 2019; Haas 2018; Held 1995).

Today, however, the postwar order is in jeopardy (Albright 2018; Zeihan 2016; Grossman and Hopkins 2016). There is a much bleaker picture across much of Europe and Latin America, and even in the United States as authoritarian leaders are exploiting the growing dissatisfaction with the liberalism paradigm, including democracy and market economies based on globalism (Berberoglu 2019; Bremmer 2018; Postelnicescu 2016; Bache 2015). On both sides of the Atlantic, economic, social, cultural, and demographic anxiety, mixed with fears regarding immigration, has been fueling nativist and protectionist ideologies and a surge in autocracy, authoritarianism, white supremacy, xenophobia, and intolerance. The popularity of extreme right-wing Euroskeptic parties and neofascism, which are opposed to liberal democracy, is becoming increasingly pronounced across the EU (Berman 2019; Brack and Costa 2019).

Within this context there is a growing concern about whether democracy can survive amid a host of new challenges that include threats of terrorism, an obsession with national security, a growing trend toward tribalism, divisiveness, anti-Semitism, Islamophobia, and a global immigration crisis (Berman 2019; Fisher et al. 2018). At the national level, the resurgence of white identity and right-wing ethno-nationalism, or often referred to as identitarianism (albeit in part due to global economic insecurity), is also challenging traditions and norms in the West by manifesting itself in the reemergence of fascism (Albright 2018). This is an ideology in which people obsess about a mythic past rooted in ethno-nationalism and a homogenous country, propaganda, "fake news," anti-intellectualism, and victimhood, therefore a nation in need of a "savior" (Gest et al. 2018).

Thus, identity politics has increasingly become part of the rebellion against liberal democracy and multiculturalism, and many argue that it is indeed replacing economic interests as a major divide among citizens. On a more global scale, after decades of playing a leading role in the international scene the United States is no longer the sole superpower in economic and political affairs (Carpenter 2019; Diamond 2019). As postwar alliances and institutions have become under attack, some analysts refer to this new global order as "Anything goes" (Friedman 2019).

Diamond (2019: 44) summarizes: "It's not just that liberal democracy is retreating under pressure from demagogic politicians exploiting the stresses of globalization, rising inequality, economic insecurity, job displacement, immigration, and so on. It's that authoritarian forces everywhere perceive that there is no longer any price to pay for ruling as nastily as they want . . . every regime is getting worse. Liberal democracies are becoming more intolerant. Illiberal democracies are electing authoritarian personalities . . . who are purging judges and locking up journalists who dare to criticize them."

Richard Haass, president of the council on foreign relations, sees the fading role of the United States in maintaining world order as negligent on behalf of the current leadership. He laments that alliances and trusted relationships between leaders in the United States and Europe, that were once cemented, have been gravely disrupted and have left a vacuum for authoritarian leaders to take advantage of and to create a new world order that is opposed to globalism and democracy (Appelbaum 2017). Underlying much of this are the underlying trends described above and the intersectionality with the immigration crisis on the U.S.–Mexico border and across the European Union (EU). Fear of foreigners and the rise of white supremacy have resurfaced in the United States and in several EU countries amid economic insecurity and an increase in racial animus.

OUTLINE OF CHAPTERS

In the opening chapter, I provide an overview of the various macro- and micro-levels of analysis to understand current immigration patterns. I also utilize a historical perspective to examine the laws and ethics of immigration and attempts by governments in the EU and in the United States to regulate immigration. The two conflicting perspectives are communitarianism and communalism. These theories and perspectives will be addressed throughout the text and serve as a framework to better understand the rise of authoritarian politics and nationalist, anti-immigrant movements throughout the world. The chapter also includes a discussion of how asylum cases are becoming increasingly difficult to win, or even present to authorities. I compare and contrast some of the changing immigration policies in both regions.

The second part of the chapter addresses the emerging/resurfacing elements of ethno-nationalism and the popularity of autocrats in both the EU and the United States. To make sense of the appeal of autocrats and neofascism, and particularly among segments of the population that is comprised of white working-class males, I apply certain social movement and critical race theories. I argue that the dynamics above are related to the broader shift toward illiberalism.

For example, the lack of integrated institutions to remedy economic crisis and regulate immigration has caused many European citizens, and the rising far-right and ultraconservative populist leaders, to question the legitimacy of the system and democracy as well. Consequently, they embrace a Euroskeptic perspective and question the sustainability of the EU. In the United States this is often referred to as "Trumpism"—a rejection of democratic liberalism, globalism, multiculturalism, and a support for nativist and "America First" ideologies. Complementing these dynamics is the growing popularity of the "Great Replacement" movement: the belief that as more countries become majority minority, whites feel they are losing their power and status.

In chapter 2, I focus on the history of Latinx immigration and examine how, historically, trends, laws, and economic needs of the United States have impacted immigration patterns. It includes a discussion of the externalization policies that in certain points of time have been used to keep "undesirable" migrants from reaching the United States to apply for asylum, and how politics surrounding the Cold War and other international events have impacted how refugees and asylum seekers are treated.

I apply theories of immigration and scholarly perspectives of human rights regarding asylum cases to serve as a framework through which to analyze contemporary dilemmas regarding immigration policy. A theoretical framework that acknowledges the structural forces that promote immigration from developing countries and considering both the push and pull factors is important. While acknowledging economic factors and labor needs, I also recognize the motivations, goals, and aspirations of the individuals and families (agency) who are responding to outside economic, political, and social forces. Doing so enables us to grasp the push and pull factors at the individual level (agency) and local/national/international level (structures and systems) and use these in a complementary way to analyze contemporary dilemmas regarding immigration policy.

In the following chapter, I analyze the growing trend toward anti-Semitism, Islamophobia, and white anxiety across Europe as much of the region has taken a surprising turn toward far-right nationalism. In some EU countries, extremist populist parties are now in power, in others they are a part of a coalition, and in a few cases they have indeed gained significant seats in Parliament. This alarming turn is one result of the fear of an "Islamist invasion" that will result in what many fear as the Great Replacement movement (whites and Christians being outnumbered by nonwhites and Muslims and Jews). Globalism is also promoted as suspect as leaders blame the increasing rates of economic inequality on immigrants and take advantage of the anxiety of white working-class men who are economically struggling and feel culturally alienated.

Also, in this chapter I provide an overview of the growing Euroskepticism throughout much of the EU in addition to the growing resentment of immigrants. Some of the reasons for this growing trend is economic insecurity and white anxiety as embedded in structural and systemic dynamics and institutions of liberal democracy and globalism, which many feel have failed them on economic, political, and social grounds. Furthermore, the mishandling of the immigration crisis during the 2014–2015 period by the European Commission has served as a catalyst for nativist and racist sentiments that have resurfaced throughout the continent, accompanied by a return toward autocratic leadership. I compare and contrast the situations in the various EU countries in terms of immigration policy. At the end of the chapter I discuss how theories of migration, social movements, and critical race theories, and varying perspectives on the laws and ethics of asylum cases can help us to better understand the struggle.

I conclude with a section that focuses on the immigrant detention camps in parts of the EU and how some countries are criminalizing any types of assistance for refugees and asylum seekers and/or advocacy work. Overcrowded camps, with deplorable health and safety conditions for both families and minors traveling alone, have caught the attention of the international community and governments are being pressured to address the issue. In spite of this pressure, however, many countries are implementing even more severe externalization policies.

In chapter 4, I update how the Trump administration uses both mainstream and social media to engage in misinformation campaigns and purposeful falsehoods to promote "Trumpism," and to exploit the anxiety that many members of the white working class feel by scapegoating Muslim and Latinx immigrants. I also look at the role of media pundits, primarily on Fox News, in setting immigration policy through their close relationship with, and influence over, the Trump administration. This chapter also discusses Trumpism in a global perspective, highlighting the global nature of the rise of Islamophobia, anti-Semitism, and white supremacy. For example, Trump has declared that large numbers of immigrants led to a decay of law order, culture, and traditional values in not only the United States but also in Europe.

Trump has also reversed post–World War II transatlantic alliances and has supported autocrats in Europe as part of his disdain for democratic liberalism. At the end of the chapter I note how social media is playing a key role in fueling white supremacy, ethno-nationalism, and hate crimes against immigrants. New information communication technologies (ICTs) and social networking sites have shifted the relevance from activists merely gaining media attention from the mainstream press to ordinary citizens who become the message creators who construct and distribute their own information. This chapter applies social movement, immigration, and critical race theories to make sense of the rise of white supremacy and hostility toward immigrants.

In the last chapter, I illustrate waves of protest activity and contentious politics (actors working outside of the formal political system and institutional processes to affect social change) in resistance to immigration policies over the past few decades. Pro-immigration rights activists have engaged in marches, demonstrations, rallies, and boycotts. Some are organized to resist pending legislation that is still being debated in Congress, while others are in opposition to laws and policies that have already been approved. I highlight the fact that protest activity increased significantly once Donald Trump was elected president, and particularly so when he introduced the Muslim ban and the zero-tolerance policy that led to the separation of Latinx families.

This chapter also includes the strong reaction among citizens to detention centers that house children and minors as a result of the zero-tolerance policy, and defiance of the policies at Immigration and Customs Enforcement (ICE) practices which are rooted in the harassment of noncriminal immigrants. It illustrates that it is a combination of citizens, businesses, faith-based groups, and politicians who have joined forces in a call for more humane policies toward immigrants and a pathway to citizenship. I further address the mobilization around Deferred Action for Childhood Arrivals (DACA) legislation and the mobilization efforts by the DREAMers—young people brought to the United States at a young age and are without documents but seeking citizenship. Migrants, with the support of others, have also protested against the inhumane conditions in some EU detention camps that are sheltering migrants.

I end the chapter with a discussion of how advocacy works at the grassroots level, with a focus on human rights groups working to reunite separated families and others that are committed to preventing deaths of migrants crossing the U.S.-Mexico border and traversing the Mediterranean Sea, are approaching the crisis of immigration through the sponsorship of relief efforts, acts of civil disobedience, and advocacy work.

Chapter 1

Theories of Migration, Social Movements, and Ethno-nationalism

In this chapter, I explore the various theories of migration at both the macro- and micro-level of analysis. I also take a historical perspective in examining the laws and ethics of immigration and attempts by governments in the EU and in the United States to regulate immigration. These include both the communitarian and the communalism perspectives. Part of this discussion are issues related to asylum cases and the increasing difficulties migrants are experiencing when they attempt to utilize this process. I compare and contrast some of the changing immigration policies in both regions.

The second part of the chapter addresses the issue of the rise (and return) of ethno-nationalism and autocrats (strongman politics) in both parts of the world, and particularly among working-class white males, and how an application of certain social movement theories and ethno-nationalism/critical race theory can refine our understanding of this dynamic.

Part of trend dynamic is the shift toward illiberalism and the challenges facing the EU and the United States. The lack of integrated institutions across the EU to remedy economic crisis and regulate immigration has caused many European citizens, and the newly minted far-right and ultra-conservative populist leaders, to question the legitimacy of the system and democracy. Consequently, they embrace a Euroskeptic perspective and question the sustainability of the EU. In the United States this is often referred to as "Trumpism"—a rejection of democratic liberalism, globalism, multiculturalism, and a support for nativist and "America First" ideologies. Complementing these dynamics is the growing popularity of the "Great Replacement" movement: the belief that as more countries become majority minority, whites feel they are losing their power and status.

THEORIES OF MIGRATION

Theories of immigration are diverse and expand across the macro- and microlevel of analysis in trying to understand the causes for, and results of migration (Haas et al. 2099; Favell 1999). Structural theories examine how individual decisions are impacted by macro-level economic and social dynamics such as individuals' search for better economic opportunities. World systems theory, in particular, views migration across countries as an inherent part of global capitalism as migrants flee from lesser to more developed countries (Sassen 1988). Historical–structural approaches to migration recognize the ways in which globalization facilitates the interdependence of economies and markets and capital mobility as export-oriented economic platforms in both manufacturing and agriculture have historically spurred workers and their families into regional and oftentimes long-distance migration (Silver 2003; Sassen 1988).

Dual labor market theory shares some similarities with world system theory as the main focus is on structural dynamics in the global economy but looks more at demand in advanced countries rather than supply from less developed countries (Haas et al. 2020; Castles and Miller 2009). The duality is rooted in a need for low-skilled jobs that stems from the refusal of workers in host countries to undertake these jobs due to low pay, unsafe working conditions, and low status attached to certain kinds of labor. Thus, employers and governments actively recruit workers from lesser developed countries as immigrants are deemed necessary to fill these positions (Haas et al. 2019).

Similarly, neoclassical economics theory focuses on economic related and macro-level variables assuming that immigrants use a cost/benefits rational analysis upon making a decision to migrate (Mansoor and Quillin 2006). In conclusion, structural macro-level theories suggest that in a globalized economy, rooted in neoliberal principles of the free movement of goods, services, and labor, immigration is often an offshoot of international trade agreements and labor needs across state boundaries (Massey 1999).

One of the shortcomings of these theories, however, is that they often fail to recognize the interconnection between contexts and individuals' motivations to migrate, such as cultural aspects of immigration including families, households, and conditions in the home country (Bauer and Zimmermann 1999; Massey et al. 1998). Another is that they cannot adequately explain why countries with similar economic and labor needs don't receive the same number of immigrants as others.

To address some of these shortcomings, and as an extension of neoclassical theory, the human capital theory uses a meso-level of analysis that includes additional variables which incorporate the sociodemographic characteristics of immigrants, level of education, occupation, age, and marital status among other factors (Collinson 2009; Quillan 2006). Network theory shares a similar perspective through its attention to the perpetuation of migration patterns over time and across physical locations despite a lack of wage differentials or recruitment policies (Castles and Miller 2009; Dustmann and Glitz 2015). Vertovec and Wessend (2005) contend that it is often kin and friendship networks created through diaspora of certain ethnic groups that facilitates the institutionalization of these networks which over time can become self-sustaining. Thus, for these theories the focus is more on agency or push factors rather than looking at structures in isolation. The following chapters examine in detail why it is important to consider how these theories can often be applied in a complementary fashion.

SOCIAL MOVEMENT THEORY

In addition to the theories presented earlier in the chapter, various social movement theories can also help us to situate the current popularity of nativism, illiberalism, and the reemergence of far-right groups and autocratic leaders. Strain theory, rooted in relative deprivation, focuses on economic grievances such as high unemployment rates among certain segments of the population that can translate into racism and scapegoating (Kitschelt 1986). There is plenty of research to support this theory. For example, Van Dyle and Soule (2002) found that farm disclosures and the outsourcing of manufacturing jobs increased the rate of active white militia organizations across parts of the United States.

McVeigh's (2009) research on the Ku Klux Klan (KKK), however, illustrates that it is not just economics that fuels hostility toward immigrants, rather it is demographic changes in local communities. He finds that when homogeneity among white Protestant groups became threatened or were perceived to be threatened beginning in the 1920s, KKK membership and mobilization activities increased. Dietrich (2014) shows that the competition between immigrants and the native population for not just jobs but also educational opportunities, neighborhoods, and political power enhances grievances across other dimensions, and Hutter (2014) also highlights that when globalization is accompanied by ethnic and racial diversity, far-right groups gain membership.

Strands of social movement theories that focus on cultural dimensions of collective behavior are also useful, and particularly those that focus on the importance of framing and collective identity. Melucci (1996) defines collective identity as an interactive shared process that links individuals or groups through sustained interaction. It illuminates how individuals come to decide they share certain orientations and grievances. Polletta and Jasper

(2001) suggest that collective identity can be a perception of a shared status or relationship, which may be imagined rather than experienced directly. Key to forging collective identity and articulating shared meanings is how individuals frame their issues to resonate with potential recruits and to build solidarity by linking participants' grievances to mainstream beliefs and values (Benford 1993).

Framing is also critical. Social movement scholars define a frame as an interpretative schema that an individual or group uses to interpret reality, on an ideological basis, by selectively omitting or emphasizing various aspects of the world (Snow et al. 1986). Frames are typically referred to as "injustice frames" that contain implicit or explicit appeals to moral principles (Ryan and Gamson 2006). For framing to be influential, organizers must persuade large numbers of people that the issues they care about are urgent, that alternatives are possible, that activists have moral standing and can be invested with agency (Tilly 1978). Snow et al. (1986) delineate that social movement actors must provide "prognostic," "diagnostic," and "motivational" frames. This means identifying problems (including attributions of blame or causality so there is a target for actions), posing solutions in a way that mobilizes participants and appeal to third parties, and agitating for a "call to arms."

The next section focuses on a specific push and pull factor regarding immigration: those migrants and refugees seeking asylum. In both the United States and within several EU countries, it is becoming increasingly difficult to be granted asylum and even more cumbersome to apply for this status due to the changes in asylum laws and policies which neglect international agreements. One of the main issues that the following chapters explore in detail is *why* people are seeking asylum in record numbers, and the roadblocks that migrants face in their attempt to apply for it, which in turn leads to the practice of illegal immigration.

PERSPECTIVES ON THE LAWS AND ETHICS OF IMMIGRATION AND THEORIES OF THE REGULATION OF IMMIGRATION

In 1948, the United Nations recognized the right for individuals to seek asylum from persecution in other countries, and the modern asylum system was created at the 1951 United Nations Convention on the Rights of Refugees (United Nation Human Rights Committee). At this convention, the participating countries agreed that accepting refugees was essential to preventing similar atrocities that occurred during World War II and established international law by which individuals would be guaranteed asylum if they were fleeing based on "a well-founded fear" of persecution on the basis of religion, race, or political beliefs (United Nations Human Rights Committee).

More precisely, the convention stated that the receiving state of asylum seekers is required to uphold the principle of nonrefoulement. This means that a refugee cannot be deported back to their country of origin if there was strong evidence of fear or a history of persecution. It was also designed under the rubric of national security concerns, while at the same time acknowledging that asylum seekers should not be detained simply for seeking asylum, which sometimes requires individuals to breach immigration rules. Additionally, although the convention prohibits the expulsion of refugees, there is no legal provision for them to enter another country (United Nations Human Rights Committee).

Some recommendations adopted (though not bound by international law) in the document focused on the protection of a refugee's family and the obligations of host governments to provide necessary measures for keeping families united and not separated at different detention facilities (Domonsoske and Gonzales 2018). Forty-eight states have ratified the United Nations Convention on the Protection of the Rights of All Migrant Workers and Members of Their Families. Ironically, countries who receive the majority of migrant workers, such as North America, Western Europe, and Australia are among those that have not ratified this (Domonsoske and Gonzales 2018).

One major complication of refugee and asylum laws is that the contemporary immigration crisis is very different than those that were being addressed in the 1940s and early 1950s when these international laws were established. Instead of fleeing state prosecution, most immigrants are now trying to escape dire economic situations, civil wars, natural disasters, climate change, and gang violence (Menjivar and Cervantes 2018; Minkin 2018). Thus, this challenges some of the structural-oriented theories of immigration that tend to focus primarily on economic factors.

According to United Nations Human Rights Commissioner, for example, the violence due to gang activity in many countries has become more deadly than military conflicts in other parts of the world. The movement of refugees is further hampered by unclear regulations that expose refugees to unforeseen tribulations, governments at odds with each other and upset with current policies (especially throughout the EU), and many citizens becoming increasingly hostile toward the influx of immigrants (Baczynska and Ledwith 2016; Cendrowicz 2015; Kim and Sundstrom 2014).

There is a political and legal dimension to how countries respond to those seeking asylum status. For example, although both American and European law requires governments to let refugees apply for asylum no matter how they arrive, the politics surrounding migration always calls for limits on the numbers of individuals and often depends on the country of origin (Kurry and Redo 2018; Kneebone 2009). One of the ways that many governments have been addressing this contradiction without breaking international law has been to prevent people from arriving or deterring them from attempting to migrate, oftentimes making the crossings too dangerous or impossible for migrants to attempt the journey (Eljechtimi 2018).

To address some of these complications on July 12, 2018, the United Nations completed an agreement to improve ways to handle the global flow of migrants called the Global Compact for Safe, Orderly and Regular Migration. The goal was to preserve the basic human rights of all migrants and to stop irregular immigration. One hundred and ninety-two countries ratified it and the United States originally participated in the negotiations but later withdrew (Specia 2018a). President Trump argued that such multinational agreements subverted the power of individual governments to control national borders (Da Silva 2018).

There is also a lack of clarity of the 1948 Universal Declaration of Human Rights in that the contradiction between the primacy of universal human rights and national sovereignty was never reconciled (Inghilleri 2012). Two of the perspectives scholars use to evaluate this dilemma are communitarianism, which embraces a restrictive approach, and cosmopolitanism which favors a more open one (Amstutz 2015). The communitarian approach views strong nation-states as most significant to ensure stability and the safety and prosperity of the host's own population.

To understand the communitarian perspective, global welfare theory argues that immigration control is impacted by the public sphere when fears of the loss of national identity, security, and perceived differences in racial, ethnic, or cultural identities motivate feelings of exclusion (Midgley 2017; Van Wormar and Link 2016; Marin 2015; Consterdine and Hampshire 2013). Traditional ideas of national identity, which were rooted in fixed demographics, come into conflict with a modern world that has been increasingly globalized. In alignment with global welfare theory, proponents of closing borders argue that is necessary to preserve a state's distinctive culture, values, and the continuity of ethnic identity (Gest et al. 2018; Hohmann 2017; Payne 2012; Laden and Owen 2007).

An opposing perspective embraces a moral dimension premised on the argument that immigrants deserve the same basic rights regardless of nationality—a liberal political theory that favors the rights of people in terms of equality, social justice, and democracy as highlighted by Hoffman and Graham (2015), Cole (2011), and Laden and Owen (2007). This is more in alignment with cosmopolitanism which appreciates the strengths of diversity that benefit the receiving country. While states' rights and human rights are the fundamental framework for immigration arguments in that most countries tried to create policies that both secured human rights and national safety

(Song 2019; Gabey and Caren 2016). This balance has shifted, however, in the current era in favor of national security and communitarianism, and this will be explored in more depth in the following chapters.

THEORIES OF ETHNO-NATIONALISM
AND CRITICAL RACE THEORY

The struggles at the international level are compounded by those at the national level in the context of the current shift toward opposition to liberal democracy, the social welfare system, and the nationalism that populist leaders have seized upon in both the EU and the United States (Albright 2018; Leruth and Usherwood 2018). In Europe, the anti-immigration, Islamophobic, and Euroskeptic dynamic has energized a strong nativist, far-right populist wave (Brack and Costa 2019; Leconte 2010). Center-right, if not alt-right governments have been replacing center-left parties that dominated most European countries since World War II (Hallahan 2018). Some of the traditionally staunchest supporters of social democracy, for example, Germany, Italy, France, and Spain, are experiencing this trend (Galston 2018).

Part of the reason for the emergence is the economic disparity which was exasperated by the 2008 global economic crisis. Leaders across Europe have blamed the increasing rates of inequality and a sense of cultural alienation, particularly among white working-class men largely on immigrants (Cohen 2019; Shaheen 2019). For some countries, this is an imagined threat rather than actual migration or presence of immigrants as far-right leaders rely on misinformation campaigns and fear tactics that scapegoat immigrants (Strickland 2018a).

Theories of ethno-nationalism offer further explanations for the trending toward extreme right-wing nationalism and the rise of neofascism. For some scholars, the explanation is rooted in economic populism (Bremmer 2018: Judis 2018; Brubacker 2017). Others argue that forms of racism, nativism, and ethno-nationalism are fluid as they are connected to particular historical, cultural, geographic, and political contexts (Garner and Selod 2014). When trying to understand ethno-nationalism in particular it is important to tease out racial and economic issues because they often get conflated. Some argue that the best explanations of ethno-nationalism are rooted in white nativism, the threat of reduced social status among white citizens oftentimes, but not always, combined with racism (Jardina 2019; Mutz 2018). The goal of nativism is to justify and reward the superiority of the "native" and racism's goal is to reinforce "white's superiority" (Herber et al. 2008; Gallindo and Vigil 2006).

Garner (2009) argues that racialization is a process that tends to attribute innate characteristics and cultural values to a certain group—a difference between in-groups and out-groups within the dynamic of a power relationship. He therefore denounces the idea that racialization only applies to relations between groups as constructed by "races." He also applies critical race theory to examine white racialized identities, stating: "The norms of whiteness are in great part dictated by identification with a code: a set of behaviors that are viewed as constituting respectability. This is bound up with self-sufficiency, community orientation, civility and work ethic" (446).

Whiteness, Garner contends, is a way of understanding the social world and which supposes that white is a position of relative privilege, albeit uneven, contingent, and situational. He therefore recognizes underlying process of racialization in addition to class-based issues, calling this "victimization of whiteness" whereby ethnic minorities are now afforded rights and privileges previously exclusive to the white working class. This feeling that they are losing their sense of national belonging, and significantly the ability to determine who belongs and who does not is particularly disturbing.

Expanding on this, Higham (1999: 384) claims that "nativism always divided insiders, who belonged to the nation from outsiders, who were in it but not of it." Focusing on the period between 1860 and 1925 in America, he distinguishes between three types of nativism. He contends that the first two stem from religious and political differences as migrants from Europe disrupted the norm of Catholicism and were coming from communist countries in large numbers. Other scholars have further linked racism to Islamophobia directed at Muslims and to anti-Semitism targeting Jews in both the United States and Europe (Garner and Selod 2014).

This is closely connected to ethno-nationalism—the perception that shared heritage which includes language, faith, and ancestry as passed down by ancestors is at the root of who "belongs." In Europe, populism based on identity issues and ethno-nationalism also has historically focused more on religion—discrimination against Islam whereas in the United States it has been expressed more by means of race and ethnicity.

The third form of nativism Higham identifies is certain groups' cultural traits posing a threat to the supposed American way of life. Expanding on this premise, Huber et al. (2008: 41) contend that "the issue of nationalism is important to nativism because it not only illuminates the process of defending national identity from perceived threats, it also engenders a fear of the foreigner." Their conception of racial nativism delineates that is not just racializing an immigrant group to influence public opinion toward anti-immigrant persuasions. Rather, it combines racialization and anti-immigrant sentiment with the manifestation of this ideology within institutions and practices to sustain white privilege and oppress immigrant minorities. Additionally, a sense of nativism is intensified during times of national crisis such as war, economic crises, or large numbers of immigrants in a short period of time (Gallindo and Vigil 2006; Portes and Rumbaut 2014).

The concept of "racist nativism" is helpful in understanding the combination of racists and anti-immigrant feelings (Lippard 2011). Huber et al. (2008: 42–43) describe this as

> "the assigning of values to real or imagined differences in order to justify the superiority of the native, who is perceived to be white, over that of the non-native, who is to perceived to be people and immigrants of color, and thereby defend the native's right to dominance. . . . The notion of whiteness was privileged because it became strategically equated to Anglo-European heritage, Western religious traditions, and other values and beliefs deemed dominant and supportive of the 'American Spirit' . . . Being an American, or being perceived as such, and thus enjoying the privileges that come with that identity, had much, if not everything, to do with being white. Whiteness, thus, became the most important requirement for profiting from the privilege of being native to US soil."

Jarret (1999) outlines four categories of how anti-immigrant sentiment is formed. One is that citizens see immigrants as a political threat. The second is a perceived threat to the cultural and social order and lack of assimilation. The third concerns environmental issues and fear that immigrants are a drain on social and financial resources. The fourth are economic concerns regarding the impact on employment rates, wages, housing, and use of social services. Chavez (2008) points to how these four myths are created and perpetuated in mainstream media, which help shape and perpetuate myths about Latinx immigrants in the United States. His covering of the 2012 and 2016 elections, for example, highlights how these narratives were used to dehumanize Latinos.

EUROSKEPTICISM, ETHNO-NATIONALISM, AND THE RISE OF AUTOCRATS

In post–World War II, most of Europe shared a consensus that forming a common community rooted in peace and prosperity through multidimensional integration was the best way to prevent another major war (Goodman 2018; Diamond and Gunther 2001). Leaders worked together to formulate various negotiations and treaties to ensure economic and political integration, and ultimately a collective sense of security and cogovernance (Friedman 2018). Out of this consensus came the EU. The EU thrived as it expanded from the six founding members to twenty-eight and became the largest economy in the world. It shared a common currency and enjoyed the highest social benefits anywhere (Goodman 2018).

While former communist countries eagerly joined the EU, assuming living standards would rise and be similar to those in Western Europe, that did not come to fruition and gave rise to right-wing reactionary forces that are consolidating political power by appealing to ethno-nationalism and a rejection of liberal democracy (Berbeloglu 2019). On the cultural front, the EU founders saw this as an experiment whereby nation-states and race-based identity could be transcended and lead to cultural integration (Fisher 2019). However, this overlooked deeply rooted national identities which were exacerbated by the 2008 economic crisis. Part of the explanation for the reappearance of nativism is that "European" identity was very much secondary for citizens who overwhelming identify with a particular European nation (Kitschelt 1995).

Over time the different structure of individual states' economies and cultural differences within the EU raised additional concerns about the legitimacy of the system as it became more apparent that the EU lacked the proper institutional apparatus to address the economic and immigration problems (Hobolt and Tilly 2014). Now, as Europeans struggle with the social and political strains set off by migration from poor and war-torn nations outside the European bloc, the contradiction between the concept of the experiment of the EU and the reality of its borders has been exposed (Thorton 2015).

The EU also has a very porous border and is therefore susceptible to high rates of refugees, and especially because it is located adjacent to the Middle East and Northern Africa, two very politically and economically unstable regions (Blinder et al. 2020). In the aftermath of the Arab Spring uprisings across the Middle East and North Africa that began in 2012, and the pursuing outbreaks of civil war, refugees fled to Europe in large numbers. The failed states of Tunisia, Syria, Libya, and Egypt that followed the overthrow of the dictators who were in power for years set off a massive humanitarian crisis which the EU was unprepared to handle (Bauman et al. 2014).

To regulate immigration is much more difficult in the EU than in the United States. In the United States, the federal government has centralized control over immigration policy, in the EU there is not a strong sense of political unity and governments have to deal not only with external borders but also have to determine how to manage the travel of migrants within the twenty-eight countries that constitute the EU (Amnesty International 2017; Chomsky 2015). Thus, unlike the United States it does not have institutions that allow it to operate as a state, and there has always been a gulf between the decision-making institutions of the EU and the parliaments and citizens of the Member States (Berman 2019; Brack and Costa 2019; Bach 3015).

More broadly, while NATO and other supranational institutions and agreements did lead to an absence of war within Europe, many citizens have become disillusioned with the new global order (Brack and Costa 2019; Leruth et al. 2018). There is a growing feeling that bureaucrats, elites, and technocrats in Brussels are out of touch and that citizens and national parliaments have little or no voice on important issues, thereby undermining the democratic vision. This mistrust is widespread. According to a 2012 poll, 83 percent of Greeks, 47 percent of Spaniards, and 39 percent of Italians reported that they felt EU countries constitute a "major threat" to their national economy (Pew Global Attitudes Survey 2012).

Thus, in addition to immigration, globalism and cosmopolitanism are another target of anger for many in the working class (Beitz 2011). Taking advantage of this anger and mistrust in the status quo which is embedded in notions of liberal democracy, autocratic leaders and strongman politics are becoming more acceptable in many parts of the world. This is manifested in a rejection of democratic rules, blatant attacks on political opponents who are claimed to not be legitimate, attacks on the media and judicial independence, a weakening of the rule of law and civil liberties (Levitsky and Zilbatt 2018). Through the attack on global institutions and international agreements, far-right nationalist groups label themselves as populists and champions of a new politics rooted in white and Christian identity and defenders of Western cultural values (Beitz 2011).

One irony is that nominally democratic nations are becoming de facto authoritarian states (Levitsky and Ziblatt 2018). Distinct from past political methods, autocratic leaders are not declaring martial law through a military coup or suspending the constitution; they can merely subvert the democratic institutions by coming to power through those very democratic institutions that are in place, thus performing subtle coups while upholding the image of democracy (Levitsky and Ziblatt 2019). They rely on the threat of real or imagined crisis (typically blamed on "outsiders" and scapegoating immigrants) to augment and centralize their power to subvert constitutional checks and balances.

WHITE IDENTITY, "GREAT REPLACEMENT" IDEOLOGY, AND THE THREAT OF NEOFASCISM

In both the United States and the EU, there has been a sharp spike in hate crimes, mass shootings, and viral attacks against immigrants, primarily against Muslims, Latinx communities, and Jews. Alt-right groups and the language that they use, which were not long ago considered to be on the margins, or even unspeakable, have now made their way into mainstream politics and discourse (the specificities of this new reality is more thoroughly documented and analyzed in later chapters). An existential threat is felt among many white working-class males, what they perceive to be the Great Replacement movement (Jardina 2019; Judis 2018). At the heart of this is a fear that Muslim and Latinx immigrants, as well as Jews are intentionally trying to have higher birth rates to outnumber whites and Christians (Bridges 2018; Williams et al. 2017; Garner and Selod 2014).

Others contend that the anger felt by white working-class people within and across societies is fueled by globalization and the disintegration of economic, political, and social traditions it brings (Bremmer 2018). To try to comprehend the construction of white working-class American and British identity, Jest (2017) compares white working-class residents in Youngstown, Ohio to those in East London UK—both communities that he calls "post-traumatic cities." He finds that although wages have stagnated and jobs (especially in manufacturing which served as the economic base in both of the cities) have been relocated overseas, the income and wealth benefits enjoyed overall by the white working class in comparison to minority groups have remained significant.

He argues that globalization has hit the working-class communities particularly had and thefore achieved status through work, income and social mobility is no longer available. For many, this has led to a sense of lost identity in terms of middle-class status. Political parties are tapping into this and exploiting the sense of alienation and frustration and pivoting toward cultural and social scapegoats which fuel the trend toward neofascism (Hochschild 2016). Furthermore, while right-wing extremists connect the loss of national identity with globalization, underpinning this is an existential threat of the "other," which needs to be countered with strongman politics (Lind 2020; Zeihan 2016).

Giroux (2018) defines the situation this way: "Fascism, with its unquestioning belief in obedience to a powerful strongman, violence as a form of political purification, hatred as an act of patriotism, racial and ethnic cleansing, and the superiority of a select ethnic or national group has resurfaced in the United States . . . If we are to understand the current resurgence of right-wing populist movements across the globe, economic factors alone do not account for the current mobilizations of fascist passions" (Karlin 2018).

CONCLUSION

This chapter viewed some of the theories of migration at both the macro- and microlevel of analysis and offers a historical perspective to examine the laws and ethics of immigration and attempts by governments in the EU and in the United States to regulate immigration, including the opposing views of communitarianism versus communalism. As this analysis illustrates, asylum cases have become much more complicated and difficult in the contemporary era as the regulations that were established in the late 1940s and early 1950s are out of synch with the complexity of today's increasingly globalized world. As governments strive to reform their laws to restrict, or at least control, irregular immigration and to ensure national security, the rights of immigrants become increasingly jeopardized.

Chapter 2

Immigration Patterns between the United States, Mexico, and Central America in a Historical Perspective

Currently there are approximately forty million people who are residing in the United States that were born outside of the country: about 54 percent are from Mexico and Latin America, 27 percent from Asia, and 15 percent from Canada and Europe (American Progress Organization 2017). The undocumented population of the United States is 76 percent Latino, and 28 percent of all immigrants are from Mexico—about half of those are undocumented. While demographic trends speak for themselves (projections are that Latinos will account for almost one half of the population in California and a handful of other states by 2050), a vibrant debate surrounds the basic question of what this means for the United States economically, politically, and socially.

The focus of this chapter is on Latinx immigration and an examination of how contemporary trends, laws, and economic needs of the United States have impacted immigration patterns. It includes a discussion of externalization policies that in certain points of time are used to keep "undesirable" migrants from reaching the United States to apply for asylum, and how politics surrounding the Cold War and other international events have impacted how refugees and asylum seekers are treated. I apply theories of immigration, social movement theories, critical race theory, and scholarly perspectives of human rights when it comes to asylum cases to serve as a framework through which to analyze contemporary dilemmas regarding immigration policy.

GLOBALIZATION, U.S. FOREIGN POLICY, AND THE IMPACT ON BORDER MIGRATION PATTERNS

Before discussing in depth, the relationship between the United States and Mexico, it is interesting to note how different this relationship is in comparison to the northern border that it shares with Canada. The border that the United States shares with Canada is the longest in the world, much of it free from any kind of Border Patrol (Portes and Rumbaut 2014). Daily, over 400,000 and $1.6 billion in goods cross through one of the 120 points of entry. Yet, it has never faced the scrutiny of the southern border. This was pointed out by a few politicians following the 2001 terrorist attacks against the United States. According to Senator Heidi Heitkamp (D) North Dakota: "The problem is that we don't know what the threats and risks are because so much attention is given to the Southwest border" (Drucker 2018).

In 2011, a former commission of U.S. Customs and Border Protection testified before the Senate Judiciary Committee that, regarding terrorism, "it's commonly accepted that the more significant threat comes from the U.S.-Canada border rather than the southern border" (U.S. Government Publishing Senate Report 114-155). A 2015 report produced by the Senate Committee on Homeland Security and Government Affairs concluded: "Some experts also believe that terrorists could exploit vulnerabilities along the northern border to carry out an attack on the U.S" (U.S. Government Publishing, Senate Report 114-1551). Despite these warnings, however, the obsession continues to be on the southern border as a site of concern. As other chapters in the text reveal, the intersection between immigration and racism is relevant.

Much of the driving force behind immigration from Latin America is, and has historically been, U.S. foreign policy. Therefore, the geopolitical context is key to understanding why the United States allows or denies certain groups from Latin American countries entry—typically altering quotas based on perceived national security interests. A historical view of immigration policies shows that beginning in the 1800s the United States has experienced multiple waves of migration in response to fluctuating demands for labor, nationalist goals of land settlement, and racialized policies. To situate the immigration trends across the U.S.-Mexico border, we can look at how the political and economic dynamics have manifested themselves between the two countries over time.

In the eighteenth century, U.S. internal and foreign policy was driven by the concept of Manifest Destiny, the belief that the United States was predestined to rule all of North America. This is well exemplified through a statement made by Senator Albert Beveridge (R-IN) at a congressional meeting in 1900. He summed up the ideology this way: "We are the ruling race of the world . . . . We will not renounce our part in the mission of our race, trusted under God of the civilization of the world . . . . He has marked us as his chosen people . . . . He has made us adept in government that we may administer government among the savage and senile peoples" (Acuna 1972).

These "savage and senile peoples" originally referred to Native Americans and would later be broadened to include any group that was not Anglo.

This ideology served to justify conquest of new territories across the United States, the system of slavery (of imported Africans), and attempted genocide (of Native Americans) for economic profit (Stone and Kuznick 2012). More specifically, in the case of Mexico, this mindset validated the conquest of the Southwest and resulted in the United States taking over one half of Mexico's territory following the Mexican American War. This was formally established under the Treaty of Guadalupe Hidalgo in 1848 (Acuna 1972).

These clearly Eurocentric viewpoints illustrate the relevancy of Bridge's (2019) and Garner and Selod's (2014) arguments regarding the intersection between racism and nativism in their use of critical race theory. They are also demonstrative of the theories put forth by Herber et al. (2008) and Gallindo and Vigil (2006) that emphasize how the goal of nativism is to justify and reward the "native" on the basis of white superiority.

While the war against Mexico was justified under the guise of "spreading civilization," the underlying issue was slavery (Chavez 2008). The illegality of slavery in Mexico prohibited the accumulation of wealth for southern farmers in the United States (though of course this was rarely mentioned publicly). The annexation of Mexican territory subsequent to the war placed not only the land but also Mexican citizens in the hands of the U.S. government (Stone and Kuznich 2012). The treaty did grant U.S. citizenship to the people living in the conquered territories of California, Colorado, New Mexico, Nevada, Texas, and Arizona, but excluded voting rights and educational opportunities on par with Anglo citizens (Acuna 2015).

After early European settlers advanced westward under the precept of Manifest Destiny, the U.S. government disseminated its policy of conquest and economic and political domination to other parts of the world south of its border. Just as businesses and political elites profited internally under Manifest Destiny by expanding slavery, annexing land, and having access to cheap Mexican labor, they later did so as a de facto foreign policy (Bonner 2016). In its efforts to create and maintain an economic empire across Latin America, the United States plundered much of it by extracting natural resources, exploiting cheap labor, undertaking military interventions, and propping up and assisting local elites who worked in alliance with U.S. business interests at the expense of their own population (Acuna 2015).

Furthermore, the Monroe Doctrine was established in 1823 to protect the Western hemisphere from any anticipated expansion of European colonization, and in 1924 President Theodore Roosevelt declared the right of the United States to exercise an "international police power" in Latin America (Bonner 2016). The Monroe Doctrine was, in part, an extension of the Manifest Destiny ideology to maintain U.S. hegemony in the region as President James Monroe stated that it was the "main duty" to spread the benefits of Anglo-Saxon civilization to less civilized populations in the

Caribbean. While originally the Monroe Doctrine was relatively passive, over time it justified interventions in Cuba, Nicaragua, Haiti, and the Dominican Republic, on ambiguous claims of corruption or inadequate governments (Putterman 2018).

It was in the late nineteenth century that the U.S. government began employing interventionist policies by financially and militarily supporting coups throughout Latin America, most of which put unpopular but powerful dictators in charge and who were partial to U.S. business interests (Immerewahr 2019). This helped the United States maintain political and economic advantages in the region and to secure countries as safe havens for U.S. investors to operate without fear of reprisal from governments or workers. For example, between 1898 and 1934, the U.S. Marines invaded Cuba four times, Nicaragua five times, Honduras seven times, the Dominican Republic four times, Haiti twice, Guatemala once, Panama twice, Mexico three times, and Columbia four times (Stone and Kuznick 2012).

Though interventionist policies were employed under the auspices of national security the reality was somewhat different. General Smedley Butler, a highly decorated marine leader who carried out many of these coups and the plundering of Latin American countries attested: "I spent most of my time as a high-class muscle man for Big Business, for Wall Street, and the bankers. In short, I was a . . . gangster for capitalism. . . . I helped make Mexico and especially Tampico safe for American oil interests" (Immerewhar 2019). The blatant military force would later be replaced by a more benign form of economic and political corporate rule under the neoliberal economic model (Gonzales 2011). Both the direct use of military intervention and the undermining of the Mexican economy offer insights into the migration of many Mexicans fleeing to the north.

The U.S. government also continually undermined or covertly overthrew those Latin American elites who did not comply with U.S. demands. The support for brutal police-state dictatorships was implemented under the banner of "defending freedom" against communism (Gonzalez 2011). This worked in conjunction with the more sinister desire to create and sustain a good climate for U.S. businesses. For instance, in 1954 the United States supported the overthrow of democratically elected president, Jacobo Arbenz in Guatemala (Gleijeses 1991).

Throughout the 1980s, the CIA continued to provide weapons and advisers to the army which was engaged in terrorist tactics and genocide amid a long entangled civil war. This was even though Congress had ordered an end to military assistance because of the atrocious human rights violations (Gleijses 1991). The repercussions, as in the case of Mexico and other Central American countries, were an outflow of citizens heading to the United States.

The Contras in Nicaragua throughout the 1980s were also illegally funded by covert operations undertaken by high-level officials in the Regan administration in their attempt to overthrow the popularly supported and democratically elected Sandinista government (Gonzalez 2011). The U.S. government has a long history of intervening El Salvador's internal affairs, going back to the 1932 rebellion over land reform initiated by Farabundo Marti (Schultz 1981). Between 1980 and 1992 a civil war between the Farabundo National Liberation Front and the military-led government ravaged the country. Under the leadership of President Ronald Reagan, the U.S. government provided military and training assistance for the Salvadoran military and death squads (Bonner 2012). The United Nations estimates that 85 percent of the 80,000 civilians who died were killed by the military and death squads (Mulligan 2004). The support of the military dictatorship has helped to sustain one of the most unequal societies in the hemisphere (Brigida 2018). With economic, political, and civil systems in tatters, desperation has driven huge swaths of Salvadorans from their home country who subsequently are seeking refuge in the United States.

In sum, the current and past patterns of migration can be explained by some straightforward and many more concealed and less obvious forms of intervention in the internal workings of Central America and Mexico that devastated local populations and served as push factors for migration.

MEXICAN MIGRATION PATTERNS AS LINKED TO LABOR NEEDS IN THE UNITED STATES

Part of the irony of the legacy of U.S. policy and the government's interaction with non-Anglo groups, which began with Manifest Destiny, is that Mexicans now stream into the very country that was once part of theirs, and where their ancestors had resided for thousands of years. In spite of this history, the U.S. response to Mexican migration has always been dictated by the state of the economy at the given historical juncture (Passel et al. 2012).

There has also always been an ambiguous and often contradictory attitude among U.S. citizens and political representatives toward Mexican immigrants. As the financial standing of the country ebbs and flows, so do common sentiments toward immigrants, and particularly the undocumented who come to be viewed as stealing jobs from citizens during economic slowdowns (Carty and Macias 2015). The message of this rather schizophrenic attitude toward Mexican immigrants held by many native-born Americans is "we need your labor but you are not welcome as citizens."

During World War I, for example, the Mexican government exported Mexican workers as contract laborers to help ease the labor shortage in the

United States at the U.S. government's request (Delgado-Wise and Marquez 2007). This worked well for the Mexican government as well because its economy was suffering from high levels of unemployment. As the U.S. economy thrived during the 1920s, the steady demand for Mexican labor continued and workers came both legally and illegally because with such great need for hired hands, employers were happy to hire workers who did not go through the proper legal channels, making it easier for both workers and employers (Hoffman and Graham 2015).

Though welcomed as workers, Mexican immigrants were suspect of being "germ carriers" and thus stripped at the border where they were bathed in kerosene (Frey 2019). Much of this rhetoric prevails today. For instance, Fox News host Tucker Carlson in 2018 stated that immigration from south of the border "makes the United States dirtier" and President Trump has referred to them as an "infestation," "animals," and "vermin" (Graham 2018). On his Fox television news show, Carlson criticized Democrats in reference to the caravans coming from Central America opining, "Our leaders demand that you shut up and accept this. We have a moral obligation to admit the world's poor, they tell us, even if it makes our own country poorer, and dirtier and more divided. Immigration is a form of atonement" (Horton 2018). This is representative of the communitarian perspective which views immigrants largely as invaders and a threat to naturalized citizens, and in alignment with Kitchelt's (1986) and Consterdine and Hampshire's (2013) conceptualization of these processes.

Strain theory as utilized by social movement scholars including McVeigh (2009) and Van Dyke and Soule (2002) is also useful in understanding these dynamics, as is Bridge's (2019) and Higham's (1999) work that delves into processes of nativism and divisions between "insiders" and "outsiders" over time in particular countries. Hushman's (2017), Payne's (2012), and Garner and Selod's (2014) theoretical work on nativism is also helpful in that they highlight how much of the anti-immigrant and racist perspectives, embedded in fear of foreigners, are often contingent on certain historical factors, one of the most prominent being large numbers of immigrants arriving in a short period of time. In turn, this leads to what Selod (2014) and Lippard (2011) conceptualize as racist nativism.

Structural theories of immigration, such as world systems theory, dual labor market theory, and neoclassical economics theory as proposed by Haas et al. (2020) and Mansoor and Quillan (2006) also help to make sense of this dynamic. The labor needs of a rapidly growing economy in a First World country became dependent on the labor of a lesser developed country. For Mexican workers, economic and financial concerns were the most decisive push and pull factors and were rooted in a rational, cost/benefit tradeoff.

Because of the need for immigrant labor, in this case the United States embraced a more cosmopolitan approach to newcomers.

Amid the Great Depression and soaring unemployment rates during the 1930s, however, there were mass deportations of Mexicans under the Mexican Repatriation program as Mexicans were accused of taking jobs from U.S. citizens. Many of those forcibly expelled from the country had lived in the United States all their lives and were in fact U.S. citizens. Of those deported, 60 percent were U.S. citizens or residents (Serwer 2018). In the 1940s during World War II, the U.S. government was once again facing a labor shortage and installed the Bracero (guest worker) program to help alleviate the situation. This program also helped to sustain the desperately needed production of U.S. agricultural goods (Serwer 2018). Under this program, workers were able to freely cross the border for seasonal work under short-term contracts and with no enforced border policies.

The post–World War II economic boom in the United States continued to provide plenty of jobs for those seeking them from south of the border and in fact, Mexican workers were actively recruited by U.S. businesses (Gonzalez 2011). Similar to the situation during World War I when braceros were in short supply, U.S. growers regularly hired those who came into the country undocumented (Chavez 2008). According to the Bracero History Archive, there were 4.6 million contracts signed by U.S. employers hiring Mexican workers over the forty-year period of the program. To ensure their return once the contracts were fulfilled, the agreement between the U.S. and Mexican governments required employers to withhold 10 percent of laborers' pay and remit that money to Mexican banks that the Bracero workers could claim when they returned. More often than not, the money was not there (Chavez 2008).

When the economic expansion of the U.S. economy slowed in the mid-1950s, many migrant workers (approximately 70,000) were deported under President Dwight D. Eisenhower's Operation Wetback—thousands of families were removed from the country by buses, trains, and ships, far into Mexican territory to hinder attempts of reentry (Hernandez 2006). With the economic downturn, organized labor blamed the financial hardship on immigrant workers, and U.S.-born workers accused immigrants of being scabs and strike breakers. These sentiments influenced public opinion and the volatile backlash against Mexican immigrants returned.

Theorists such as Dietrich (2014), Hutter (2014), and Jarret (1999) would posit the rise of these public opinions on the basis of a perceived drain on economic and financial resources. As was the case in the 1930s, deportation proceedings of Operation Wetback were invasive and, in some ways, inhumane. Under the program, hundreds of Border Patrol agents and state and local police went house to house checking the immigration status of residents. Here we witness a shift back to the communitarian lens.

Despite the aggressive efforts, Operation Wetback was ultimately a failure in terms of stopping the flow of Mexicans into the United States (Hernandez 2006). This was mostly due to the influence of powerful agribusiness interests in Congress that were reliant on Mexican labor. Political officials and law enforcement tended to turn a blind eye toward immigration offenses to appease their wealthy donors (Chavez 2008). After a backlash from American farmers who depended on the cheap labor the immigrants provided, the program was reinstated.

The main accomplishment of Operation Wetback was the media coverage that it received and installing the derogative term "wetback" into American discourse and insinuating that immigrants were a national security threat. As Chavez (2008) illustrates in his work on the impact that mainstream media has on creating narratives and thus influencing public opinion, myths are created and perpetuated to dehumanize immigrants. Similarly, to negate any sympathy toward Mexicans, Border Patrol agents began using the term "criminal aliens" rather than unsanctioned laborers as they had been previously defined. A regional supervisor in 1956 issued a directive saying that they wanted to avoid "a picture in the minds of public and courts of a poor, emaciated, Mexican worker," and replace it with "criminal alien" or "border violator," creating images of immigrants as criminals (Hernandez 2006).

Social movement theorists accentuate the relevance of the framing of narratives to influence public opinion. As Tilly (1978) and Snow et al. (1986) argue, for framing to be impactful those controlling the narrative must persuade large numbers of people that the issues at hand are urgent and solutions are possible through agency. This was the intent and outcome of the language used to describe undocumented workers, as well as the media portrayals of them. However, because there were so few immigrants who had been convicted of a crime the authorities needed a new reason to explain why Border Patrol was investing so many resources to control the borderlands (Fernandez 2012). This racialization of Latinx immigrants, which began with Operation Wetback by viewing them as threats and problems, resonates strongly in the United States today. Bridges (2019) and Garner (2014) have keen observations on how the conflation of nativism and racism is fluid, in that it corresponds to the political, historical, and geographical situation.

Historically, the high level of unemployment in Mexico, accompanied by the need for labor in the United States, created logical reasons for migration as Haas et al. (2018) and Castles et al. (2009) put forth as key structural explanations for migration. Once again, the United States was seeking low-skilled workers from a less developed country to take jobs that American citizens are unwilling to do, and this fits the model of neoclassical economics theory which highlights that employment opportunities are a driving force of immigration. The cross-border agreement through the Bracero program, which facilitated circular paths of immigration, is also best understood through the lens of macro- and structural-level theories that focus on the dynamics of the world system, and the relationship between developed and developing countries.

THE MEXICAN ECONOMY IN THE CONTEXT OF NEOLIBERALISM AND THE IMPACT ON IMMIGRATION TRENDS

On the Mexican side of the border, in an attempt to remedy its own economic crisis during the 1960s, the Mexican government initiated an export-oriented model of production called Border Industrialization Program (BIP), which was installed to diversify Mexico's economy (Wilson and Wood 2016). One key component of this program was the creation of free trade zones in border cities throughout Mexico. Under the BIP, investors from the United States readily moved in and the region was flooded with U.S.-based corporations that were able to prosper off of cheap Mexican labor (Carty and Macias 2014). This time, however, the exploitation of labor occurred within Mexico rather than in the United States.

This set the stage for what would eventually become a thriving maquila industry in the 1980s and 1990s, under which foreign-owned and foreign-managed factories imported materials and equipment duty- and tariff-free for the purpose of assembly and then export of the finished product (Wilson and Wood 2016). The end of the Bracero program ten years earlier had led to very high unemployment rates on the border, and thus the BIP was also designed as a mechanism to provide desperately needed jobs for Mexicans living in border regions. This did much to benefit U.S.-based corporations but little to boost the Mexican economy or assist Mexican workers due to the extremely low wages that laborers were paid (Bacon 2015).

The passage of North American Free Trade Agreement (NAFTA) in 1994 between Mexico, the United States, and Canada further exacerbated the already difficult economic conditions and wreaked havoc on Mexico's economy. One of the most controversial parts of the agreement was the elimination of Article 27 which had been written into the Mexican Constitution in 1927 following the 1910 revolution (Castillo 2004). The Ejido (communal land) system guaranteed that certain tracks of land would be controlled by the indigenous Mayan population for local production and could not be sold to foreign corporations. This system was dismantled to make way for foreign corporate-controlled agriculture for export, disenfranchising and displacing thousands of local farmers. Additionally, government subsidies for sowing corn were eliminated by the Mexican government as part of the treaty while U.S.-based agribusiness corporations enjoyed generous subsidies granted by the U.S. government (Harvey 1998).

The result was that local farmers in Mexico could no longer survive economically by growing corn or other traditional agricultural commodities because of the dumping of cheap corn on the domestic market by large agribusiness corporations in the United States (Gonzales 2011). Small farmers simply could not compete with the mechanized output of U.S. agribusiness. As a result, Mexico's grain imports from the United States tripled from 1994 levels, while real prices for Mexican corn fell more than 70 percent and the domestic market was destroyed (Bacon 2015). While the access of imported goods allowed for cheaper products to enter Mexico, the subsidies provided to U.S. farmers generated an unbalanced trade policy that drove scores of Mexican farmers to border cites to look for jobs in the maquila industry, or to cross the border into the United States in search of work (Carty and Macias 2014).

This is yet another example where world system and neoclassical theories of immigration are helpful. The free movement of goods, services, and labor as a consequence of the NAFTA agreement, in conjunction with labor needs in a wealthier country relying on a workforce from a lesser developed country in close proximity, played a large role in migration cycles. NAFTA therefore served to reinforce the maquila sector that flourished in border towns like Tijuana and Ciudad Juárez. Juárez has become the world's largest border community and has the highest concentration of maquila workers in the country with over 300 factories (Bacon 2015). While these factories (*maquiladoras*) provide jobs for those who are no longer able to work in the agricultural sector due to competition from foreign businesses, most pay less than the minimum wage.

In sum, NAFTA created and sustained the already extant cycle of poverty and migration. Ninety percent of Mexican household incomes either stagnated or declined since the passage of NAFTA, and in 2004 the minimum wage was equivalent to less than four dollars per day in the United States— this is among the lowest in the world (Chang 2013). Rather than providing new job opportunities in Mexico, it fueled immigration across the border at even higher rates. When NAFTA was implemented, 4.6 million Mexicans were residing in the United States; by 2013, this number exploded to 13 million (Chang 2013).

NARCO-TRAFFICKING AND THE WAR ON DRUGS

Another international agreement between the United States and Mexico that augmented the array of problems within Mexico and provided incentive for Mexicans to flee the country is the War on Drugs. This emerged as a collaborative effort between the United States and Mexico to destroy the drug cartels under the umbrella of national security (Gonzalez 2011). The joint policy is an indirect consequence of NAFTA; transporting drugs into the United States became very easy for narco-traffickers because illicit goods can easily be hidden alongside legitimate cargo (Marosi 2010). Given the exponential increase in trade between the United States and Mexico, due to NAFTA, checking every truck, car, or service vehicle is an impossible task for any law enforcement or customs agency. Ironically, the United States is currently the largest consumer of illicit drugs coming from Mexico and has been conducting its own, failed internal War on Drugs for decades (Payani 2020).

Additionally, since NAFTA undermined the livelihood of growing basic traditional commodities such as corn or beans, there is now a pervasive incentive among peasants to grow illicit crops that garner higher profits (Marosi 2012). Given the ongoing economic and social crisis in Mexico, and lack of employment opportunities and hope for the future, illegal activities and organized crime have become alluring choices in terms of making money and providing status for much of Mexican youth. This contributes to the failing efforts to curb drug trafficking and has led to escalating violence throughout Mexico, fueled by the growth of drug cartels.

In Mexico, the War on Drugs officially began in 2006 under President Felipe Calderón's six-year term, which has been characterized by many Mexicans as *el sexenio de la muerte*, or the six years of death (Gonzalez 2011). By the end of Calderón's term in office, according to the National Institute of Statistics and Geography of Mexico, an estimated 120,000 people had been killed due to drug-related violence. A major reason for the surge in violence is Calderón's lack of necessary resources to battle the cartels through traditional forms of law enforcement; he therefore deployed 50,000 military troops to civilian areas instead (Payani 2020).

The assassination of drug lords resulted in the splintering and acceleration of organized crime, giving rise to dozens of new cartels that swiftly engaged in turf wars, increasing the violence and narco-trafficking throughout the country (Castles and Miller 2009). In 2008, amid the explosion of violence and drug trafficking, President Barack Obama proposed the Merida Initiative with the acquiescence of the Mexican government. Under the plan, Mexico received money from the United States for weapons to enable the government to combat the flourishing drug cartels (Castles and Miller 2009). The overall goal was to disrupt organized crime by providing Mexico with weapons and to create new and more efficient forms of border security through the militarization of the border.

The Initiative, however, backfired as these weapons were used against the police and military by the cartels themselves which led to a civil war that killed hundreds of thousands of Mexicans (Bonner 2012). The narco-trafficking and criminal activity also led to a huge bottleneck for Mexicans legally trying to flee their country. Due to a lack of visas available, and Mexicans not receiving asylum status, illegal crossings became inevitable. According to the U.S. Executive Office for Immigration Review, in 2011, 6,100 Mexicans applied for asylum with only 294, or 5 percent, receiving it (U.S. Department of Justice 2016).

REFUGEES FROM CENTRAL AMERICA AND CUBA

Since the initiation of the Cold War immigrants fleeing communist governments were accepted as refugees and asylum seekers, viewed by the U.S. government as oppressed individuals. Cuban immigrants were welcomed in the early 1960s because they were categorized as refugees escaping the communist revolution. The Cuban Adjustment Act of 1966 allowed for anyone who emigrated from Cuba to seek residency after one year of residing in the United States (Hinckley 2016).

This first wave of Cubans tended to be wealthy and well educated (thus naturally ideological opposed to communism) and integrated into mainstream American society with relative ease (Hinckley 2016). Because the shared perception was that these Cuban refugees had something of value to contribute to the United States, the government had a cosmopolitan approach in welcoming the migrants. Thus, they were viewed as adaptable to the "code" of being white, and therefore not subject to the racism that most other immigrant groups faced. They fit the code of respectability as they were mostly well educated, self-sufficient, civil, and had a community-based orientation—characteristics that Garner (2012) points out in defining the "us versus them" narrative among native citizens when judging immigrants.

A second wave of Cuban immigrants took place in the late 1970s which consisted of a different demographic. Thousands of Cubans attempted to get asylum by taking over Latin American embassies due to dire economic conditions and political repression and in 1980 President Fidel Castro announced that anyone who wanted to leave was free to do so, departing from the Port of Mariel (Berg 2015). This was known as the Mariel Boatlift that lasted between April 15 and October 18. The agreement was mutually terminated by the U.S. and Cuban governments in late October 1980 (Capo 2017).

During the boatlift, approximately 125,000 Cubans fled (Glass 2009). What Castro did not relay to Cubans, but was announced through U.S. media outlets, was that one of the conditions required was that the refugees have someone pick them up in the United States upon arrival. Castro did, however, tell Cubans that they could bring others with them. These "others" included some who were mentally ill and prison inmates who were released (Glass 2009). In response, the U.S. government put many of the refugees in detention centers on military bases across the country. This second wave, thus, encountered a communitarian view upon their arrival to the United States.

Many people that did not suffer from mental illness and who were not criminals were detained as well and remained at the facilities as they waited to be sponsored (Hinckley 2016). Thousands of family members rushed to Florida hoping to connect with relatives. The Carter administration maintained the open-door policy toward Cuban immigrants (those who were not detained) and immediately granted them refugee status (Gonzalez 2011). This policy was widely approved by U.S. citizens. Thus, this wave of Cuban immigration can be best explained by meso-level and cultural-oriented theories of immigration. They note that in many cases it is social reasons, and not primarily economic ones that influence migration flows. These can include, among many other variables, family connections, seeking better education opportunities, and conditions in the country from which migrants are fleeing.

In 1996, the United States created the "wet foot dry foot" policy. This meant that Cubans who made it to U.S. shores were given legal residency and a path to citizenship through their expedited "legal permanent resident" status; those captured at sea were returned to Cuba or a third country (Blizzard and Batalora 2020). The acceptance of those who made it to the United States, though illegally, was predicated on an attempt to undermine the communist Castro regime. In the late 1990s immigration patterns changed. The term "dusty foot" referred to those who arrived in the United States not by sea but through Mexico. The Department of Homeland Security (DHS) allowed most of the "dusty" Cubans to apply for immediate parole, affording Cubans a privileged position relative to other immigrants in the United States (Cobb and Knight 2008). In 2017, President Obama ended the "wet foot dry foot" policy and made Cuban immigrants "subject to removal" just like all refugees from other countries (Blizzard and Batalora 2020).

On the other hand, during the 1980s the Reagan administration's view of El Salvador and Guatemala as buffers against communist revolutionaries had negative repercussions for asylum claims (Chavez 2008). The United States ignored the brutal death squads that governed and terrorized the local populations with impunity because these countries represented "freedom," and sustained a safe haven for U.S. investment. As a result, the United States granted political asylum to less than 3 percent of Salvadoran and Guatemalan asylum seekers (American Immigration Council 2018).

The thousands of immigrants fleeing for their lives were labeled as "economic" refugees by the government and subsequently deported. To consider them as political refugees would be to acquiesce to the notion that the United States was supporting governments that were persecuting their own people (Frelick et al. 2016). This highlights the communitarian versus cosmopolitan dichotomy as intertwined with perceived national security issues.

Though peace accords were signed in El Salvador in 1992 and in Guatemala in 1996, the root causes for the communist uprisings and of the violence that ensued, primarily stemming from severe poverty, grave class inequality, and a lack of democracy and basic human rights, were never addressed (Mersky 2005). Thirty-five years later land and wealth distribution in the region are among the most unequal in the hemisphere, and according to the UNHCR for Guatemala, El Salvador and Honduras have some of the highest homicide rates of any country in the world that is not officially at war (United Nations Human Rights Organization 2019).

More recent intervention in Central America is also partly to blame for the exodus of migrants fleeing to the United States. For example, in 2009 the Obama administration supported the military coup in Honduras which expelled the democratically elected government of Manuel Zelaya from the country (Mohammed and Alexander 2019). This resulted in a period of rule by the right-wing National Party, restoring the brutal repression of the previous Honduran regimes. President Obama refused to refer to it as a military coup because if he were to do so the United States would be compelled by law to withdraw military funding from the military regime. Honduran president Juan Orlando Hernandez, a close ally of the United States, was reelected in 2017 in an election that was vehemently condemned all throughout the hemisphere except the United States. Honduras is now a country of 9.2 million where over 6 million live in poverty and has been labeled the "murder capital of the world" (Mohammed and Alexander 2019).

The destabilization of El Salvador, Guatemala, and Honduras, known as the Northern Triangle, is one of the leading factors driving the most recent influx of immigrants coming to the United States, and unaccompanied minors that began in 2014 (Appleby et al. 2020). The number of these rose by 25 percent from 2015 to 2017 according to Pew Research Center (Pew Research Center 2018). In 2016, the Office of the United Nations High Commission for Refugees (UNHCR) estimated that at least 53 percent of those fleeing the Northern Triangle qualified as refugees.

The flood of young immigrants from Central America, many trying to reconnect with family members, challenges the structural-level theories premised on the assumption that economic issues are the main pull factor.

Emotions are clearly a driving force in this case, serving as both a push and pull factor for these young migrants who are making an extremely dangerous and long journey with no clear prospects of employment once reaching the United States. Thus, this cycle of immigrants supports the findings of immigration theorists Castles and Miller (2009) and Vertovec and Wessend (2005) who advocate for the inclusion of network theory in deciphering immigration push and pull factors.

Despite the fact that this part of Central America has become deadlier than some of the military conflicts taking place in other parts of the world, today migrants from the Northern Triangle experience denial rates of approximately 80 percent according to the Transactional Records Access Clearinghouse (TRAC) at Syracuse University (Appleby et al. 2016). UNHCR (2018) summarizes the situation this way: "violence and persecution generated by transnational organized crime, gang-related violence, and drug cartels in some parts of Central America are likely to be the primary cause behind the increasing numbers of asylum seekers from Central America seeking international protection in the United States" (United Nation Human Rights Commission 2018).

Akin to the case in Mexico, and as the UNHCR statement makes clear, the destabilization of Central American countries has also left a large vacuum for nonstate actors such as drug cartels, gangs, and other terrorist organizations to fill. The huge extortion rates that gangs demand leave people living in fear throughout both Mexico and Central America. Washington Office on Latin America cites figures showing that: Salvadorans pay an estimated $400 million a year in extortion fees, Hondurans pay around $200 million, and Guatemalans an estimated $61 million (Beltran 2017). In El Salvador, in 2018, 70 percent of businesses were forced to pay extortionists, and those who do not pay are commonly assassinated (Beltran 2017).

U.S. BORDER PATROL, IMMIGRATION POLICY, AND THE ASYLUM PROCESS

The Southwest region of the United States has always been a porous border. Throughout much of the area, beginning in the 1800s, Border Patrol agents were mostly unemployed or underemployed and landless white men from the border region, the "Texas Rangers" and border militias were originally established during the gold rush to protect against perceived threats to white political power (Fry 2019). Being a Ranger as part of a militia gave them an opportunity to use their power against the perceived enemy who they tended to blame for their economic difficulties. The government and employers fed this mindset, and not surprisingly race was at play as well. After the Mexican

American War of 1848, Rangers continued to act on these racial assumptions against Mexicans and indigenous peoples in defense of white and European-based identity and control of the Southwest. The threat of reduced social status, therefore, led to an embracement of racist nativism, as predicted by Jardina (2019).

Mutz (2018) also theorizes that the mindset that the superiority of "natives" must be defended at certain historical junctures when social or economic status is questioned or declining and leads to the default position of nativism which seeks to justify white superiority. Midgley (2017), Van Wolmart and Link (2016), and Herber et al. (2008) also find this dynamic in their work. The fact that most Rangers were recruited from those who were struggling economically also validates McVeigh's (2009) analyses of the KKK in the United States through the application of strain theory.

Militias on the border continue to thrive. The Southern Poverty Law Center (SPLC) identified 216 active militia groups in 2018 (Southern Poverty Law Center 2019). Armed border vigilantes seek and detain migrants on the Southwest border declaring that their goal is to "do the job our government refuses to do" and "protect America" from "tens of millions of invading illegal aliens who are devouring and plundering our nation" (Holthouse 2005). One of the most recent and infamous militias, the Minutemen, was created in 2005 to patrol the Arizona-Mexico border. Members would, through violent means, catch and detain migrants until official Border Patrol agents arrived (Fikes 2018).

In April 2019, another group formed called the United Constitutional Patriots. This group also kidnapped and illegally detained migrants. The leader was arrested after live broadcasting, via Facebook, the detainment of groups of migrants. These groups are a good example of the importance of both framing (and in particular the manifestation of the injustice frame that citizens are being taken advantage of) and collective identity (law-abiding U.S. citizens) in mobilizing and recruiting members to a cause.

In terms of *formal* Border Patrol efforts, over the past two and a half decades the federal government has spent billions of dollars on border control efforts, implementing hundreds of miles of fencing, increasing deportations and detentions at alarming rates, and solidifying punitive sanctions against undocumented workers (Cantu 2018). However, none of these measures have resulted in concrete results and the U.S. government remains perplexed by the magnitude of the problem. In an attempt to address the immigration crisis in a comprehensive way, the U.S. government initiated Immigration Reform Corrections Agreement in 1986.

This reform bill regularized the status of nearly three million undocumented individuals in exchange for increased enforcement along the border and legislated sanctions against employers who knowingly hired undocumented workers (Ngai 2004). Yet, it did not deter future entries into the country as the need for Mexican labor remained. "Prevention through Deterrence" in the 1990s led to the construction of more walls and employment of more agents to patrol border cities (Cornelius 2004). This was an attempt to force migrants to take riskier paths through the dessert, many of whom would die due to the elements, and importantly to the government for them to remain out of the public eye to avoid controversy.

Operation Hold the Line in 1993 also impeded immigration at busy and visible parts of the border with a special focus on El Paso and Juárez to stifle border crossings, hoping that it would deter other immigrants from attempting the journey north, and led to an even further increase in Border Patrol agents (Cantu 2018). Another effect of blocking popular routes is that it made migrants more dependent on coyotes and professional smugglers, thus enhancing cartel-aligned human trafficking networks. Consequently, this resulted in high rates of kidnappings, extortion, and deaths as immigrants were increasingly forced to cross clandestinely, thus becoming easy and vulnerable targets for coyotes (Cantu 2018).

In 1994, President Bill Clinton implemented Operation Gatekeeper in anticipation of the influx of immigrants heading to the United States due to NAFTA, and to try to hinder it. This established a more extensive wall in San Diego County, where most crossings were taking place and further militarized the border and the Immigration and Naturalization Service was put in charge of stemming the tide (Cottam and Marenin 2005).

This eliminated circular immigration which caused many Mexicans to overstay their visas. Additionally, the policy forced migrants to cross through new locations and use new ways to enter the United States. In 2009, Princeton University professor, Douglas Massey, in his testimony before the Senate Judiciary Committee, elaborated on the unintended outcome of Operation Gatekeeper. He stated: "From 1965 to 1985, 85% of undocumented entries from Mexico were offset by departures and the net increase in the undocumented population was small. The build-up of enforcement resources at the border has not decreased the entry of migrants as much as discouraged their return home" (Massey 1999).

Border Patrol once again ratcheted up significantly following the 9/11 terrorist attacks in 2001 (Christi and Bergeron 2011). It became part of the U.S. Customs and Border Protection under the newly created DHS. Another DHS entity, ICE was established to arrest, detain, and process removals away from the border—meaning in local communities. As part and parcel of the war on terror that followed the 9/11 attack, President Bush directed U.S. attorneys to adopt an "enforcement with consequences" strategy in 2005. As a result, attorneys prosecuted more than 50,000 cases of migrant unlawful entry or reentry. The next year President Bush sent 6,000 National Guard troops to the border to enforce Operation Jump Start to assist Border Patrol, mainly by constructing additional fencing (Fry 2019).

Another consequence of these efforts was that immigration-related offenses became the leading type of federal prosecution (Cantu 2018). The DHS started referring more cases to the Justice Department for prosecution than all of the other federal crime-fighting agencies, the U.S. federal government began spending more money on border and immigration enforcement than on all other law enforcement combined, and prosecution for illegal entry or reentry rose from 12,500 in 2002 to over 85,000 in 2013 (Human Rights Watch 2013). By 2015, prosecutions for unlawful entry and reentry accounted for 49 percent of all federal prosecutions and the federal government had spent at least $7 billion to detain unlawful border crossers (Cantu 2018).

Despite the harsh measures, the number of migrants asking the United States for asylum rose nearly 70 percent between 2017 and 2018 according to the DHS—almost 60 percent were people in families with small children (Nixon 2018b). This is very different than previous waves of immigration which tended to consist of young males crossing the border in search of work. According to U.S. Customs and Border Protection, between October 2018 and April 2019 there was a 347 percent increase of apprehensions of family units who crossed the border illegally in comparison to the same time frame between 2017 and 2018 (Friedman 2019).

Therefore, theories that focus mainly on structural forces due to economic and labor issues are insufficient to understand this mass exodus. The reason for the spike in immigration across the U.S.–Mexico border in these instances is clearly due to the harrowing conditions in the countries that migrants are fleeing from, despite the hostility from the receiving country. This is why theories that are more oriented toward agency and cultural and social variables serve as an important complement to macro-level theories.

RETURN OF ETHNO-NATIONALISM
IN THE UNITED STATES

While the United States has a reputation (in part mythical) as a country built on immigration and welcoming those looking for a better life or escaping harm, there is also a rise of an anti-immigration, nativist outlook there. The United States is indeed the home to more immigrants than any other country in the world and historically it has resettled more refugees than any other country, showing global leadership (Rush 2019). It played a major role in responding to the huge refugee crisis following World War II when national boundaries were redrawn which resulted in massive population shifts and accepted over a half a million refugees escaping the horrific conditions in Europe (Kaplan 2018).

The United States also responded to the outpouring of refugees fleeing other dire conflicts including the Vietnam War, the Cuban crisis, and those fleeing the communist uprisings during the Cold War and took in especially large numbers of Koreans, Chinese, and Eastern Europeans (Kaplan 2018). According to the Office of Refugee Resettlement, the United States has resettled more than three million refugees since 1975, thus demonstrating a policy of welcoming refugees and a responsibility to assist those in economic, political, or social turmoil. However, there were also times throughout history when the United States had not been welcoming, at least toward certain groups. For example, in the late nineteenth century the United States began implementing exclusionary policies when it came to immigration and by 1924 Congress had largely adopted a "whites only" immigration system, banning all Asian immigration through the National Origins Act, establishing quotas for the number of immigrants allowed to enter from anywhere other than Northern and Western Europe, and pointedly discriminating against Southern and Eastern Europeans (Garcia 2008). The Act reduced general immigration to less than 15 percent of pre–World War I levels and made "undocumented" immigration common for the first time (Garcia 2008).

Legislation in 1965 that mandated an evenly distributed quota system of 20,000 persons per country and preferences for family members was another key change to the U.S. immigration policy (Ngai 2004). This greatly impacted Latinx immigration as it meant that no country could account for more than 7 percent of the 140,000 employment-based green cards each year which are much more difficult to obtain than visas for permanent residency. The policy led to the longest wait to attain citizenship status in the world and has been particularly troublesome for individuals from countries such as Mexico, China, India, and the Philippines that have historically had the highest levels of migration to the United States (Ngai 2004). The unintended consequence of this quota system was a large increase in unauthorized entries.

Additionally, the notion of "getting in line" was no longer a real option for many as the regulations became incredibly complex and the system dysfunctional for those who would like to conform to the legal system but find it overwhelmingly confusing and the waiting period unrealistic. For example, in 2016 the State Department estimated that 5 million people were waiting abroad, indefinitely, for approval of temporary visas (Bier 2016). There are also lawyer's fees that are required and which many, as they are coming to the United States out of economic despair, cannot afford.

While historically the United States has made some restrictions on immigration, an intense sense of hostility toward immigrants is on the rise. Today, for the first time in the United States there is an absolute decline in the nation's white non-Hispanic population, and there are more children who are minorities than those who are white at every age up to nine years old (Brookings Institute 2018). Thus, the United States will have the first minority white generation born in 2007 and later, thereby challenging the power, status, and privileges that have historically been afforded to whites. These demographic shifts can in part explain the increase in white anxiety and nativist sentiments, though these are not necessarily new.

The United States indeed has a long history of nativism rooted in racism and fear of other cultures and ethnic groups. For instance, President Benjamin Franklin, fearful of German immigrants arriving in large numbers in Pennsylvania in the 1750s, warned that "Few of their children in the country learn English . . . The signs in our streets have inscriptions in both languages . . . Unless the stream of the importation could be turned they will so outnumber us that all the advantages we have will not be able to preserve our language, and even our government will be precarious" (Hightower 2018).

In the past decade, we have seen a reemergence of this fear of the "other." The election of the country's first black president, Barack Obama, played a role in sparking this through the emergence of the Tea Party (whose white nationalist beliefs were key to its mobilization), and gave it a platform for a racist backlash (McAdam 2018). Parker and Barreto (2013:3) summarize, "We believe that people are driven to support the Tea Party from the anxiety they feel as they perceive the America they know, the country they love, slipping away, threatened by the rapidly changing face of what they believe is the 'real' America: a heterosexual, Christian, middle class (mostly) male, white country."

This sense of white anxiety is well documented. For example, in a 2016 poll, 57 percent of white Americans said, "discrimination against whites is as big of a problem today as discrimination against blacks and other minorities" (Gonyea 2017). This is fueling the Great Replacement movement in both the United States and Europe: the existential threat about the changing demographics in which whites will be outnumbered. This has led to several acts of mass shootings and hate crimes that will be covered in some of the following chapters. The next section revisits trends at the international level to explore the growing rejection of liberal democracy which is being replaced by far-right wing populism and Euroskepticism which stems, in part, from white anxiety.

EXTERNALIZATION POLICIES AND GROWING HOSTILITY TOWARD ASYLUM SEEKERS

Liberal political theory, as espoused by Cole (2011), suggests that the rights of people engrained in a sense of moralism and cosmopolitanism are beneficial for both immigrants and the receiving country. This perspective recognizes the strengths of diversity that immigrants bring to society. On the other hand, the communitarianism perspective upholds a restrictive approach to immigration on the basis that only strong nation-states can ensure the stability, security, and prosperity for its citizens, and through the forces of globalization come under siege and challenge states' unique culture, values, and ethnic identity. Part of this ideology is global welfare theory, which many immigration scholars, including Consterdine and Hampshire (2013) and Miller (2005), purport that immigration policy is often affected by public opinion and particularly when citizens begin to feel alienated economically, politically, or socially and thus resist newly arriving immigrants.

One way to decrease immigration is to make it impossible for migrants to reach their destination. The externalization policies of the United States have traditionally targeted migrants from Haiti, Cuba, Mexico, and Central America (and after 9/11 those coming from majority Muslim countries). These include interdiction, visa prescreening before arriving in the United States, detention in transit countries, and providing foreign aid for a third state hosting of refugees during asylum processing (Frelick et al. 2016).

The first broad scope of externalization policies began during the 1990s under the Clinton administration when it initiated the Interdiction of Illegal Aliens Act. This was aimed mainly at the huge influx of Cubans trying to make it to the United States by sea (Hinkley 2016). Since the Cold War had ended Cubans were now labeled as economic refugees, rather than political ones, as the argument about national security no longer held weight (Berg 2015). Most were sent to Guantanamo Bay for processing and deportation.

President Clinton also authorized the indefinite detention of Haitian refugees who were fleeing widespread violence and the reign of terror following the 1991 coup against Jean-Bertrand Aristide. They were sent to Guantanamo Bay naval base where they were allowed to apply for asylum (Frelick 2007). In 1992, however, President Bush signed the Kennebunkport Order which allowed the U.S. Coast Guard to intercept Haitian vessels and send those fleeing the country back to Haiti without processing any asylum claims (Berg 2015).

In 2014, President Obama implemented Operation Coyote and Operation Coyote 2.0 to try to stem the flow of the unaccompanied minors fleeing from the Northern Triangle. As part of the effort, the government sent DHS personnel to Mexico and Northern Triangle countries to try to increase the apprehension of human smugglers (Frelick et al. 2016). Also, in 2014, under pressure from President Obama, Mexico began to employ its Programa Frontera Sur (Southern Border Program) to help curb the tide of unaccompanied minors crossing Mexico seeking asylum in the United States (Silva 2020). Check points were set up along the most frequented transit routes and Mexico worked to deport Central Americans before they could reach the United States. According to Human Rights Watch, after its implementation in 2016 asylum was granted to less than 1 percent of those minors apprehended (Frelick et al. 2016).

In addition to sending DHS agents to the border, the U.S. Customs and Border Patrol (CBP) launched a Dangers Awareness Campaign (Semple 2018b). This was a public service announcement throughout major cities in the United States and Central America to raise awareness about the dangers of the journey and informing those attempting to cross that they would not be granted automatic asylum. It also warned about the exploitation of coyotes and cartels in their human trafficking efforts, in addition to those who succumb to the brutal terrain. The main target of this campaign was families of unaccompanied minors, warning them about some of the rumors coyotes may be spreading about certain benefits refugees would be receiving in the United States upon arrival. The messages, however, were largely ignored due to the desperate conditions in the countries from which migrants were fleeing (Semple 2018).

IMMIGRATION POLICY UNDER THE TRUMP ADMINISTRATION

The anti-immigration measures have become increasingly draconian following the election of President Trump in 2016. He ran on a campaign that promised a Muslim ban and resisted the idea of granting asylum to Syrians, stating that they would pose a security risk (Jackson 2017). Once in office he put into place the executive order, "Protecting the Nation from Terrorist Entry Into the United States," that is, the Muslim ban on the basis of ensuring national security. However, between 1975 and 2015 no terrorist acts had been undertaken in the United States by foreign-born extremists from the countries on the list (Iran, Libya, Somalia, Syria, and Yemen). Midgley (2017), Garner (2014), and Selod (2014) speak to this connection between ethno-nationalism (as proposed by these policies) and religious and political divides, and in particular the Islamophobia trend over the past several years.

The Trump administration also terminated the Central American Minors Program that allowed refugee children from Northern Triangle countries to enter the country to reunite with their parents who are in the country legally, as well as the temporary protected status for 200,000 El Salvadorans, 57,000 Hondurans, 50,000 Haitians, and smaller numbers of Nicaraguans, Sudanese, and Nepalese (Kerwin 2018). In 2017, President Trump also ordered a six-month phase out of President Obama's DACA (also known as the DREAMers) executive order that he called unconstitutional (Dinan 2018).

Federal judges in New York, California, and Washington, however, by means of a nationwide injunction ordered that the main parts of the program remain as the case made its way through the courts, and it was revised by the Supreme Court in 2020. In August 2019, Judge Bates from the district of Columbia called the rationale for its termination "arbitrary and capricious" (Higgins 2020). Additionally, in November 2018 the Ninth Circuit court of appeals in San Francisco ruled against the administration and upheld the injunction against Trump's attempt to revoke deportation protections of the 700,000 DREAMers. It also questioned the "cruelty and wastefulness of deporting productive young people to countries with which they have no ties" (Dickerson 2020). The courts' rulings exemplify the importance of taking into account the morality and ethics of migrants' cases and their contribution to society which is a central argument of liberal political theory, critical race theory, and the cosmopolitan approach to immigration. In the summer of 2020, the Supreme Court ruled against the end of the program which was a huge blow to the Trump administration.

The Trump administration has also greenlighted ICE to ratchet up its activities in local communities. During 2018, approximately 27,540 citizens were questioned by ICE—five times as many than the last year of the Obama presidency (Earnshaw and Carlson 2018). The administration's directives as to how ICE should operate and who should be targeted pivoted significantly from the previous administration under President Obama. Obama said "felons not families, criminals not children, gang members, not a mom who is working hard to provide for her kids" should be the select target of ICE activities. Trump, on the other hand, encouraged ICE to "take off the gloves," and named Jeff Sessions (later forced to resign by the president)—one of the most anti-immigration lawmakers in Congress—as the head of the Justice Department (Earnshaw and Carlson 2018).

Additionally, under the Trump administration several politicians, once on the fringe when it came to immigration policy, are now driving mainstream dialogue. Sessions, for example, argued that the United States should reinstate the 1924 law which, "slowed down immigration significantly . . . and created really the solid middle class of America, with assimilated immigrants, and it was good for America" (Earnshaw and Carlson 2018). In November 2019, the SPLC published information depicting how over 900 emails shared by Stephen Miller, Trump's senior immigration adviser and who served as an aid between 2015 and 2016 for Sessions, demonstrated his inclinations of white nationalism through his collaboration with the right-wing media outlet, Breitbart news (Goldberg 2019).

During his tenure as an aid to Trump, Miller advocated for the Muslim ban, the separation of families, and fought to drastically cut refugee admissions. He also advocated the execution of "dramatic, highly visible mass arrests that they argued would help deter the soaring influx of families" (Sacchetti 2017). ICE acting director, Thomas Homan told House Appropriations Committee's Homeland Security in 2017 "If you're in this country illegally . . . you should be uncomfortable . . . You should look over your shoulder, and you need to be worried" (Sacchetti 2017).

The quotes by these high-ranking officials demonstrate Garner's (2012) assessment of what constitutes the perception of white privilege, superiority, and fear of immigrants' ability or willingness to assimilate to the unspoken "White/Anglo" code to be considered an American. This rhetoric is also what Bridges (2019) and Huber et al. (2008) theorize as important to protecting white superiority—racism veiled as patriotism and pride in heritage, culture, and certain norms and behaviors.

In July 2018, Attorney General Sessions reversed President Obama's policy that extended protection to some victims of domestic abuse and criminal violence who were seeking asylum. He explained, "Asylum was never meant to alleviate all problems—even serious problems—that people face every day all over the world" (Mcardle 2018). Homeland Security adviser Kristen Nielsen (who resigned in April 2019), in a statement to Congress in May 2018 had declared, "Asylum is for people fleeing persecution, not those searching for a better job, yet our broken system, with it debilitating court rulings, a crushing backlog and gaping loopholes, allows illegal migrants to get into our country anyway, and for whatever reason they want" (Mcardle 2018).

Secretary of state, Mike Pompeo on the basis of national security concerns announced a new cap of 30,000 immigrants allowed to enter the United States in 2019—the lowest yearly total since the refugee program began in 1975 (Johnson 2018b). Critical of this policy, and cognizant of the role the United States has fueling the immigration crisis, the director of Win Without War, Stephen Miles declared, "At a time when the world is facing the largest displacement crisis in recorded history, it is unconscionable that the Trump administration would further dismantle the US Refugee Admissions Program by setting a cap of 30,000 refugee admissions for fiscal year 2019—the lowest resettlement cap in the program's history . . . . the US has a direct moral responsibility to open its doors, not slam them shut, given that our own nation is an active combatant in many of the very conflicts and humanitarian crisis driving the global refugee crisis" (Davis 2019). In 2019, the White House declared that it would accept only 18,000 refugees in 2019, down from 30,000 preciously assured and Obama's 110,000 in 2016 (Goldberg 2019).

Additionally, while the Trump administration has restricted the number of refugees from Africa, Asia, and the Middle East (which Trump referred to as "shithole countries") it did not reduce these from European countries (O'Keef and Gearan 2018). This rejection of immigrants from certain countries, and use of national security concerns as the basis for capping immigration overall, is indicative of the perspective of global welfare theory and the communitarianism perspective in that refugees and asylum seekers are only welcome if they add value to the well-being of the country. This supports the theories of Amstutz (2015) and is also suggestive of what Mutz (2018) refers to as the justification and reward for white superiority and is embedded in the Anglo-Saxon code that Garner (2009) points to within his framework of critical race theory.

THE CARAVANS FROM CENTRAL AMERICA AND ADDITIONAL EXTERNALIZED METHODS

Because of the border dynamics over the past few decades, which have militarized the border and cut off the logistical roots through externalization policies and which force migrants to make their journey across more dangerous and remote terrain, most migrants rely on coyotes who charge exorbitant fees. According to the DHS, ten years ago immigrants coming from Central America and Mexico paid between $1,000 and $3,000; they now pay up to $12,000 for the same journey (Lee 2019). In fact, the smuggling business is so lucrative that in 2019 eighteen marines, those assigned to protect the border and uphold U.S. immigration policy, were charged with smuggling undocumented immigrants into the United States (McGlughlin 2019).

Thus, to avoid the high costs and for safety reasons, many have joined the yearly, and now semimonthly caravans to request asylum either in Mexico or in the United States. These are organized by a number of nongovernmental organizations (NGOs), the main one being Pueblo Sin Fronteras, which is a transnational advocacy group (Accedo 2018). It provides migrants with temporary travel documents that protect them from deportation. When the caravan from Honduras approached the U.S. border in 2018 with nearly 6,000 travelers, President Trump chastised the Mexican government for not doing enough to thwart the migrants' efforts before reaching the U.S. border and applied more extensive externalization policies. In April 2018, he ordered the deployment of the National Guard to the Southwest border in an attempt to turn the caravans back (Accedo 2018).

In September 2018, the U.S. government also started to offer foreign assistance funds to assist Mexico in paying for plane and bus fare to deport the thousands of migrants who arrived in Mexico (Harris and Ahmed 2018). Kristen Nielsen, Secretary of Homeland Security, stated that anyone who intended to apply for asylum in the United States should instead seek protection in Mexico and the Trump administration sought to disqualify migrants who did not first seek asylum in Mexico first (a "safe third country agreement") before entering the United States (Leurt and Yates 2018).

This "Remain in Mexico" policy was put into place in December 2018, first in San Diego, CA, at the San Ysidro port of entry and then in El Paso, Texas. It was implemented, according to the Trump administration, as a deterrent to other immigrants who hope to make it to the United States (Kanno-Youngs and Averbuch 2019). Formally referred to as "Migration Protection Protocols," this has had drastic consequences for asylum seekers. For example, as was covered by the mainstream press and subsequently went viral, Oscar Ramirez, twenty-five years old, died with his two-year old daughter tucked under the back of his shirt while crossing the Rio Grande (Ahmed et al. 2019). He had arrived in the border city of Matamoros, MX, only to find that the international bridge was closed indefinitely. The image of his and his daughter's drowned bodies, face down on the shore of the river sparked outrage over the increasingly aggressive directives to stymie the efforts of migrants trying to cross the border through legal points of entry.

Though Attorney General Jeff Sessions called for those members of the caravan seeking asylum to follow the law and go to official ports of entry to request assistance, when they did so they were blocked by Border Patrol agents claiming that they were unable to process them, and many were left stranded for weeks on international bridges trying to cross the border (Villegas and Uyhas 2018). The sinister hopes of those making policy are that if migrants are stuck in Mexico with slim chances for asylum, they will return home.

The Mexican government did grant migrants one-year humanitarian visas so that they could reside and work in Mexico while they waited for their court hearing in the United States (Ahmed et al. 2019). However, increasing pressure on the Mexican government Trump threatened to use emergency powers by imposing tariffs of up to 25 percent on all goods imported from Mexico if President Obrador did not stop the flow of Central American migrants crossing Mexico to reach the United States. The day before Trump's proclamation, 1,036 migrants surrendered to Border Patrol—the largest group ever apprehended at the border (Ahmed et al. 2019).

As of February 2020, as a result of the Remain in Mexico policy, according to Dylan Corbett who is the executive director of the Hope Border Institute in El Paso, TX, "of the 7,000 asylum cases that have been completed in the El Paso sector since the policy was implemented, only 15 individuals received asylum—a denial rate of more than 99%" (Long-Garcia 2020). According to Syracuse University tracking over that same time period in 2019 the average denial rate was 50 percent in New York, Los Angles, San Francisco, Houston, and Miami, which together assessed more than 85,000 cases (TRAC 2019).

Highlighting the pressure on Mexico and blaming the Democrats for failing to protect the border, Trump declared, "I want to thank Mexico. Twenty-seven thousand soldiers they have. But think of how bad that is—think of it—where we use Mexico because the Democrats won't fix our broken immigration system" (Ramos 2019). In October 2019, the Mexican Ministry of Foreign Affairs announced a 56 percent decline in number of Central American immigrants crossing Mexico between May and August due in large part to the deployment of the National Guard (Ramos 2019).

In late July 2019, attempting to put pressure on the Guatemalan government to thwart caravans organizing in or going through Guatemala, Trump threatened to tax money that migrants sent home to relatives in Guatemala and on Twitter he threatened other Central American countries as well tweeting, "We have today informed the countries of Honduras, Guatemala, and El Salvador that if they allow their citizens, or others, to journey through their borders and up to the United States, with the intention of entering our country illegally, all payments made to them will STOP (END)!" (Semple 2018). In October 2018, President Trump stated that he would suspend aid to the Honduran government if it did not stop migrants crossing its border. In late September, Honduras signed an agreement requiring migrants to apply for and be denied protections in Honduras before petitioning for U.S. asylum and that same year the DHS signed a two-year agreement with Guatemala to assign eighty agents to monitor checkpoints on its northern border (Semple and Villegas 2019).

In July 2019, Guatemala signed another agreement mandating that asylum seekers ask for asylum in their country before moving forward north (Semple and Villegas 2019). Ironically, a U.S. State Department alert made dangers of Guatemala clear in a warning for U.S. travelers declaring on its website: "Violent crime, such as armed robbery and murder, is common. Gang activity, such as extortion, violent street crime, and narcotics trafficking is widespread. Local Police may lack the resources to respond effectively to serious criminal acts" and the Migration Policy Institute called the Guatemalan asylum system "embryonic" (Adams 2019).

The passage of many of these recent laws, and threats to the Mexican and Central American governments, is disturbing in that the U.S. asylum laws guarantee that immigrants are allowed to seek asylum regardless of how they arrive at the border. Therefore, these externalization policies contradict the history of both U.S. and international law. In June 2019, a union that represents DHS employees stated in a court filing that the Remain in Mexico policy in fact violates international law and "abandons our tradition of providing a safe haven to the persecuted" and "undermines the purpose of asylum" (Zaveri 2018).

Other "prevention through deterrence" methods have been more extreme and include violence. In private conservations with aids, Trump suggested fortifying a border wall with a water-filled moat, stocked with snakes or alligators and an electrified wall with spikes on top, and recommended that aids seek a cost estimate for the project (Shear 2018). He also publicly mused about the possibility of U.S. soldiers shooting migrants if they threw rocks, and only rescinded this idea when aids informed him that it would be illegal to do so (Shear 2019).

Another agenda the Trump administration has pushed is expedited removal, under which immigration agents would solely make decisions pertaining to asylum cases and the onus is on individuals suspected of being in the country illegally to prove otherwise (American Immigration Council 2020). He proclaimed on Twitter that he wanted the power to immediately reject people seeking asylum at the border before they could plead their cases in front of an immigration judge stating, "We cannot allow all of these people to invade our country. When somebody comes in, we must immediately, with no Judges or Court Cases, bring them back from where they came," thus calling for a denial of due process (Kugle 2018). Because expedited removal through fast-track deportations allows ICE to quickly deport someone without going through an immigration judge, asylum seekers have little or no time to consult with a lawyer and collect documents.

For 15 years, expedited removal was approved only if undocumented individuals were discovered within 100 miles of the Canadian or Southwest border and if they had been in the country for less than two weeks (Kanno-Youngs and Dickerson 2019). In late July 2019, however, the Trump administration changed this policy drastically, declaring that it would speed up deportations if individuals could not prove that they were in the United States more than two years. Additionally, in fiscal year 2018, migrants who were deported by DHS under the expedited process were held an average of eleven days in detention in comparison to fifty-one days in 2019 (Kanno-Youngs and Dickerson 2019).

ZERO-TOLERANCE POLICY

In April 2018, the Trump administration implemented its zero-tolerance policy. Sessions described the plan of action this way: "If you cross the Southwest border unlawfully, then we will prosecute you. It's that simple . . . People are not going to caravan or otherwise stampede our border. If you are smuggling a child then we will prosecute you, and that child will be separated from you as required by law. If you don't like that, then don't smuggle children over the border" (Jordan 2020). Like previous measures, this was devised to punish those seeking asylum and deter other potential immigrants. Trump also ordered an end to the "catch and release" policy, under which immigrants who had not committed any crimes were released to the community while awaiting hearings in immigration court rather than being detained (Beech 2018).

TRAC, however, showed that "as of the end of May 2019 one or more removal hearings had already been held for nearly 47,000 new arriving families seeking refuge in this country. Of these, almost six out of every seven families released from custody had shown up for their initial court hearing .... multiple hearings are usually required before a case is decided. For those who are represented, more than 99 percent had appeared at every hearing held" (TRAC 2019).

As a result of the zero-tolerance mandate, families who crossed the border were separated from their children because minors cannot be held in criminal custody. They were therefore located to shelters while their parents or other adult relatives were detained waiting for their asylum case to be heard by a judge (Jordan and Dickerson 2019). The callousness of the administration when referring to the policy was notable. Former White House chief of staff, John Kelly stated that family separation is a "tough deterrent" and that "the children will be taken care of—put in foster care or whatever" (Mark 2018). When an audio recording was publicly released of children crying and screaming as they were being separated from their parents Sessions' response was that "we cannot and will not encourage people to bring children by giving them blanket immunity from our laws" (Shear and Gibbons-Neff 2018).

Many critics of the policy felt that the obsession with the caravan was a ploy used by Trump and other Republican candidates prior to the 2018 midterm elections to ignite fear among the citizenry (Olmstead 2018). They also note that illegal border crossings have been declining for nearly two decades, and in the 2017 fiscal year border crossing apprehensions were at their lowest point since 1971. Amid the public outrage and massive demonstrations and protests against the zero-tolerance policy and the resulting separation of family members, President Trump signed an executive order on June 20, 2018, to end it, though he kept parts of it by indefinitely detaining families as a unit in temporary detention centers while parents proceeded through immigration courts (Valverde 2018).

The order also still mandated that all adults crossing illegally be prosecuted. In September 2018, the administration announced a new regulation that would eliminate the 1997 *Flores v. Reno* settlement which mandated that children held in detention must be released to a licensed care program within twenty days with living conditions appropriate for minors and assurance of provisions for education (Valverde 2018).

In September 2019, a federal judge refused proposed regulations that would allow the U.S. government to detain families for indefinite periods of time, upholding the Flores agreement that concluded the government is required to release children as quickly as possible (Jordan 2020). Therefore, thousands of families were released to await trial in random shelters and overcrowded detention centers run by nonprofits, private prisons, and security and defense companies while their children were sent to other facilities (Cantu 2018). As of early January 2019, approximately 12,400 migrant children were being held in about 100 permanent sites and temporary facilities as their parents were going through immigration proceedings (Barker and Kulish 2019).

The separation of families proved to be a logistical and political nightmare for those who proposed it and were tasked with implementing it (Dinan 2018). Sometimes parents were not informed what was happening to them and/or their children. The Inspector General for DHHS (Department of Health and Human Services) found the government did not create a centralized database to track children or any kind of procedures that could match the children with their parents. During a July 2018 court filing, the Trump administration admitted that more than 463 parents were separated and deported while the children remained in U.S. custody facilities (Miroff 2018).

The attempt to reunify children with their parents, as dictated by the District Court of Southern California in July 2018 was a disaster. The DHHS issued a report admitting that the agency failed to keep records of the locations of parents and children after they were separated (Dickerson 2018). In January it released another report which disclosed that thousands more children had been separated from their parents for months before the policy was publicly announced. At a Senate Judiciary Committee hearing in late July, officials said they were given few instructions and had no plans for reuniting the families when the policy was announced (Nixon 2018a).

Representatives from the DHS and lawyers who were let into the children facilities for inspection documented that infants and toddlers were often cared for by children as young as eight years old (Romero 2019). The DHS inspector also reported that facility lights were kept on 24 hours a day and that in some cases migrants had to stand as there was no room to sleep on the floor; those lucky enough to find space were sleeping on concrete. They submitted eighty declarations from doctors and lawyers who were also allowed to inspect the facilities attested that they witnessed "children wearing clothing stained with vomit or breast milk," and "babies are being kept in these freezing cold conditions, and some of them have only a diaper and a T-shirt to wear" (Romero 2019).

In June 2019, an attorney from the ninth circuit court decreed that the government was responsible to provide "safe and sanitary conditions," including soap, toothbrushes, and suitable sleeping arrangements (Kanno-Youngs and

Dickerson 2019). One judge asked the defendant who was trying to justify the conditions, "Are you arguing seriously that you had not read the agreement as requiring you do something other than what I described: Cold all night long. Lights on all night long. Sleeping on the concrete floor and you get an aluminum blanket?" (Blow 2019). The Office of the United Nations High Commissioner for Human Rights concluded that the Trump administration was guilty of "a serious violation of the rights of the child" (Kanno-Youngs and Dickerson 2019).

Another impact of the legislation is that Trump's agenda has resulted in the highest level of detained immigrants in history (Mervosh 2019). Immigration courts under Trump have approved asylum cases at the lowest rate in nearly two decades, and according to the Department of Justice, part of the reason is that the system became overwhelmed due to the zero-tolerance measure. The website TRAC Immigration highlighted that the backlog of pending asylum cases grew from 262,799 in 2010 to 908,522 in 2019 (Jordan 2019). Both the policy changes and huge caravans have resulted in a major backlog at the border. Also, during the Trump administration parole rates for those waiting for their case to be heard went from 90 to less than 1 percent (Jordan 2020). The number of detained migrant children hit its highest level that same year due to the increasing number of border crossings policies that hinder them from being released to family members (Dickerson et al. 2018).

Metering is another act of legislation that has fueled the bottleneck in immigration courts and keeps asylum seekers stuck in border cities on both the U.S. and Mexico side. This policy limits the number of people who can apply for asylum in a single day (Dickerson et al. 2018). A new policy of fingerprinting all household members and sharing that information with ICE has caused many relatives to avoid trying to sponsor a relative because of the mixed-status homes they live in. In 2018, ICE agents arrested at least forty-one unauthorized immigrants who had come forward to take custody of unaccompanied children (Dickerson 2018b). With the humanitarian crisis on the U.S.-Mexico border growing, Trump moved several hundred border agents from their positions at ports of entry on the border to help assist processing migrants seeking asylum (Semple and Villegas 2019). This caused further delays at the legitimate border crossings which caused yet another humanitarian crisis.

In response to the bottleneck on the border and in asylum courts, in late September 2019 the Immigration Judges' Union filed two complaints against the Justice Department: the cases judges must review per year are far beyond reasonable and frustration over the lack of judges to use their discretion in asylum cases. Summarized by the union president, Ashley Tabaddor stated: "The current state of affairs is that the judges have been completely deprived in their practice to exercise independent decision-making authorities" (Kanno-Young and Averburich 2019).

Following zero tolerance and the separation of families in October 2019 came the "public charge" policy (U.S. Citizenship and Immigration Services 2019). Judges in four states issued injunctions which barred the Trump administration's attempt to withhold green cards and social services such as Medicaid from those who use public benefits because they do not have health insurance or may seek to access them in the future (Jordan 2019). Judge George Daniels went so far as to say, "the rule is simply a new agency policy of exclusion in search of justification. It is repugnant to the American Dream of the opportunity for prosperity and success through hard work and upward mobility" (Jordan 2019).

This new policy is yet another example of strain theory regarding competition for economic resources proposed by Judis (2018) and McVeigh (2009). It also highlights Garner's (2014) conceptualization of the "victimization of whiteness" and theories that contend one way to maintain nativism and racism is through institutions and deciding who belongs in the country which are significant variables according to Higham (1999) and Huber et al. (2008).

CONCLUSION

The narrative of the migrant is complex and misunderstood. People are not merely crossing the border for a better life per se, but are escaping dire economic, social, and violent conditions created in part by international policies on both sides of the border. Some policies have been imposed on Mexico as dictated by U.S. foreign policy. Others have been implemented with the support of the Mexican government. U.S. foreign policy initiatives, including Manifest Destiny, the Bracero program, BIP, the maquila industry, Operations Wetback and Gatekeeper, and the War on Drugs, make it difficult for immigrants to survive in a globalized world in which they do not have any significant choice or voice. Thus, this chapter calls on us to critically examine the structural economic and political policies that are in place. While the media and political pundits typically paint a different picture, the fact is that migrants are merely a symptom of these structural conditions that lead to a lack of economic security and personal safety. Thus, the *conditions*, not the people, are the "problem."

Chapter 3

Anti-immigrant Sentiments and the Rise of Euroskepticism

The number of migrants seeking asylum in Europe has increased almost 4,000 percent over the past ten years and the rate of arrivals continues to grow; the Syrian war alone had brought over three million refugees to Europe by late 2014 (Bauman et al. 2014). One repercussion is that nearly 7,800 migrants applied for asylum in 2018 as compared to 4,835 in 2017 (Amaral 2018). Attitudes among citizens toward immigrants have waxed and waned over time. While overall immigrants were welcomed following World War II, by 2018, according to the Pew Global Attitudes Survey, citizens in many EU countries currently feel that the influx of refugees will "increase terrorism and take jobs and social benefits away from residents" (Amaral et al. 2018).

This is accompanied by a rise of populist leaders who are suspect of the EU, migrants, and Islam and run on campaigns that promise a new era of white nationalism. Leaders have also blamed the increasing rates of economic inequality, which has steadily been expanding across Europe, on immigrants and globalism, and prey on white working-class men who are struggling economically and feel culturally alienated (Cohen 2019). For some countries this is an imagined threat rather than actual migration or presence of immigrants due to misinformation campaigns and fear tactics as far-right parties and coalitions manipulate fears that scapegoat immigrants (Strickland 2018a).

Like the United States, the EU has been using externalized policies to stem the tide of immigrants by paying some countries to keep asylum seekers away from Europe (Stevis-Gridneff 2019). For example, Brussels funds the Libyan Coast Guard to intercept migrant boats before they reach international waters (Michael et al. 2019). Spain pays Morocco (Eljechtimi 2018). Other countries, including Italy and France, have curtailed or outright abolished search-and-rescue missions, restricted aid groups, and closed ports to emergency rescue vessels (Boffey and Tondo 2018). Italy also enlists Libyan militias to stifle migration across the Mediterranean, and Greece has built borders with Turkey, Spain with Morocco, and Hungary with Serbia (Michael et al. 2019).

This chapter begins with an overview of the growing Euroskepticism throughout much of the EU. Some of the reasons for this growing trend are hostility toward immigrants and white anxiety. Others are more structural in nature as citizens increasingly feel that liberal democracy and globalism have failed them on economic, political, and social grounds. I begin the chapter by addressing the rise and decline of liberal democracy in general. I also illustrate how immigration is being expressed in individual European countries, and how immigration policies, and mishandling of the immigration crisis by the European Commission, have served as a catalyst for nativist and racist sentiments combined with an ideology of ethno-nationalism that have resurfaced throughout the continent, accompanied by a return toward autocratic leadership.

THE RISE AND DECLINE OF LIBERAL DEMOCRACY IN EUROPE

Europe has taken a surprising turn toward far-right nationalism. Leaders of this movement have gained power in Hungary and Poland and are part of coalition governments in Austria and Italy, and have seats in parliaments in Germany, the Netherlands, Spain, and France (Berman 2019). Much of this is a result of the growing Islamophobia and white anxiety. In Spain, for example, the leader of the Vox Party has warned of an "Islamist invasion" (Gathmann 2019) and in France the National Front Party proclaims that the French will be outnumbered by Muslim immigrants and the country will be dictated by Shariah law (Erlanger 2018b).

This is an extraordinary turn from the post–World War II era. In the wake of the World War II, European leaders sought an alternative to protectionist and nationalist policies to secure peace and economic prosperity in the continent. They agreed to intercontinental treaties that would integrate the region through a system of cogovernance that led to the creation of the EU (Friedman 2018). Consisting of twenty-eight countries it became the largest economy in the world, shared a common currency (the euro), and enjoyed the highest social benefits anywhere (Goodman 2018). For decades social democracy, globalization, and liberalism flourished in the region. However, as it became noticeable that the benefits of the EU consolidation were not equally shared among and within countries, and the surge of immigrants diminished economic resources, many began to embrace ethno-nationalism in opposition to globalism and liberal democracy (Berbeloglu 2018).

One main driving force for these responses was the austerity measures imposed by the EU leadership in response to the 2008 economic crises. These policies imposed by the "troika"—the European Commission (created to enhance efficiency within the bloc), the International Monetary Fund, and the European Central Bank played a major role in creating the distrust that spread throughout the continent (Scharpf 2010). The drastic measures devastated the peripheral countries and North European countries resented the bailout of their Southern neighbors (Ellion and Atkinson 2016).

Across the bloc, southern countries such as Greece, Spain, Portugal, and Italy traditionally were the most pro-European integration (Lubbers and Scheepers 2010). Now, however, most resent the EU for austerity imposed on them and what they perceive as a lack of democratic legitimacy (Torreblanca and Leonard 2013). Habermas (2013) summarizes the anti-immigrant, anti-establishment sentiment stemming from the economic crisis as follows: "What unites European citizens today is the Eurosceptic mindset that has become more pronounced in all of the member countries during the crisis, albeit in each country for different and polarizing reasons" (Habermas 2018). However, at the crux of the tensions, at the macro-level is the austerity measures and the economic hardship it has caused especially for those in the working and lower classes.

The growing Euroskepticism, therefore, can in part be explained by strain theory that Van Dyke and Soule (2002) and McVeigh (2009) use to interpret growing antigovernment and anti-institution sentiments in the United States. Other theories that recognize the growth of economic populism, as applied by Joseph Stiglitz (2018) and Judis (2018) are also appropriate in terms of the reaction of limited resources, given the sudden and massive increase of immigrants in a short period of time.

In sum, most ordinary European citizens feel that they are not being represented by their elected officials. Hobolt and Tilly (2014: 14) verify, "When people hold the EU responsible for poor performance, but cannot hold it accountable for that performance, they become less trusting of its institutions as a whole." Thus, the German Bundesbank is another central point of contention and distrust for many Europeans who feel like the institutions view their concerns with condensation. For example, in 2011 when the prime minster of Greece suggested citizens should be allowed to have a referendum to determine if they would be willing to accept the austerity measures decreed by the bankers in Brussels, most elites in the media and intellectual arenas advised them to follow the orders prescribed by the "experts" (Chomsky 2015).

Resentment against Brussels continued to grow over the next few years as representatives on both the left and right discredited it or came to see it as corrupt. This led to a vacuum that autocratic leaders could exploit (Hobolt and Tilly 2016). Chomsky (2017) argues that the rise of right-wing parties in Europe is largely a result of the willingness of the centrist parties to tolerate economic and social policies that have been decimating many middle- and working-class citizens. Trade deals and international alliances that hurt working-class people and increased rates of immigration led to competition for traditionally white jobs, schools, neighborhoods, and political power which fueled the resentment (Scheers et al. 2002). This effect is theorized by Hutter (2014), Dietrick (2014), and Mutz (2018).

These dynamics also embody the predictions of certain theories of immigration and the conditions under which ethno-nationalism emerges and thrives. The economic crisis has resulted, at least in part to a growing sense of white anxiety, exclusion, and loss of cultural and national identity—what Garner (2014, 2009) refers to as the "victimization of whiteness." They also highlight the importance of many of the contentions of Huber et al. (2008) and Rumbaut and Portes (2006) that outline how spikes in the fear of "other" occur during economic and other types of crisis, and especially when there is an influx of large numbers of immigrants in a short period of time. These forces underlie the communitarian perspective, as outlined by Condenstine and Hampshire (2013) and Cole (2011) toward immigration across much of the EU.

IMMIGRATION AS A CATALYST
TO EUROSKEPTICISM

Europe's response to the influx of refugees following Arab Spring exposed its vulnerabilities and particularly so when large numbers of Libyans migrated to Italy and then more from Syria to Greece (Kinglsely 2018a). When thousands of migrants arrived seeking asylum in Europe through the Greek islands there was no way to efficiently respond. Countries on the perimeter complained that due to the proximity of travel routes they were condemned to take on a disproportionate amount of the burden (Brack and Costa 2019).

This crisis challenged the Schengen zone that was created in 1985. This area is comprised of twenty-six European nations with the purpose of facilitating global integration and trade across Europe (Cunha et al. 2015). One of the oversights is that the agreement established internal borders but did not include a common external border. Thus, borderless internal travel without safeguards against an external border caused problems for much of the area since once inside, there is little to deter refugees from traveling to their preferred destination. Article 80 of the Treaty on the Functioning of the European Union maintains that sovereign states are required to adhere to their obligations, which include migration and asylum rights (European Think Tank 2011). Under the law, the EU country where immigrants first arrive is responsible for registering them and determining whether they are refugees. It also stipulates that other countries could return any migrants who crossed into them from the country of first arrival (Cunha et al. 2015). However, during the immigration influx following Arab Spring and other crises, most countries did not register immigrants and allowed them to cross borders, and they could not be returned if they were not tracked.

In 2015, prime minister of Germany, Angela Merkel warned that if European countries did not fairly share the burden, then opportunistic leaders could exploit the issue to dismantle Europe's freedom of internal movement (Harding 2015). Germany, Austria, and Sweden initially took on more than their share, while others agreed to admit much fewer than required—most notably the Czech Republic and Hungary (Grant and Domokos 2011). In order to address this, the European Commission proposed a quota system to distribute immigrants around Europe according to a common system based on national population, gross domestic product, past asylum loads, and assimilative capacity. However, this was rejected by many Member States which created temporary borders to impede immigrants' entry (Cunha et al. 2015).

Once public opinion turned from welcoming refugees and asylum seekers to resentment toward immigrants, Merkel pressured the European Commission to scrap the Dublin Agreement (Eddy 2018a). The Dublin Agreement demarcated which EU Member State would be responsible for the asylum application process and typically the responsible Member was the state through which the refugee first entered in the EU (Grant and Domokos 2011). In 2015, eight nations within the Schengen area (Austria, Denmark, Hungary, Belgium, Germany, Norway, Slovenia, and Sweden) tightened their border regulations. Since 2015 European leaders have cut unauthorized migration to Europe by 90 percent (Specia 2018a).

A report conducted by the RAND Corporation summarizes the situation this way: "The Schengen Member State notifications seeking to justify the reintroduction of internal border controls point to a political climate in which there is a loss of trust in the ability of (other) Member States to effectively guard the external borders, process asylum applications and cooperate together in the fight against terrorism and other serious crimes. Trust among the public in the EU also seems to have been undermined by the failure of the Union to effectively address the deficiencies exposed by the refugee crisis" (Paoili 2016).

THE EU'S REACTION TO THE IMMIGRATION CRISIS

Italy

Though Italy was one of the founding members of the EU and was its fourth-largest economy until its recent economic collapse, the leaders and its citizens have joined the growing number of Euroskeptic, nationalistic countries (Edwards 2019). In doing so, it abandoned the traditional left of center political position it has maintained for decades. Much of this can be explained by anti-immigrant positions that have opened a space for alternative parties and populist demagogues.

The Northern League (a regional separatist party that is anti-immigration, nationalist, xenophobic, and has an "Italian first" agenda) and the Five Star Movement (which ran on an antiestablishment platform and garnered the most seats) were both highly successful in the March 2018 elections. The two parties had consolidated power and agreed to work toward a common strategy which includes renegotiating their membership in the EU, abandoning the euro, deporting undocumented immigrants, and ending the sanctions against Russia (Horowitz 2018a).

Italy was in fact the first country to vote against the EU as a governing bloc (Erlanger 2018a). There are a few reasons for the shift toward Euroskeptic populism in Italy. To take advantage of the anti-immigrant reaction that was simmering, during the 2014 election Interior Minister Matteo Salvini ran on a platform of expelling all undocumented immigrants for economic reasons. He accused undocumented migrants of taking jobs from young Italians and advocated extreme measures including "a mass cleansing, street by street, neighborhood by neighborhood" and argued on Twitter that "unchecked immigration brings chaos, anger and drug dealing, thefts, rapes and violence" (Embury-Dennis 2018). On Facebook he posted an image of older Italians searching for food through garbage bins with African immigrants criticizing Italian rice. He has also encouraged Italian women to have more babies as part of his "Italy First" stance (Horowitz 2018a).

This is a clear example of the Great Replacement theory being activated by a populist leader accompanied by a communitarian attitude toward foreigners. The underlying message is that a strongman in power will restore law and order and keep Italian citizens safe from outsiders. The "us versus them" mentality is amplified through Salvini's messaging and framing of the issues, an important aspect of social movement theory as espoused by Snow et al. (1986) and Ryan and Gamson (2006). The "outsider" versus "insider" also solidifies a sense of collective identity which Melulcci (1996) and Benford (1993) agree are important to motivate citizens to action and influence public opinion. The urgency that Salvini is inferring, and the undertones of morality, strengthens both the framing and sense of collective identity which Tarrow and Tilly (2006) also point to as key variables mobilizing citizens to action. It further exemplifies racist nativism as discussed by April Schueths (2014) and the perceived drain on economic resources that Stiglitz (2018) and Jarret (1999) emphasize.

Though immigration is a major factor, there are other variables that also need to be considered. Historically, political corruption and scandal have been a constant concern and there is clearly a loss of legitimacy regarding the government and the previous parties—only 15 percent of citizens say that they trust the government and 3 percent support the traditional parties (Momiglian 2018). The 2008–2009 recession that spread across the EU hurt Italy (and especially the lower and middle class) particularly hard. Italy now has the largest public debt in the EU. This was followed by a two-year recession between 2012 and 2013 that led to further disgruntlement among the lower classes (Elliot 2018). Currently, one-third of Italians below the age of twenty-five are unemployed which is double the average of the EU (Edwards 2017). As Hutter (2014) and Jurdis (2018) would argue, these trends often lead to anti-immigrant sentiment.

Like many countries across the EU, immigrants are the primary scapegoat for the economic difficulties Italy is facing. After Pope Francis visited migrants on the Island of Lampedusa (off the coast of Italy) in 2013, and the Italian government adopted a humanitarian policy to rescue migrants from the Middle East and Africa crossing the Mediterranean Sea, public opinion supported the asylum seekers (Hooper 2013). This changed when many Italians started to resent the fact that Italy was one of the major receiving countries of migrants, feeling a sense of loss to be able to control their borders.

Before Salvini took power Italy traditionally organized rescue missions for refugees in the sea and allowed private rescue boats run by NGOs to operate off of the coast of Libya to transport refugees to Italian ports (Scherer and Di Giogio 2014). After coming to power, however, Salvini ordered the Coast Guard to stop the assistance and put measures in place to forbid entry to private rescue boats, claiming that rescue operations only encourage more migrants to attempt the journey (Povoledo 2018). Additionally, the collaboration between the Italian government and the Libyan Coast Guard to monitor immigrants crossing the Mediterranean Sea has resulted in migrant ships being intercepted and forced back to Libya. Libyan militias, as part of the smuggling trade, also deter rescue boats from working close to the Libyan coast. Italian forces have systematically searched and seized rescue boats on the premise that they are involved in human smuggling (Tondo 2019).

To gain support for his policies Salvini pointed to the economic burden Italy was shouldering for the rescue operations. For example, in 2013–2014 the operation Mare Nostrum (in which Italian military ships served as the front line in rescue operations), which was an Italian military rescue operation that saved around 150 people from drowning, cost the government $10 million (Fioretti 2014). The government ended the operation and with emphasis Salvini said "enough! Saving lives is a duty but transforming Italy into an enormous refugee camp isn't . . . We're closing the ports" (Larger 2018).

By enacting externalization policies, Italy also gave out thousands of travel permits to encourage Tunisians to flee beyond Italy to other parts of Europe and offered economic aid for Tunisians who were willing to return home, and also provided resources to aid Tunisia's border control efforts (Hendow 2017). As noted in chapter 2, a similar policy has been implemented by the U.S. government granting bus passes and plane tickets to send immigrants back to their country of origin.

The externalization policies have had a devastating effect on migrants who, as a result, are sometimes stranded at sea for weeks. In late June 2018, a rescue ship that was carrying over 200 African migrants was refused entry to the Italian port. It was eventually able to dock in Malta after being stranded for a week in the Mediterranean Sea when eight European countries, on humanitarian (not legal) terms, agreed to receive the asylum seekers (Povoledo 2018). To legitimize his actions of not accepting the rescue ship, Salvini once again claimed that Italy would no longer be "Europe's refugee camp" (Fioretti 2014). On Twitter he called Malta's acceptance, with the assistance of the other countries, a success for the Italian government and for his deterrent efforts. Engaging in a similar approach, in the United States President Trump has thanked Mexico for using its National Guard to thwart refugees from Central America making it to the United States.

In yet another instance, three ships carrying migrants, including two navy vessels and one run by doctors without Borders, were accepted by Spain after Italy refused them entry to its port in Sicily. Salvini also hailed this as a "victory" for his party (Povoledo 2018). There have been several other instances of rescue ships being denied access to Italian ports over the past few years. In a reversal, however, the courts ruled against Salvini's order to block access for refuges on rescue ships on the basis that international maritime law acknowledges that anyone at sea who is in distress must be helped.

These efforts are further examples of Italy's hard-line communitarian perspective toward refugees, upheld by theories used by Consterdine and Hampshire (2013) and Miller (2005). Salvini points to the economic distress migrants put on the economy, thus appealing to sense of injustice for Italian citizens. This is illustrative of theories that explain nativist and racist tendencies and how it is linked to ethno-nationalism as proposed by Bridges (2019), Garner (2012), and Higham (1999). The message is that national identity must be protected from foreigners and one way to manifest this is by invoking the ideology of communitarianism into the institutions and legal workings of society as contended by Bridges (2019), Jardina (2019), Mutz (2018), and Huber et al. (2008).

Social movement theories also help us make sense of the trajectory of Europe's stance toward immigration. Salvini's condemnation of undocumented immigrants and blaming them for Italy's economic difficulties is indicative of strain theory—Italian citizens being deprived of jobs, better wages, and social services due to the influx of immigrants. His perspective also supports McVeigh's (2009) and Van Dyke and Soule's (2002) analyses which apply strain theory.

Furthermore, his reference to immigrants bringing chaos, drugs, crime, and violence was a successful use of framing that influenced public opinion toward a rejection of immigrants. However, his approach and overall ideology is currently being challenged by the emerging "sardines" social movement that opposes Salvini's hostile attitude toward immigrants and the EU. This grassroots effort among citizens and immigrants is calling for a shared sense of humanity and respect toward all residing in Italy. This resistance mobilization will be further analyzed in chapter 5.

In other new developments, in late January, Luigi Di Maio, leader of the Five Star Movement quit his position as the party fell into chaos. Additionally, a few days later Salvini's League Party lost a significant regional election in an endeavor to instigate the collapse of the Italian government so that he may steer the country toward a harder right-wing and populist ideology (Horrowitz and Povoledo 2020).

France

The main frustrations in France are embedded in Euroskepticism, though anti-immigrant feelings are also strong. For example, President Emmanuel Macron boasted about how many immigrants have been expelled or refused entry, and like Salvini, began refusing the entrance of migrant ships. In November 2019, France began a regimen of trying to attract skilled immigrants while closing the door on others and implemented a policy under which immigrants would have to wait three months before qualifying for nonurgent health care (Onisi 2019). This is comparable to the "public charge" legislation in the United States and desire for skilled immigrants, preferably from countries where whites are a majority.

France is like many other countries in the EU in that there is a divisive tension between those who live in the countryside and smaller cities and those in metropolitan areas. Many of the latter feel disdain toward the urban elites running the country, whom they feel do not understand the struggles of the working class (Felix 2019). This was highlighted when Luigi Di Mario met with a group of organizers from Yellow Vests in France and declared that "a new Europe is being born" (Felix 2019). The French government called its ambassador back to display its disdain for these organizing efforts—the first time it has done so since Mussolini declared war in 1940.

The Yellow Vest movement and recent protests across the France are more rooted in strain theory than hostility toward immigrants per se, but there is a noticeable trend toward communitarianism and reliance on externalization policies targeting migrants. The eagerness to welcome highly skilled migrants exemplifies the foundation of dual labor market theory which focuses on demand for certain kinds of labor in more advanced countries rather than on supply in less developed countries as argued by Donato and Massey (2016), Quillin (2006), and Silver (2003). It can also be understood under the lens of human capital theory advanced by Sassen (1988) who considers variables such as the sociodemographics of immigrants, level of education, and occupation among other factors driving immigration patterns.

And finally, Jarret's (1999) theory of ethno-nationalism and Judis' (2013) theory of economic anxiety are useful in that there is a growing fear in France about immigrants being a drain on economic and social resources which the current protests focus on—though not outright targeting immigrants for grievances. At this point, the main target of consternation is President Macron and what many feels as him being out of touch with the everyday struggles of French citizens.

Poland

Akin to the situation in France, in Poland the debate about globalization and liberal democracy has created a division between the conservative-leaning countryside in Eastern Poland and more liberal-leaning citizens in the cities and suburbs (Santora 2019). Many in rural areas feel left behind while other parts of the country that have embraced Western values and capitalism are enjoying a much higher quality of life and wealth. Strain theory helps explain the situation in Poland where the anticipated benefits of joining the EU were offset by the economic inequality that resulted between rural and urban areas. Most Polish citizens had become accustomed to the generous social policies and safety net that the Soviet Union provided. When these benefits were reduced or eliminated, skepticism toward the EU and an anti-immigrant sentiment proliferated. Mutz (2018) and Hutter (2014) note how when there is increased competition for access to jobs, schools, and other various social services, raced-based and anti-immigration attitudes tend to escalate.

On a campaign slogan of "Poland for Poles," the far-right Law and Justice Party, represented by Jaroslaw Kaczynski, came to power in 2015 (Santora 2019). His message of national pride resonated with those who felt that they were not sharing the benefits of economic growth (Berendt 2018). Beyond an ideology of ethno-nationalism, an anti-immigrant posture was also part of his platform. Kaczynski warned voters that migrants are bringing "dangerous diseases" and "various types of parasites" to Europe. Poland took a firm stance against the EU in its attempt to distribute quotas of immigrants. It has, however, been accepting immigrants, mostly Christian, from Ukraine. Prime Minister Mateusz Morawiecki explained the policy by stating, "We want to reshape Europe and re-Christianize it" (Santora 2019). During an Independence Day march, some carried banners that read, "White Europe" and "Clean Blood." The interior minister commented on it saying it was a "beautiful sight."

Unabashedly proclaiming a sense of communitarianism, and thus playing on the fear of loss of national identity and perceived differences in racial, cultural, and ethnic senses of belonging, Kaczynski's framing of anti-immigrant rhetoric is designed to stir up a sense of collective identity among Poles to the exclusion of migrants. The banners, and their approval by one of the highest-ranking officials, demonstrate that many Poles feel comfortable expressing their hostility toward those who are of a different heritage. The demonstrations in Charlottesville in the United States, discussed in the next chapter, in which marchers shouted, "blood and soil" and "Jews will not replace us," and President Trump claiming that there were "fine people on both sides," demarcate similar trends resonating on both sides of the Atlantic.

Explaining the interconnections between racism and ethno-nationalism, Heber et al. (2008) and Gallindo and Vigil (2006) note the parallel efforts to justify the superiority of the natives, that is, white citizens. This is further combined with economic populism by exploiting the feeling that working-class Poles were being excluded from the benefits of economic prosperity as theorized by Judis (2018). Garner (2012) and Higham (1999) also specify how nativism is often rooted in religious, not just racial differences. Davis (2011) further recognizes how historically in Europe religion was the main driver of identity issues and ethno-nationalism.

Since coming to power Kaczynski has curtailed the independence of the judiciary and the news media to promote his right-wing, anti-EU, anti-immigration agenda. Poland was the first member nation to be threatened with having its voting rights suspended because the European Commission determined that it had failed to uphold the core values of the EU (Boffey and Davies 2017). In October 2018, Europe's highest court ordered the government to reinstate more than two dozen judges who were dismissed in a purge which Kaczynski organized and carried out (Boffey and Davis 2017). These are similar to the illiberalism advocated by the Trump administration in the United States.

There has been additional backlash against his autocratic approach to governance. In November 2018, his Law and Justice Party suffered a major defeat in municipal elections and especially in mayoral races (Berendt 2018). Not relenting, the Law and Justice Party took over the independent media to spread propaganda for the 2019 election through government control, claiming that the media was dominated by the liberal elite. This correlates with the Trump administrations' insistence that independent media is "fake news," as will be discussed in detail in the following chapter.

Spain

Spain has also shifted toward a nationalist and ultraconservative populism
and away from its long history of socialist leanings in part due to increasing waves of immigration that the country was not prepared for (Faber and
Seguin 2019). It became a prime destination for migrants from Africa once
Greece, Austria, Hungary, Italy, and France started to close their borders and
greatly reduced the number of immigrants they would accept (Minder 2019).
In 2018, more migrants arrived by sea to Spain than any other European
country.

The Socialist Party suffered a major setback during the 2018 election
when right-wing parties won enough votes to replace members of the party
from power in the nation's largest region for the first time since the rule of
the dictator, General Francisco Franco (Minder 2019). The ultranationalist Vox Party, which made it for the first time into Parliament, is rooted in
an anti-immigrant, nationalist ideology and promotes traditional values and
Catholicism. It ran on a campaign to "make Spain great again" and called
for the abolition of the 2007 "law of historical memory" which mandated the
removal of General Franco's symbols from public places. Vox also advocated
for the building of walls around two of the Spanish enclaves in North Africa
to exclude immigrants from entering Spain (Caparros 2019).

The 2019 election, which had the highest turnout since the 1970s also
showed the growing political polarization within Spain as the Socialist Party
strengthened its hold on government (Minder 2019). This is similar to the
push back in Poland in the last elections and the mobilization against Salvini
in Italy. Prime Minister Pedro Sanchez declared that the Socialist Party sent a
message to the world that "it is possible to win against regression and authoritarianism" (Minder 2019). Yet, in November 2019, the Vox Party did become
the third largest party, doubling its seats in Parliament. The rise, sustenance,
and support of nationalism is in part a response to the Catalan secessionist
movement, which Vox responds to with an emphasis on fatherland and questioning who legitimate citizens are, as well as a sense of victimhood at the
hands of outsiders (Caparros 2019).

Once again religion is a key variable in promoting ethno-nationalism
through nationalist ideology. The framing of "make Spain great again"
conjures up a feeling that Spaniards are being left behind in their own
country at the expense of foreigners. Vox's call for reintegrating Franco's
symbolic presence in Spain is very similar to the struggles in the South in
the United States over Confederate statues that many see as an acceptance,
if not glorification of slavery. One of these struggles culminated in the clash
in Charlottesville, VA, which left one young woman dead and several others injured. Islamophobia, prevalent in Spain, is pointed out by Garner and
Selod (2014) as a prominent form of racism in Europe, which oftentimes is

conflated with nativism and ethno-nationalism. This combination of racist and anti-immigrant feelings is also at the crux of the work of Schleuths and Lippard (2011), Huber et al. (2008), and Galinda and Vigil (2006).

Turkey

Turkey is one of the key points of entry for many immigrants trying to reach Europe by sea, and a particularly popular route for Syrians, Afghans, and Iraqis. At the peak of the immigration influx in 2015, about 850,000 migrants arrived in Europe through Turkey, which ultimately took in two million Syrian refugees alone (Cendrowicz 2015). To ease the situation in 2016, the EU struck a deal with Turkey to stem the flow of immigrants in return for about $6 billion in aid (Cendrowicz 2015), thus relying on externalization policies of immigration. Under President Tayyip Erdogan, Turkey completed a border wall and imposed restrictions on Syrians traveling from Lebanon or Jordan.

Erdogan, who has been in power for sixteen years, has made dramatic constitutional and institutional changes to enhance his position as an autocrat. When first elected he made major changes to political and civil life by pivoting away from the parliamentary system. He did this by centralizing and increasing his executive powers which opened a space for him to exert control in nearly all areas of life. He eventually took control over the army, cracked down on civil liberties, fired or detained tens of thousands of civil servants, and closed over 1,000 schools (Malsin 2016).

After an attempted military coup in July 2016, which resulted in over 200 deaths Erdogan declared a three-month state of emergency and purged and arrested tens of thousands of citizens. He shut down 131 media originations and issued warrants for the arrest of approximately ninety journalists who he charged with being implicated in organizing the coup. The government has imprisoned more journalists than any other country despite the fact that most of the media is under the control of his hard-line supporters (Malsin 2016).

However, these strongman politics are being challenged (as mentioned, this has been the trend in Poland and Spain as well). Erdogan and his Justice and Development Party lost control of Ankara, the capital of Turkey and Istanbul, which is the financial center, in their worst defeat since Erdogan has been in power. Though part of this may be in reaction toward his style of government as an autocrat and clamp down on civil liberties, the fact that the economy has been devastated most likely also played a significant role.

Hungary

Another practical port of entry for immigrants is Hungary. Paradoxically, Hungary had previously been perceived as a role model for the potential of newly burgeoning democracies in the post-Cold War era after the collapse of the communist bloc. It aggressively started to build Western-style political institutions and established a robust market economy (Friedman 2013).

However, this has recently been reversed. In 2010, the Fidesz Party, under the leadership of Viktor Orbán won a "supermajority" in Parliament and he has used this leverage to push through an agenda rooted in illiberalism through legal and bureaucratic measures. Once in office he declared, "the era of liberal democracy is over. Rather than try to fix a liberal democracy that has run aground, we will build a 21st century Christian democracy." He further elaborated, "The danger is threatening us from the West. The danger comes from politicians in Brussels, Berlin and Paris" (Cohen 2018).

When running for a fourth time Orbán promised to protect Hungarian culture from outsiders proclaiming, "Hungary First," claiming that Hungary was losing its sovereignty in an attempt to instill fear among Hungarian citizens (Santora and Bienvenu 2018). He framed the presence of immigrants as posing a terrorist threat and Muslims in particular of undermining Christianity. He also chastised the policy of the quota system in clear opposition to the idea that immigration is a human right and warning that this would destroy the nation-state of Hungary. Orbán also posted billboards across the country featuring a long line of immigrants trekking through the countryside with a message reading "STOP" (Santora 2018b). At one rally he declared, "Massive migration goes together with the increased terrorist threat," and repeatedly spoke of Muslim immigrants as undermining Christian traditions and values (Gorondi 2017).

By controlling the media, he also dictates the framing of the narrative and builds a strong sense of collective identity, key concepts that are central to cultural strands of social movement theory. In doing so, he has successfully persuaded Hungarians that there is an immigration crisis, and therefore gaining acceptance of his anti-immigrant policies, though indeed there have been few migrants trying to enter Hungary since 2015. In a radio interview, Orbán contested that Hungary has a moral duty to refuse to take in refugees or asylum seekers, opining that, "In Brussels now, thousands of paid activists, bureaucrats and politicians work in the direction that immigration should be considered a human right. That's why they want to take away from us the right to decide with whom we want to live. It's my personal conviction that migration leads in the end to the destruction of nations and states" (Scheppele 2015). By conflating issues of race with civilization and culture, Orbán's message obfuscates the fact that the backlash against immigration is indeed rooted in racial undertones.

Since elected he has made legislative changes which have weakened democratic institutions such as the media and the courts, and has undermined the country's checks and balances, though all done so in a technically democratic fashion. He has also shimmied the electoral system, appointed loyalists to key positions in the judiciary, and eroded the independence of the news media (*The Economist* 2018). A very similar trend is occurring in the United States under President Trump. Purported to provide a counterweight to "progressive" news outlets, in December 2018, Orbán waived competition regulations to allow loyalist media owners to "donate" hundreds of newspapers, television channels, radio stations, and websites to a central fund controlled by three of his closest supporters (Walter 2019).

Orbán has one of the most hostile attitudes toward democratic liberalism, globalization, and cosmopolitanism, again, an outlook he shares with Trump. For example, he accuses George Soros, who is an extremely wealthy donor to the Democratic Party in the United States and an international philanthropist, as someone who promotes global liberal democracy and therefore an enemy to the sovereignty to Hungary. In fact, while running for office Orbán's anti-immigration campaign included a "Stop Soros" law which legislated that any NGO receiving foreign funding would have to pay a 25 percent tax on their contributions (Paris 2018). This law targeted agencies that were assisting asylum seekers, and refugees in particular. At one of his rallies Obran, referring to Soros proclaimed, "We are fighting an enemy that is different from us . . . not national but international; does not believe in working but speculates with money; does not have its own homeland but feels it owns the whole world" (Paris 2018).

Soros had created the foundation to spread democracy globally, promoting justice, free speech, political freedom, and human rights in more than 100 countries (Mervosh 2019). Under the threat of legal sanctions, the foundation was closed in 2018. Patrick Gaspard, president of Mr. Soros's Open Society Foundations declared: "Migration is clearly being used by the Hungarian Government as a political diversion. The ultimate objective is to intimidate civil society and muzzle independent critics, including those who receive some of their funding from Open Society" (Dunai 2018).

The "Stop Soros" legislation was also condemned by global agencies and human rights groups, including the United Nations and Amnesty International. Director of Amnesty International Europe, Gauri van Gulik stated, "Criminalizing essential and legitimate human rights work is a brazen attack . . . It is a new low point in an intensifying crackdown on civil society and it something we will resist every step of the way" (Romo 2018). Ironically, in 1998, while trying to break from the Soviet Union after its collapse Orbán sought funding from the Soros Foundation to study how, using grassroots organizations, Hungary might be able to make the transition from a dictatorship to a democracy (Mervosh 2018).

There is no doubt of Orbán's anti-immigration and anticosmopolitan perspective. His rhetoric is exemplary of using nativism to encourage Hungarian citizens to think about who belongs and who does not, and who gets to decide. Having an international enemy, an outsider who does not understand their ordinary lives builds a sense of solidarity through collective identity and antagonism toward those who do not share their heritage, traditions, and culture. Garner's (2014) conceptualization of critical race theory is instructive for the attention it gives to power relations under the rubric of racialized identities and the unspoken, yet powerful consequences of the code of whiteness. Through his control of media and posting billboards, and therefore framing, Orbán is able to distort the reality of the immigration situation within Hungary. This is central to the work of Jardina (2019) and Mutz (2018) who examine the conflated nature of racism, nativism, and ethno-nationalism.

The Central European University, located in Budapest and which was founded in Hungary after the collapse of the Soviet Union to champion the principles of democracy and free society, was also closed in December 2018. Summarized by the president of the University, Michael Ignatieff said, "C.E.U. has been forced out. This is unprecedented. A U.S. institution has been driven out by a country that is a NATO ally" (Santora 2018b). The governmental body of the EU responded to what it views as the establishment of a near dictatorship. In September 2018, European lawmakers voted to seek retribution against Hungary for violating democratic norms—this was the first time that the European Parliament has undertaken such a measure, and Fidesz was suspended from the EU's most powerful political coalition in March 2019 (Santora and Erlanger 2019). Orbán reacted by claiming EU lawmakers wanted to overrun Hungary with immigrants and destroy Hungarian culture (Kingsely and Erlanger2018).

Orbán's government also changed the constitution to make it illegal to "settle foreign populations" in Hungary, a rebuke of attempts by the EU to encourage Hungary to admit small numbers of refugees who had been living in other European countries (Kingsley 2018a). Under the new laws Hungarian citizens who assist migrants in an attempt to legalize their status by distributing information about the asylum process or providing them with financial assistance could result in a twelve-month jail term. As I address in chapter 2, these fear tactics are also common in the United States. For example, according to the Council of Europe, "refugees in Hungary have been caged, starved and denied legal representation" (Kingsley and Erlanger 2018). Critics claim that the government, unable to deport those who have been denied asylum, is trying to make conditions unbearable so that they will self-deport.

Germany

Surprisingly, with its past of history of fascism which culminated in the Holocaust, Germany has joined the populist wave of nationalism as well.

Recent surveys show that the Holocaust and what happened under fascism is not in current memory of many young people and some are in fact dismissive of the Holocaust (Wynne 2018). The coleader of the AfD, Alternative for Germany Party, called the Nazi era "a mere bird poop of history" (Benhold 2019). In 2017, the party became the first far-right party to enter Parliament since World War II and now it sits in every state legislature in the country.

As is the case in many other countries, the welcoming of immigrants waxes and wanes contingent on the health of the economy. Immigrant labor was welcomed in the 1940s and 1950s because it was essential to the postwar reconstruction of Germany (Payani 2020). These workers, however, were perceived as the "inferior" race and were denied the political, social, or civic benefits of living in Germany. Most German citizens assumed they were merely temporary workers, but when immigrants began to settle in the host country, and the economy and employment opportunities slowed, cultural racism flourished (Payani 2020). Immigrants came to be seen as not just biologically inferior, but also unable or unwilling to assimilate, and therefore posed a threat to the identity of the nation.

Hence, for a limited time Germans adopted a cosmopolitan stance toward migrants. Structural theories of immigration, especially those developed by Mansoor and Quillin (2006), can refine out interpretation of immigration patterns as there was a good match for individuals in poorer countries seeking better economic opportunities and a need for labor in redeveloping Germany. Dual labor market theory and the work of Donato and Massey (2006) and Masoor and Quillan (2006) is instructive as well in that there was a demand for work that many Germans deemed beneath them.

When the economy slowed, however, racist and nativist attitudes emerged. The racism was rooted in white superiority, and nativism from a feeling a loss of national identity, as outlined by Herber et al. (2008) in their theorizing of ethno-nationalism. Economic anxiety also prevailed which further helps understand white anxiety rooted in economic populism which Judis (2018) focuses on in explaining the dynamics of ethno-nationalism. Additionally, the criticism of immigrants rooted in the fear of lack of assimilation lends credence to critical race theory.

In 2015, at the height of refugees fleeing countries that were suffering a humanitarian crisis as a result of the Arab Spring uprising, Prime Minister Merkel stated that she would allow all immigrants into Germany who could reach it, which resulted in over one million refugees, a vast majority of them from Syria, pouring into the country seeking asylum (Hutton 2015). That year it was processing tens of thousands of refugees crossing the Austrian border, and most located in low-income neighborhoods where housing and other resources were scarce which caused class tensions. The question once again arose about whether the new immigrants would be willing to or capable of assimilating and reintroduced contingent concerns about national identity among the local population. The Bracero program in the United States, covered in chapter 2, raised similar concerns.

As public opinion shifted, and the sheer number of immigrants turned German citizens against Merkel's welcoming stance, she conceded to build border camps for asylum seekers and to tighten the border with Austria. The camps or "transit centers" were distributed at various points along the border and through which those seeking asylum would be screened and would be sent back to the original host country where they first registered (Eddy 2018). This is comparable to the "Remain in Mexico" and "safe third countries" agreements introduced by the Trump administration, addressed in the previous chapter.

Like many other parts of Germany, citizens in Bavaria initially clapped at train and bus stations to welcome the immigrant caravans as they arrived. Public facilities were transformed into temporary camps to assist the immigrants and citizens set up and organized kitchens to help feed the new arrivals. Public opinion changed, however, when the number of immigrants soared. Merkel's policies, in turn, made her vulnerable to the political ambitions of others (Connolly and Le Blond 2018).

For instance, the Premier of Bavaria, Marcus Solder warned that Germans must prioritize their own citizens and ran on a platform of "Germany for Germans," border security, law and order, and a rejection of liberal democracy. He declared, "Asylum tourism must end . . . we have to consider our own people, not always focus on the whole of Europe" (Bennhold 2018). Referring to the events in Bavaria Gerald Knaus, the director of the European Stability explained, "This is not about economics. It is about identity and a very successful populist P.R. machine that is rewriting history. The Bavarian revolt was rooted in nativist anger. Most of the changes in attitude have occurred near the border where AfD has been most active and has successfully stricken fear into much of the local population. One of these fears is the Islamitization of the area (Bavaria is mostly Roman Catholic) as well as crime and terrorism" (Serhan 2018).

In fact, Bavaria is wealthier and more conservative than most parts of Germany and the unemployment rate is roughly 3 percent (Bennhold 2018). Thus, the surge of anti-immigrant attitudes cannot be explained by economic strain, but rather by racial anxiety and fear of challenges to German national identity that the AfD Party was able to tap into through successful framing techniques. This supports McVeigh's (2009) analysis on the emergence and popularity of the KKK in the United States.

Anti-Semitism is also on the rise, not just in Germany but across the EU and the United States, which is also fostering racial and immigrant resentment. For example, in a 2018 EU survey of European Jews, 85 percent of respondents in Germany characterized anti-Semitism as a "very big" or "fairly big" problem and 89 percent said the problem has become worse in the last five years (Cohen 2017). Overall, reported anti-Semitic crimes in Germany increased by almost 20 percent in 2018. Another survey by the Allensbach Institute found that in 2018, 55 percent of AfD supporters believe that Jews have "too much influence on the world" as opposed to the 22 percent of the average overall population (Salzborn 2018).

Dietrich (2014) and Hutter (2014) address the insider/outsider dynamic with the insiders, or natives, assumed superior yet threatened by alternative traditions, cultures, and values. They also recognize that when globalization intensifies, and immigrants arrive in large numbers changing the demographic landscape of the country, membership of extremist and far-rights groups increases. Nativist identity has certainly taken over in Bavaria despite a robust economy. Thus, this challenges the link between economic populism and anti-immigrant sentiment. Clearly in Germany, Islamophobia and Anti-Semitism played a key role in the changing of public opinion toward immigrants. This trend supports the work of Hushman (2017), Portes and Rumbaut (2006), and Higham (1999).

Britain

Though Britain has been least affected by the immigration and debt crisis, it is one of the most Euroskeptic countries and has also embraced a fear of, and hostility toward, immigrants. In 1948, due to a major labor shortage, tens of thousands of people were encouraged to come to Britain from its colonies in the Caribbean to help in postwar efforts to rebuild the country (Elliot and Humphreys 2015). The "rebuilders" were part of what was called the "Windrush Generation," named after a passenger liner that brought most of the migrants to Britain (Miles 1989). Since the colonies had not yet gained independence many of their passports were marked "Citizen of the UK and Colonies," and therefore most of the workers assumed that they would naturally become British citizens upon arrival (Hodges 2018).

However, at the end of the labor shortage, and when the rebuilding efforts were nearly completed in the early 1960s, the British government passed laws that restricted migration from the Commonwealth. Harsher immigration laws were passed by Prime Minister Teresa May in 2012 that also targeted these groups (Hodges 2018). These decreed that immigrants must document their right to government benefits by proving their legal status. Most of the workers, however, were given permission to enter Britain based on their parents' passports and thus never had to apply for travel or immigration documents, assuming that their status was legitimatized (Kimiko 2018). Additionally, the Home Office failed to keep records confirming their status, and thousands of landing cards from the 1950s and 1960s were destroyed by British immigration officials.

This situation is very similar to the now "public charge" policy in the United States which limits undocumented immigrants' rights to health care and screens incoming immigrants for their ability to pay for health care or likelihood to need any kind of social services. Another similarity is how immigrants were treated under the Bracero program as they were perceived to be temporary workers but not citizens, and even after a couple of generations not considered American. These dynamics are supported by Garner's (2014) analysis which argues that ethno-nationalism is fluid and connected to particular historical, cultural, geographical, and political contexts.

The first wave of immigrants in Britain was welcomed by a cosmopolitan attitude as Amstutz (2015) outlines as one of the key theories of immigration. This is also in part explained by world system theory advocated by Silver (2003) and Sassen (1988) given the relationship between the more developed and less developed countries. It can also be understood through the lens of dual labor market theory that Haas et al. (2020), Miller (2009), Castles et al. (2009), and Borjas (2008) put forth in recognizing how the supply and demand on the international market for labor was beneficial to both countries and migrants' decisions to relocate to Britain were based on a cost/benefit calculation. The second wave of immigrants, in contrast, experienced a mindset of communitarianism. Conderstine and Hampshire (2013) and Miller (2005) argue that despite economic concerns a sense of exclusion tends to prevail when national identity and culture are under real or perceived threat.

As anti-immigration and Euroskepticism gained momentum across the Britain, in June 2016, through a referendum, the majority of British citizens voted to leave the EU (Evans et al. 2017). This is a cause of major concern for the EU as London is a permanent member of the United Nations Security Council and dedicates significant military and diplomatic forces regionally and globally. Prime Minister Theresa May resigned after her attempts to negotiate the break were rejected by Parliament three times. Britain formally left the EU on January 31, 2019, as the Conservative Party, led by Boris Johnson, won the election in a landslide victory as he had promised a quick and decisive departure from the EU.

Some contest that the driving force behind the vote was the "left-behind" citizens—older, white, and working class who felt that distant bureaucratic elites in Brussels hold most of the power and are out of touch with their reality and concerns and that the UK was losing control of its borders (Scuria 2017; Goodwin and Heath 2016). For example, in 2014, 77 percent of British respondents said they favored a reduction of immigrants (Bernstein 2016) and others note the economic inequality that became increasingly pronounced amid fiscal austerity policies dictated by Brussels (Dorling 2016).

Strain theory is applicable to the economic anxiety that many British citizens felt which led to their support of Brexit. Thus, the Brexit mobilization once again displays the prominence of communitarianism as theorized by Midgley (2017), Van Wormart and Link (2016), Marin (2015), and Amstutz (2015) as many British citizens became convinced that they were losing control of their borders, but also their indignation toward Brussels and a postindustrial economy which was leaving many behind.

As mentioned, on January 31, 2019, Brexit was finalized. However, Britain's hope that its departure might influence other countries to exit as well backfired as the remaining twenty-seven countries quickly solidified their support for the bloc (Erlanger 2018a). According to many reports, the 2016 vote was less about economic anxiety and more about a struggle for British identity and a longing for what is perceived as a loss of national sovereignty (Castle 2020). As part of the deal, Europeans living in Britain no longer have long-term permission to stay and work, leaving younger people fearful for their futures.

In February 2020, President Johnson announced that low-skilled workers would be barred from Britain in an attempt to curtail overall immigrations as was promised as part of Brexit by Johnson beginning in January 2021 (Castle 2020). Only skilled workers who can prove that they speak English will be allowed into the country. The reversal is notable in that unlike other countries like Germany and France, in 2004 it welcomed citizens from former communist countries that had joined the EU. After the Brexit referendum migrants from within the EU dropped dramatically, but this was offset by those coming from outside the bloc (Castle 2020). Employers in industries such as construction and the food industry who rely on low-skilled immigrant labor are bewildered by the policy. One of the managers of the Pret fast-causal food chain stated in 2017 that only one in fifty applicants for jobs in its restaurants was British (Edwards 2017). This echoes what world renowned chef, Anthony Bourdain described as being the case in the United States in the previous chapter.

Sweden, the Netherlands, and Denmark

Another unanticipated political change has occurred in Sweden, which is by and large a racially and culturally homogenous country with one of the most generous social welfare systems in the EU and has enjoyed a reputation as a "moral superpower" (Erlanger 2018a). During the 2015–2016 immigration crisis, Sweden took in more migrants per capita than any other EU country (Becker 2019), and it was the first country in Europe to grant permanent resident permits to asylum seekers from Syria. During the Syrian civil war, 96 percent Syrians who fled to Sweden in 2013 were granted asylum. In 2015, it also accepted 163,000 asylum seekers, most arriving from Afghanistan, Somalia, and Syria (Becker 2019). One oversight, however, was that it did so without considering how newly arriving migrants could or should be integrated and assimilated into Swedish society.

As other immigrant groups tended to do in cities across Western Europe, new arrivals mostly clustered in low-income neighborhoods and Swedish citizens questioned their ability to assimilate. Facing poor job prospects and rampant employment discrimination many immigrants began to internalize their perceived "otherness" and embrace the stereotypes of being unwilling or incapable of assimilation (Bittner 2018).

In alignment with a growing anti-immigrant stance and the Social Democrats' inability to deal with the issue of assimilation, the Eurosceptic Sweden Democrats Party increasingly gained influence and challenged the Social Democrats Party, who was the frontrunner in almost every election since 1917. Until recently the Sweden Democrats (founded in 1988) were categorized as a racist fringe of Swedish politics with ties to neo-Nazis and a racist movement called Bevara Sverige Svenskt (Keep Sweden Swedish) and have called for a repatriation of all immigrants who arrived in Sweden since the 1970s (Anderson and Erlanger 2018).

Despite a thriving economy and low unemployment, the Sweden Democrats argue that immigration should stop and that resources should go to refurbishing the welfare state which is strained by an aging population and the influx of immigrants (Crouch 2014). In 2014, Sweden began implementing stiffer border controls and immigration laws, which drastically reduced the number of immigrants. In 2015, when most asylum seekers were unaccompanied minors, migration laws shifted once again as ports of entry were temporarily closed and a valid passport was required to enter the country (European Network against Racism 2014).

In 2018, the Sweden Democrats achieved another major political gain by securing 18 percent of the vote (Teitelbaum 2018). Much of the surge had to do with anti-immigration sentiment rooted in both economic and racist anxiety. One ad depicted a white woman trying to collect benefits while being pursued by niqab-wearing immigrants pushing strollers. The party also called for the "preservation of Swedish DNA" and ethnic purity (Teitelbaum 2018). Salvini's campaign in Italy used a similar type of framing—"native" citizens going without basic necessities while foreigners are privileged. This appeals to the Great Replacement ideology that foreigners are having more children and need more resources, and thus pose a threat to the homogenous culture, religion, and heritage of the country.

This anti-immigrant, anti-Semitic, and Islamophobia is broad and vast throughout the EU. For example, in a December 2018 survey on experiences and perceptions of anti-Semitisms in Europe, the EU Fundamental Rights

Agency found that 89 percent of Jews living in Austria, Belgium, Denmark, Germany, France, Hungary, Italy, The Netherlands, Poland, Spain, Sweden, and UK stated that anti-Semitism has been increasing in their country over the past decade, and more than a third feared being physically attacked (Cosse 2019).

In another study undertaken by the European Network against Racism in 2018 in Sweden, it concluded that "there is a distinct ethnic hierarchy where ethnic Swedes see themselves as far superior to non-European ethnics" (European Network against Racism 2018). Additionally, a 2016 Pew Research Center survey revealed that the Netherlands scored the lowest across the EU in terms of approval of different races and ethnic groups' arrival to improve the country. According to the report, "Racism and Xenophobia in Sweden," conducted by the Board of Integration, almost 40 percent of Muslims said that were subject to verbal abuse (Drake and Poushter 2016).

The situation in Sweden also speaks to economic populism as the government intuits that it must provide for its own citizens ahead of immigrants, as many immigration theorists contend is especially true when there is a large, quick, and unanticipated wave of new immigrant arrivals. It is further representative of Jardina's (2019), Mutz's (2018), and Garner's (2014) work that illustrate how a real or perceived loss of status among whites, and the presumed norms of whiteness, are threatened, which often leads to a heightened embracement of ethno-nationalism. Youth, which drive most of the movement within the Sweden Social Democrats, use similar tactics of those employed by white supremacist groups in the United States (discussed in the next chapter), in terms of conscientiously repackaging blatant racist ideology for it to have a more patriotic and respectable appeal.

For example, while Jimmie Akesson, who is the leader of the Sweden's Democratic Youth Party has stated that Muslim refugees posed "the biggest foreign threat to Sweden since the Second World War" for public appeal, he and other leaders insist on a "zero tolerance" about promoting extreme xenophobia and racism (Crouch 2014). The group has also purged members who had been exposed by the media as having extreme views and they encourage participants do dress "presentably" at public demonstrations. The framing of their message also focuses almost exclusively on assimilation and threats to the social welfare system, rather than racism or white superiority.

This trend of the growing popularity of extreme and far-right groups has emerged in the Netherlands and Denmark as well. In the Netherlands, far-right politicians claim that Christians are under an attack by immigrants who threaten the security, culture, and identity of the country (Crisp 2018). The far-right leader of the Netherlands, Geert Wilders, when voted into power expressed that Europe will not exist "as a predominantly white-skinned,

Christian or post-Christian, Roman-law-based kind of society" a few decades from now (Crisp 2018).

He also warned in 2015 of "masses of young men in their 20s with beards singling 'allahu akbar' across Europe" and labeled their presence as "an invasion that threatens our prosperity, our security, our culture and identity" (Barry and Sorensen 2018). This ideology of economic populism that Judis (2018) notes is combined with elements of racism and nativism which reinforce white and Christian superiority that Jardiana (2019) and Gallindo and Vigil (2018) emphasize.

In 2018, Denmark created new laws for those living in "ghettos" which overwhelmingly are populated by low-income Muslims (Barry and Sorensen 2018). Under these laws "ghetto children" are required to be separated from their families for at least 25 hours a week for mandatory instruction in "Danish values." If parents do not have their children attend, the government can stop their income assistance. While this tactic is not as extreme as the separation of families, zero tolerance, and public charge policies employed on the U.S.–Mexican border, this still causes stress and anxiety in immigrant communities. This clearly underscores the importance of Garner's (2014) work on critical race theory: the insistence on norms of whiteness consisting of particular behaviors mandated as respectable according to the dominant group.

DETENTION CAMPS IN THE UE AND THE CRIMINALIZATION OF IMMIGRANT ASSISTANCE

The last chapter noted that the wretched conditions in the refugee camps and detention centers on the U.S.–Mexico border are suspected of being created in part to deter asylum seekers, or to at least prolong the process as to discourage other potential migrants seeking asylum. There is a similar dynamic in the EU. As mentioned previously, Greece hosted very large numbers of asylum seekers who arrived by sea initially, but the migrant camps that they created were not adequate to provide basic human needs (World Report 2019). Authorities were overwhelmed and most unaccompanied children were placed in camps with adults in "protective police custody" or detention in "risked homelessness facilities" (Human Rights Watch 2019). Greece's EU-backed policy of confirming asylum seekers who arrived by sea to the Aegean islands stranded thousands of immigrants living under these conditions.

The most overcrowded and desperate refugee camp in Europe is on the island of Samos Greece where migrants (a vast number of them unaccompanied minors) are stuck in limbo in an attempt to make it to mainland Greece (Horowitz 2020). However, both the government in Greece and

UE countries are unwilling to take responsibility for the migrants and therefore hear their asylum cases. While the camp has a maximum capacity to hold 648 people there are over 3,000 migrants residing there without basic provisions or medical treatment. On the Greek Island of Lesbos, at the Moria camp, more than 15,000 asylum seekers live on the site designed for 3,000 (Churchill 2019). A regional authority inspection in September 2018 concluded that the Moria camp, the largest on the island, presented a danger to public health and the environment, and called on the government to address the issues or close the camp (Nellas and Kantouris 2019). While the government transferred tens of thousands of asylum seekers from the islands to mainland Greece it did not end the confinement policy for new arrivals.

In February 2020, police fired tear gas on disgruntled migrants marching from the camps to town to protest their wretched conditions (Human Rights Watch 2020). In fact, the Council of Europe's Committee for the Prevention of Torture visited Greece in April and issued a preliminary report expressing concerns about inhuman and degrading treatment in psychiatric establishments and migrant detention centers (Council of Europe 2020). Similar to the reports of conditions in migrant shelters for asylum seekers from Mexico and Central America in the United States, migrants sleep in tents in freezing temperatures, without hot water and little food as they wait for months for their asylum cases to be heard. Less than 15 percent of asylum-seeking children in the Lesbos camp had access to education on the islands, and only half on the mainland were enrolled in public schools (United Nations Refugee Agency 2020).

To deal with the continuing influx of immigrants from Turkey, Greece has recently created a floating net barrier to impede boats smuggling immigrants between the two countries (Kitsantonis 2020). This is similar to the walls that have been erected to separate European countries and, on the U.S.–Mexico border. In response, Massimo Moratti, the Amnesty International's research director for Europe, stated that this is "an alarming escalation in the Greek government's ongoing efforts to make it as difficult as possible for asylum-seekers and refugees to arrive on its shores" (Kitsantonis 2020). This is yet another example of "prevention through deterrence" policies that are applied in other EU countries as well as in the United States.

Migrants crossing from North Africa to get to Spain also face substandard conditions in arrival facilities and obstacles to apply for asylum. The Council of Europe called on Spain in September 2018 to improve conditions and protection measures for migrants and asylum seekers, particularly unaccompanied children in the North African enclaves of Ceuta and Melilla (Canas and Saiz 2018). The UK also faces a difficult situation dealing with how to provide for migrants seeking asylum.

More than 27,000 immigrants were detained in 2017 as those trying to apply for asylum increased amid the recent policy of not enforcing a time limit for migrants' cases to be heard (Townsend 2019). It has refused to mandate maximum time for both child and adult immigration detention, which is similar to the policy under the Trump administration in the United States. The UK, in fact, is the only country that does not have a limit on how many immigrants can be held in detention and some have been detained over two years. Detention centers that used to hold 475 people now have a capacity of 3,500, many of those being unaccompanied minors.

To deal with the overcrowding, Britain has implemented "fast-track" processing to decide asylum cases quickly, like the policy implemented in the United States whereby immigrants are denied legal aid or representation, and bail hearings. Criticisms are that immigrants are kept in prison though they have not committed a crime, there is no judicial oversight, there are huge delays from being released, and the conditions are horrendous. The government relocated only 220 unaccompanied children from other EU countries out of 480 (Townsend 2019).

In France, many of the migrants who are trying to get to Britain have been stranded in the Channel port of Calais (known as the "jungle"), which quickly came to be considered a slum. It was cleared in late 2016 due to the horrific health and safety conditions. After pressured to visit the camp by human rights activists, President Macon introduced a new policy of offering shelter, assistance, and integration for those deemed to be eligible to remain in France (Morin 2018). However, he also guaranteed a higher rate of expulsions of those perceived to be illegally in the country. He stated, "There will be no reconstruction of the 'the Jungle' or tolerance of illegal settlements in or around Calais . . . To Stay in Calais and built makeshift shelters and even set up squats is a dead end. The alternative is clear; people can get to the reception centers where everyone's case will be examined and those who have the right, given asylum in our country" (Willsher 2018).

THE CRIMINALIZATION OF ADVOCACY WORK

The criminalization of assistance to aid migrants is another trend that has been scrutinized by human rights groups and immigration activists in the EU, similar to policies undertaken in the United States (which were discussed in the last chapter). In Hungary, for instance, Parliament passed legislation to criminalize services, advice, and support to migrants and asylum seekers (Nelson 2018). It also limited daily entry of asylum seekers to 1–2 seekers per day, leaving thousands stranded in poor conditions in Serbia (Nelson 2018). This has been implemented in the United States as noted in the previous chapter, under the "metering policy." In the Netherlands, the government attempted to limit accommodations for newly arriving asylum seekers arguing that local authorities were increasingly meeting demand, and during the year closed multiple shelters claiming that there was no longer a need for them as demand had been met.

CONCLUSION: FAR-RIGHT GROUPS AND THE RESURGENCE OF WHITE NATIONALISM IN THE UNITED STATES

There are clear ties between the developments in the United States and the EU. For example, Steve Bannon, the once chairman of the alt-right Breitbart .com website and former campaign adviser to Donald Trump has created an international mobilization to promote the globalization of nationalism, what he calls "The Movement." The purpose, according to him, is to elect right-wing nationalist and populist politicians in both the United States and across Europe (Kudnani 2019). Declaring that he is creating a war room to replicate the unexpected election of Trump in 2016, and the importance of framing the message through various media outlets, Bannon explains, "It's what we did for Trump in the U.S.: writing op-eds, booking people on media, surrogate media—all that" (Fisher 2019). The growing popularity of the Movement is a result of the trends toward illiberalism and Euroskepticism that have been growing for several years, which Bannon is cleverly exploiting. Anti-immigrant sentiments combined with white anxiety are a perfect mix to fuel Bannon's movement. The antiglobalism ideology, due to frustration with Brussels and growing inequality only adds fuel to the fire.

Indicative of his communitarian ideology Bannon stated, "Brexit and Trump were inextricably linked in 2016, and they are inextricably linked today. Working-class people are tired of their 'betters' in New York, London, Brussels telling them how to live and what to do" (Cohen 2019). There is a parallel between Trump and Brexit. Like Trump, Johnson undermines the rule of law and democracy as he dismissed Parliament away for five weeks and banished twenty-one Tory lawmakers of the Labour Party. Johnson agrees, stating, in reference to Trump, "Imagine Trump doing Brexit. He'd go in bloody hard. There'd be all sorts of breakdowns, all sorts of chaos. Everyone would think he'd gone mad. But actually, you might get somewhere. It's a very, very good thought" (Castle 2020).

Speaking at the Open Future in 2018, an economic forum for ultraconservative right-wing populists, he praised Hungary's Viktor Orbán and Italy's Matteo Salvini, two of the most extreme anti-immigrant and Euroskeptic leaders, saying they were trying to get the "sovereignties of their countries back" (Castle 2020). Expressing a blatant nativist perspective, at a meeting with one of the leaders of the Vox Party in Washington, DC, Bannon argued that "it's very important that a party exists in Spain, based on the sovereignty and identity of the Spanish people and willing to defend its borders" (Loucaides 2018). Indeed, this nationalist ideology has found fertile ground in the United States, which is the topic of chapter 4.

Chapter 4

Immigration and the Rise of White Supremacy

This chapter applies social movement, immigration, and critical race theories to immigration and the rise of white supremacy. There also is a focus on how the Trump administration uses both mainstream and social media to engage in misinformation campaigns and purposeful falsehoods to exploit the anxiety that many members of the white working class feel by scapegoating Muslim and Latinx immigrants. I also look at the role of media pundits, primarily on Fox News, in setting immigration policy through their close relationship with, and influence over, the Trump administration. The chapter further discusses Trumpism in a global perspective; his claims (and he makes similar ones about the United States) that allowing immigration leads to a loss of law and order, culture, and traditional values, reversing the post–World War II trans-atlantic alliances and refusing to participate in new ones, and embracing an overall stance of illiberalism.

The latter part of the chapter highlights the global nature of the rise of Islamophobia, anti-Semitism, and white supremacy, much of which has resulted in a growing popularity of nativism and hate crimes. I note the links between extreme politicians and autocrats gaining prominence in Europe and the threat of the destruction of Western civilization held among substantial segments of the population.

As introduced in chapter 1, there are a variety of social movement theories that can refine our understanding of the rise of white nationalism and anti-immigrant feelings. Strain theory, the concepts of collective identity and framing are all important. However, resource mobilization theory, which views the media as a critical tool in activists' repertoire, needs to be updated. A major change has taken place over the past several years in terms of how information is produced, distributed, and consumed due to the introduction of the internet and social media platforms. This, in turn, has altered the terrain of establishing collective identity and the farming of messages. New ICTs and social networking sites have shifted the relevance from activists merely gaining media attention from the mainstream press to ordinary citizens who become the message creators, or Mojos (often referred to as mobilize citizen journalists), who construct and distribute their own information (Carty 2015).

Henry Giroux emphasizes the importance of the communication field, and consequently the political environment, in motivating contentious politics. He summarizes, "Alternative newspapers, progressive media, and a profound sense of the political constitute elements of a vibrant, critical formative culture within a wide range of public spheres that have helped nurture and sustain the possibility to think critically, engage in political dissent, organize collectively, and inhabit public spaces in which alternative and critical theories can be developed" (Karlin 2018).

In essence, he argues that it is the media ecology that can accelerate serious political discussions and debate, and ultimately facilitate displays of collective behavior. He is among many theorists whose perspective was mainly focused on the use of media to promote democracy and ideologies that were representative of groups on the left. He was also referring to print media. The digital revolution, however, has advanced a new repertoire at the disposal of both those who challenge the status quo and those who support it. One of the benefits of new ICTs for organizers on both the left and right spectrum of politics is that they enhance the ability of organizers to recruit new members or at least encourage support for a particular cause.

THE DIGITAL REVOLUTION AND ITS IMPACT ON POLITICAL AND SOCIAL MOBILIZATION

Indeed, theorists have long noted that social networks, relational ties, and friendships are an invaluable resource by serving as a conduit of information and as a channel through which to recruit people to a cause. New ICTs expand the potential of these networks to develop and mutate exponentially, and especially through weak ties across diffuse networks and among individuals who might not receive this information through any other communicative format (Giungi 1999). Contrary to what some theorists feared, that the advent of digital ICTs would replace collective identity and weaken the capacity for collective behavior in real communities, mediated forms of communication often complement those based on face-to-face interaction and have a positive effect on political participation and activity.

The instantaneous peer-to-peer sharing also allows technologically enabled networks to serve as hybrids in that they do not result in mere "clicktivism" but rather encourage viewers of information to engage in contentious politics

(Carty 2015). New media technologies also substantially shift the way that activists can create, distribute, and consume information, which broadens the public sphere of communication and allows organizers to quickly and cheaply reach a critical mass, in contrast to the one-to-many flow of information through mainstream media (Kahn and Kellner 2003). This is demonstrative of what Alberto Melucci refers to as the "intermediate public space" through which individuals can politicize issues through dialogue outside of the authorities (Melucci 1996).

Additionally, Fufekci (2013) argues that new digital technology and social media can facilitate the development of community in spite of physical distance, creating virtual public spheres and encouraging new organizational structures of social movements in a collective cause. The virtual infrastructure of this new media ecology therefore helps to build networks of coordinated action that are loosely articulated and decentralized. Boulainne's (2009) findings, for example, illustrate that the dissemination of information, peer to peer through electronic mediums increases the likelihood of participation in protests activity, and what Jenkins (2006) calls the "spillover effect."

THE RISE OF ANTI-IMMIGRANT IDEOLOGY AND WHITE SUPREMACY

The application of the social movement, immigration, and critical race theories are useful in understanding recent dynamics related to the increase of nativist sentiments, the organization of groups that promote an anti-immigrant agenda, and the carrying out of protest activity or hate crimes. Framing includes narratives that migrants are criminals, introduce health risks, and refuse to assimilate. Other frames are that through programs such as DACA or family sponsorship, politicians reward bad behavior and encourage illegal immigration.

During economic downturns immigrants are scapegoated (i.e., framed) as taking citizens' jobs, responsible for stagnant wages, and are an overall economic drain on society. They are also accused of ethnic balkanization—refusing to assimilate to dominant American customs, traditions, and language (Buchanan 2014). This is true on both sides of the Atlantic. Thus, strain theory as utilized by McVeigh (2009) and Van Dyke and Soule (2002) helps us to better comprehend this resentment. Jordan's (2019), Mutz's (2018), Deitrich's (2014), and Hutter's (2014) work are also helpful in deciphering this trend.

Political scientist Samuel Huntington (2009 in *Foreign Policy*), for instance, justifies this anxiety by stating, "The persistent flow of Hispanic immigrants threatens to divide the US into two peoples, two cultures, and two languages. Unlike past immigrant groups, Mexicans and other Latinos have not assimilated into mainstream US culture, forging instead their own political and linguist enclaves . . . and rejecting the Anglo-protestant values that built the American Dream. The United States ignores that at its own peril." This perspective becomes particularly manifest during times of social instability. These frames, as perpetuated through media outlets, influence public opinion and even more importantly on immigration policy (Cargile et al. 2014). While Huntington refers specifically to the United States, the same dynamic is prevalent in many countries in the EU.

For example, because of the rhetoric and narratives about Muslims, and especially post 9/11 that centered on fear mongering, many in the United States exaggerate perceptions of Muslims' presence and power, which adds to anxiety of an existential threat. A 2016 survey showed that Americans believe 17 percent of the country is Muslim, yet it is around 1 percent (Pew Research Center 2017). These faulty perceptions are not restricted to the United States. In France, citizens think the proportion of Muslims is four times greater than what it is, and in Britain triple (Pew Research Center 2017). According to the media research institute, Media Tenor, 80 percent of (television) news coverage of Muslims is highly negative. A 2018 survey by the Institute for Social Policy and Understanding found that perpetrators of violence who were perceived to be Muslim received seven times more media coverage than non-Muslims (Hussain 2018). On the Fox News program, Fox & Friends in 2010 cohost Brian Kilmeade claimed that "all terrorists are Muslims." These erroneous assumptions highlight the importance of framing and its effect on public opinion as proposed by Cargile et al. (2014).

Additionally, Flores (2018) finds that Trump's negative statements during his campaign and once in office negatively affected public opinion toward immigrants and particularly among Republicans and individuals without college degrees. This is also true in much of Europe. For example, Flores also argues that his rhetoric of "Make America Safe Again" implies that immigrants threaten safety. Her research supports Koopmans and Olzak's (2004) work that analyzes far-right wing violence in Germany, finding that national media coverage of immigration issues, rather than competition between immigrant and native groups for resources, fuels attacks against immigrants.

THE POWER OF MEDIA IN FRAMING MESSAGES: FOX NEWS AND THE SPREAD OF TRUMP'S ETHNO-NATIONALISM

Consequently, the spread of misinformation through media outlets is also a part of framing, constituting immigration as a wedge issue to rally Trump's base of supporters. For instance, while running for office Trump character-ized immigrants as criminals, causing unemployment and declining wages for native-born citizens, and referred to them as "animals" and "vermin" (McClewnen 2018). During his 2019 State of the Union address, he portrayed El Paso (a border town where he wants to build a wall to keep immigrants out) as having "extremely high rates of violent crime" and was "one of our nation's most dangerous cities" until the government built a "powerful bar-rier" (Qiu 2019).

The El Paso County Commissioners Court challenged the White House on the basis of what it considered spreading misinformation and lies about a "crisis situation" on the U.S.-Mexico border. The resolution that the court released stated that "no crisis exists" and that "fiscal year 2017 was the lowest year of illegal cross-border migration on record" (Qiu 2019). In fact, crime was at historic lows before fencing began in 2006, and then rose again over the next four years after the fencing was constructed. El Paso's (Republican) Mayor, Dee Margo chastised Trump on CNN contending that Trump's depiction of her city is "not factually correct." She also tweeted, "El Paso was never one of the most dangerous cities in the US" and Representative Veronica Escobar accused Trump of spreading "falsehoods" (Qiu 2019).

Fox News is often targeted as a news outlet that relies heavily on report-ing and commentary filled with falsehoods and misinformation as a way to influence public opinion and shape policy. For example, on his television show, "The O'Reily Factor" Bill O'Reilly asserted that the Deferred Relief and Education for Alien Minors (DREAM) Act (which would allow undocu-mented college students to pay in-state tuition) was discriminatory toward white students—though not acknowledging that there are also undocumented students who are indeed white (Cohen 2019). Fox & Friends hosts have called what many have referred to as cages (the detention centers holding children of immigrant parents) as "tender age shelters" and Laura Ingraham called them "summer camps" (Egan 2019). Political pundit Ann Coulter went fur-ther claiming that the children detained at the border were "child actors," and warned viewers against falling for their lies or to show compassion (Chasmar 2018).

Lambasting multiculturalism and acceptance, Fox & Friends host, Brian Kilmeade stated that "the Swedes have pure genes because they marry other Swedes. Finns marry other Finns, so they have a pure society. We keep mar-rying other species and ethnics . . . They end up in schools on Long Island and, some of which are MS-13!" (Media Matters 2019). During the 2014 influx of unaccompanied minors, media pundits and celebrities also framed immigration as a threat to the legitimacy of the electoral system. Laura Ingraham described the situation as one in which the government was "traf-ficking illegal immigrants from one part of the country to another part of the country to further erode American wages and further forward their goal of ultimate amnesty and changing the electoral and cultural landscape of the United States" (Durkin 2018).

Ann Coulter, at a Conservative Political Action Conference in 2014 stated, "Amnesty goes through, and the Democrats have 30 million new voters. I just don't think Republicans have an obligation to forgive law-breaking just because the Democrats need another 30 million voters" (Titus 2014). In 2017, on the Carlson Tucker show Tucker added, in reference to Democrats, "Their political success does not depend on good policies but on demographic replacement, and they'll do anything to make sure it happens" (Grynbaum and Sullivan 2019).

In April 2019, Carlson called Central Americans "border jumpers" and Coulter on Jeanine Pirro's Fox News show said that to stem the flow "you can shoot invaders." In a broader context, on her Fox New show host Laura Ingraham lamented, "It does not seem like the America we know and love doesn't exist anymore. Massive demographic changes have been forced on the American people. And they are changes that none of us ever voted for, and most of us don't like. From Virginia to California, we see stark examples of how radically, in some ways the country has changed. Now, much of this is related to both illegal and legal immigration, that of course progressives love" (Pannetta 2019).

In a similar vein, conservative political pundit, Rush Limbaugh on his radio show explained that "the objective is to dilute and eventually eliminate or erase what is known as the distinct or unique American culture. This is why people call it an invasion. There's something behind this, folks, all these caravans amassing. This just doesn't happen organically. This is part of a targeted political project to flood this country and to paralyze the Trump administration" (Clark 2020). In 2018, Carlson opined, "This is really destroying one culture and replacing it with the new foreign culture" (Clark 2020).

The comments made by these political pundits and talk show hosts support what Jardina (2019) and Mutz (2018) view as ethno-nationalism being rooted in white nativism and the threat of the declining social status among white citizens. They are also indicative of Bridge's (2019), Herber et al.'s (2008), and Gallindo and Vilgil's (2006) contention that nativism is used to justify and reward the native race and reinforce white superiority. Garner's (2014) analysis, employing critical race theory is also relevant given his focus on white racialized identities and the norms of whiteness within a code that native citizens claim immigrants do not belong to. Garner (2014) also highlights the process of racialization which supposes whites sustaining relative privilege, and when threatened manifests itself as the "victimization of whiteness" as a consequence of rights being distributed to others who were formerly excluded from receiving them. Ultimately, white citizens are losing a sense to dictate who belongs and who does not.

Theories that focus on economic populism as being at the root of nativism are also key in explaining the hostility toward immigrants. Garner (2012), for example, focuses on class-based issues related to processes of racialization. A poll by the Public Religion Research Institute and the Atlantic in May 2016 reported that 48 percent of white working-class Americans agree that "things have changed so much that I often feel like a stranger in my own country" (McHugh and Jordans 2017).

As resource mobilization theory points out, media is a powerful tool in the arsenal of social movement actors and invaluable in controlling the narrative of contentious issues through framing. Through its broadcasting Fox News successfully identifies prognostic, diagnostic, and action frames that Snow et al. (1986) refer to. It also demonstrates Benford's (1993) emphasis on the importance of linking grievances to mainstream beliefs and values, and Ryan and Gamson's (2006) focus on injustice frames to sway public opinion and mobilize support. Through these efforts the network also helps to foster a sense of collective identity through an "us versus them" mentality which is at the core of Melucci's (1996) work.

IMMIGRATION POLICY SET BY MEDIA PUNDITS

There is often a blurring between politics, news, and entertainment which also can enhance the spread of misinformation. Almost two dozen regular guests on Fox News have or still do hold positions in Trump administration (Chokshi 2019). Conservative Fox News commentaries, many critics argue, serve not only as a mouthpiece for the White House by supporting the president's agenda or reacting to it, but in fact play a role in setting it. According to *New York Times Magazine*, in the context of Hannity's influence it claims, "The call to the White House comes after ten o'clock most weeknights, when Sean Hannity is over. On some days they speak multiple times, with one calling the other to inform him of the latest developments" (Rogers and Nixon 2018).

An analysis by Politico supports this. It demonstrates that Trump has a tendency to "live tweet" based on Fox's coverage of what they are reporting and often uses their precise language (Berver). For instance, on one segment Judd stated, "Our legislators actually have to stand up . . . they can go the nuclear option . . . they need to pass laws to end the catch-and-release program that'll allow us to hold them for a long time." A bit later President Trump tweeted, "Border Patrol Agents are not allowed to properly do their job at the Border because of ridiculous liberal (Democrat) laws like Catch & Release. Getting more dangerous. 'Caravans' coming. Republicans must go Nuclear option to pass tough laws NOW" (Berver 2019).

While the caravan from Central America to the United States happens every year, Trump was unfamiliar with it until he heard about it on Fox News, where anchors referred to it as a "small immigrant army" (Media Matters 2018). Reacting to the coverage, Trump tweeted out messages of hordes of dangerous migrants invading the border and demanded that the Mexican government stop the immigrants or else he would end funding and trade negotiations (Rogers and Nixon 2018). When a reporter asked Trump who influenced his decision to declare a national emergency when he failed to get funding for the wall on the Southwest border, which was at the core of his campaign message, he named conservative media personalities and frequent guests on Fox News talk shows such as Sean Hannity, Rush Limbaugh, Tucker Carlson, and Laura Ingram (Lee 2019).

Their previous attacks on the president for caving politically to Congress convinced Trump to refuse to sign a bill that did not include funding for the wall, which led to a record thirty-five-day government shutdown (Lee 2019). Trump also defended anchors and political pundits on Fox News, Tucker Carlson and Jeanine Pirro in 2019 when they were criticized for making bigoted statements. His message to them was to "stay strong." Pirro had made disparaging remarks about representative Ilhan Omar, suggesting that because she is a Muslim, she may practice Shariah law and not be loyal to the United States (Cummings 2019). Carlson made comments on a shock-jock radio program referring to Iraqis as "semiliterate primitive monkeys" (Grynbaum 2019). On air Carlson portrayed himself as a victim of a liberal "mob" in their pursuit to silence conservative voices. On his behalf Trump tweeted, "The Radical Left Democrats, working closely with their beloved partner, the Fake News Media, is using every trick in the book to SILENCE a majority of our Country" (Grynbaum and Rogers 2019). Garner (2012) classifies this type of mindset as the "victimization of whiteness" under the rubric of critical race theory.

Trump constantly discredits media outlets aside from Fox News and often frames the mainstream media as the "enemy of the people." On Twitter he wrote, "The Press has never been more dishonest than it is today . . . They are totally out of control . . . The New York Times reporting is false" (Grynbaum and Sullivan 2019). He also claimed (while fielding questions from reporters in Britain) that "CNN is fake news . . . I don't take questions from CNN." He then called on a White House correspondent from Fox News saying, "Let's go to a real network" (Jamieson 2017). On Twitter Trump referred to "fake news" 273 times in 2019—a 50 percent increase from 2018. He accused the *New York Times* of treason and said that *Washington Post* reporters "shouldn't even be allowed on the grounds of the white house." The Trump campaign also revoked press credentials of journalists from the *Washington Post*, Politico, and BuzzFeed News during this 2016 campaign (Grynbaum 2019).

However, demonstrating Trump's assumption that Fox must be loyal to him and frame issues in a way favorable to him, in October 2019, he criticized the network over a Fox poll that measured attitudes toward his impeachment trial. On Twitter he wrote "@FoxNews is much different than it used to be in the good old days," and Fox is "letting millions of GREAT people down! We have to start looking for a new News Outlet. Fox isn't working for us anymore!" (Koblin 2019).

In another retaliation against the press in February 2019 at the summit between the leaders of the United States and North Korea in Hanoi, Vietnam, the White House barred four American journalists from covering the dinner between Trump and Kim Jong-un. This was in retaliation after two reporters, in an earlier interaction with Trump called out questions to him about his former attorney's testimony against him in court (Grynbaum and Rogers 2019). This broke a long-standing precedent set by all other U.S. presidents in their meetings with foreign leaders while traveling abroad, and especially with those who do not allow or restrict freedom of the press.

The White House Correspondents' Association responded by a direct statement which read, "This summit provides an opportunity for the American presidency to display its strength by facing vigorous questioning from a free and independent news media, not telegraph weakness by retreating behind arbitrary last-minute restrictions on coverage" (Grynbaum and Rogers 2019). Trump's attacks on American news organizations have also been cited by press advocates for emboldening foreign autocrats who censor, threaten, jail, and assault journalists. In fact, intimidation and vilification of the press is now a global phenomenon as many journalists have been jailed or killed (Committee to Protect Journalists 2020).

Mr. Sulzerger, the editor of the *Times*, has urged Trump to abandon the "enemy of the people" terminology due to more and more world leaders mimicking his statements and cracking down on independent journalism. He stated, "In demonizing the free press as the enemy, simply for performing its role of asking difficult questions and bringing uncomfortable information to light, President Trump is retreating from a distinctly American principle. It's a principle that pervious occupants of the Oval Office fiercely defended regardless of their politics, party affiliation or complaints about how they were covered. As I have repeatedly told President Trump face to face, there are mounting signs that this incendiary rhetoric is encouraging threats and violence against journalists at home and abroad" (Grynbaum and Sullivan 2019).

THE TRUMP ADMINISTRATION'S CRITICISM
TOWARD EU IMMIGRATION POLICIES

As mentioned previously, Trump and his supporters are also hostile toward Muslim immigrants. While running for the presidency he called for a "total and complete shutdown" of Muslims entering the United States. He constantly spoke of President Barack Obama being a secret Muslim and distributed misinformation about Muslims being behind the 9/11 attack (Abdelaziz et al. 2019). When there were debates about funding for the border wall on the southern border that he desperately wanted, he made the claim via Twitter that there were "prayer rugs" (i.e., implying Muslims were infiltrating the United States from the southern border) found along the border (Oprysko 2019).

Trump extends this anti-Muslim perspective in comments he has made about Muslim refugees in Europe. At a rally in Florida in February 2018, for example, he shared the following declaration with the audience: "Who would believe this? They took in large numbers. They're having problems they never thought possible" (Lacapria 2017). He was insinuating about a terror-related episode involving Muslim immigrants in Sweden, and the supposedly high crime rates due to the presence of the immigrants.

Swedish leaders and citizens alike were at a loss as to what he was referring to. He later admitted he got his (mis) information from Fox News (Lacapria 2017). Trump also claimed London mayor Sadiq Khan was responsible for "spiraling crime" and terrorism because he allows too many immigrants into London (Dunn 2018). Referring to Germany he declared, "The people of Germany are turning against their leadership as migration is rocking the already tenuous Berlin coalition. Crime in Germany is way up. Big mistake made all over Europe in allowing millions of people in who have so strongly and violently changed their culture" (Langsdon 2018). However, according to government statistics as of May 2018, crime in Germany was down almost 10 percent from 2016 to 2017 (Langsdon 2018).

Trump has also described migration as a major contributor to what he considers a breakdown of law and order in Europe and that it is destroying its culture. Alluding to what he sees as white culture being threatened by invaders and a threat to the ethno-national majority he stated, "Allowing the immigration to take place in Europe is a shame. I think it changed the fabric of Europe and, unless you act very quickly, it's never going to be what it was and I don't mean that in a positive way. So I think allowing millions of people to come to Europe is very, very sad. I think you are losing your culture. Look around. You go through certain areas that didn't exist ten or fifteen years ago" (Li 2018).

In November 2017, Trump retweeted three videos that were posted by the leader of the far-right British political party, Britain First (Waterson et al.

2017). They purported to show the effects of mass Muslim migration in Europe and consisted of titles such as "Muslim Migrant Beats up Dutch Boy on Crutches!", "Muslim Destroys a Statue of Virgin Mary!", and "Islamist Mob Pushes Teenage Boy off Roof and Beats Him to Death!". The assailant in one video that he shared, in fact, was not a Muslim migrant and the other two videos depicted four-year-old events with no explanation. At least one of the videos, which originated in the Netherlands, was found to be completely false (Waterson et al. 2017).

The retweet was universally condemned among U.S. allies and a spokesperson for Prime Minister Theresa May declared, "It is wrong for the president to have done this. Britain First seeks to divide communities through their use of hateful narratives which peddle lies and stoke tensions. They cause anxiety to law-abiding people. British people overwhelmingly reject the prejudiced rhetoric of the far right, which is the antithesis of the values which this country represents: decency, tolerance and respect" (Waterson et al. 2017). In response to May's comments criticizing the retweets, Trump encouraged her to "focus on the destructive Radical Islamic Terrorism that is taking place within the United Kingdom" on Twitter. The White House also defended the tweets by saying it doesn't matter if the videos are accurate because Muslims pose a "threat" (Waterson et al. 2017).

Asked about Trump's retweets on CNN's "New Day," former director of national intelligence James Clapper said he found the tweets "bizarre and disturbing." He elaborated, "I think it causes friends and allies to question where he is coming from with this. So it has all kinds of ripple effects both in terms of perhaps inciting violence or encouraging anti-Muslim violence, and as well as causes, I think our friends and allies to wonder about the judgment of the President of the United States" (Jackson 2017). This once again highlights the significance that the framing of an issue can have on public opinion and policy that social movement theorists such as Benford (1993) and Snow et al. (1986) underscore.

These comments also represent how Higham (1999) defines fear of immigrants as an important factor of critical race theory as citizens can assert that outsiders jeopardize a shared sense of heritage, language, faith, ancestry, and cultural traits. Bridges (2019) and Huber et al. (2008) also argue that nationalism is important to nativism because it both illuminates the process of defending national identity from perceived threats, and simultaneously engenders a fear of foreigners. Racist nativism theories put forth by Midgley (2017), Hushman (2017), Schueths (2014), and Lippard (2011) further note that when the supposed superiority of the native status and domination is threatened, there is often aggressive action to challenge it. Jarret's (1999) work also points to how real or perceived threats of cultural and social order lead to anti-immigrant sentiments as does the analysis of Dietrich (2014).

INCREASING HATE CRIMES AND SOCIAL
MEDIA AS A TOOL OF WHITE SUPREMACISTS

White supremacy and ultranationalism are currently among the greatest domestic security threats in the United States and are increasingly growing in other Western countries as well. In 2009, the Homeland Security Department predicted that the economic downturn, the increasing use of social media, and the election of Barak Obama would make a race-driven extremism a serious threat to national security (Belew 2019). The SPLC recorded a significant increase in hate crimes during the 2016 presidential campaign, and another large spike after Trump was elected president (Weiser 2019). According to FBI crime data, there was a 26 percent increase in white supremist hate crimes in the last quarter of 2016 during the election compared to the same time frame the previous year, and the number of white supremacist murders more than doubled in Trump's first year of office (Wills 2019). Anti-Semitic crimes rose by 57 percent between 2016 and 2017 in the United States, which represents the largest increase in a one-year time frame, and incidents of white supremacist propaganda such as posting fliers or vandalizing synagogues and mosques increased 182 percent in 2018 (Weiser 2019).

This is a global phenomenon. In 2018, anti-Semitic attacks killed more Jews around the world than in any year in decades. In the first two quarters of 2019, there was a 40 percent increase in anti-Semitic incidents compared to the same time period in 2016 according to Anti-Defamation League (Watkins and Corasaniti 2019). In 2017, the New York City Commission on Human Rights surveyed over 3,000 Muslim, Jewish, and Sikh residents and found that 38 percent claimed they had been verbally harassed or taunted because of their race or faith (Nasa 2018). Almost 10 percent said they were victims of physical assault and a similar figure said they had their property vandalized or defaced.

In 2019, the FBI reported that of its 850 pending domestic terror investigations, about 40 percent involved racially motivated extremism. In 2017 and 2018, it had made more arrests connected to domestic terror than to international terrorism, and hate crimes reached a nine-year high in 2017. Michael McGarrity, an official in the FBI's counterterrorism division testified before Congress in June 2019 that, "Individuals adhering to racially motivated violent extremism ideology have been responsible for the most lethal incidents among domestic terrorists in recent years" (Watkins and Corasanititi 2019).

Since 2002 there have been three times as many deadly far-right terrorist attacks than jihadist attacks (Reitman 2018). In 2018, the FBI reported that hate crimes spiked in 2017 and nearly 60 percent of victims of hate crimes were targeted based on race and more than 20 percent based on religion. According to data compiled by the University of Maryland's Global

Terrorism Database, the number of terror-related incidents has more than tripled in the United States between 2013 and 2017, and the number of those killed by hate crimes quadrupled (University of Maryland Global Terrorism Database 2017).

These recent trends illustrate that immigration has replaced terrorism as a top concern in the United States. In 2018, hate crimes against Latinos were at their highest level since 2010 (Hassan 2019). Most of the violence has been against Latinos, followed by Muslims and Arab Americans. The SPLC reported the number of hate groups is at a record of 1,020 in 2018, and that alt-right groups have killed far more people since 9/11 than any other category of extremist (Reitman 2018). During a congressional hearing in the wake of the Charlottesville riot in 2017, the director of the FBI, Christopher Wray told lawmakers that the bureau had about 1,000 open domestic terror investigations, which is about the same number of investigations open on the international terrorist group ISIS.

A George Washington University study tracked a 600 percent increase in the followership of American white nationalist accounts on Twitter between 2012 and 2016, the followers of these accounts overtaking those of pro-ISIS accounts as the leading radical users of the platform (Bennett and Powell 2019). The Anti-Defamation League found that 71 percent of the extremist-related fatalities in the United States between 2008 and 2019 were committed by members of far-right or white supremacist movements (Anti-Defamation League 2020).

The racist rhetoric used by Trump—calling Mexicans "rapists" and "criminals," and his attempt to ban immigrants from Muslim-majority counties—may be emboldening groups and individuals that hold similar bigoted attitudes to express and act on their beliefs, assuming that this is acceptable and legitimate in the new political and cultural terrain (Horowitz et al. 2015). The director of the SPLC's Intelligence Project, Heidi Beirich stated, "This president is not simply a polarizing figure but a radicalizing one. Rather than trying to defuse hate encourage unity, as presidents of both parties have done, President Trump elevates it—with both his rhetoric and his policies. In doing so, he's given people across America the go-ahead to act on their worst instincts" (Conley 2019).

Trump also suggested in March 2019 there may be violence by his supporters if his policies are not supported. A few days later Representative Steven King of Iowa posted on Twitter a cartoon/meme referring to a possible modern-day U.S. civil war (Abramasky 2019). King, in fact, has a long history of xenophobia. In 2005, he introduced a bill that would have made English the official language of the United States and sued the Iowa Secretary of State for posting voting information on an official website in languages other than English; in 2006 he called the deaths of Americans at the hands of undocumented immigrants "a slow motion Holocaust"; he embraced the birther conspiracy against President Obama and tweeted a cartoon of him wearing a turban, and in 2018 stated he did not want Muslims working in meatpacking plants in Iowa because, "I don't want people doing my pork that won't eat it let alone hope I go to hell for eating pork chops" (Gabriel 2019).

While many of his statements (and those made by other lawmakers and political pundits) are clearly racist, he often prioritizes either culture or civilization to conflate, or perhaps confuse his message. In an interview with Steve Bannon in 2015, for instance, he claimed, "We have a right to protect our borders, our culture and our civilization." At the Republican National Convention in 2016 he stated: "I would ask you to go back through history and figure out where are these contributions that have been made by these other categories of people you are talking about. Where did any other sub-group of people contribute more to civilization?" and he tweeted, "Cultural suicide by demographic transformation must end" (Crowley 2017).

As one of the authors of "How Democracies Die," Steven Levitsky laments, "violent talk, can, at minimum, encourage lone-wolf violence. It can also slowly normalize political violence, turning discourse and ideas that were unsayable and even unthinkable into things that are sayable and thinkable" (Lenohardt 2019). Indeed, the framing of the issues and intolerant rhetoric has resulted in violence and death. One of the most egregious white supremist events took place in August 2017 when white nationalists gathered in Charlottesville, VA, for a "Unite the Right" march, chanting "blood and soil" and "you will not replace us" and throwing up stiff-armed Nazi salutes (Roose 2019). The rally is a great example of nativist racism and its relationship to white superiority that Gallindo and Vigil (2006) refer to: defending the natives' right to dominance, as well as Huber et al. (2008) and Jarret's (1999) theories pertaining how a perceived lack of assimilation among immigrant groups is envisioned as a threat to the cultural and social order.

The following day an alt-right supporter drove his car into a crowd of counter activists, killing one and injuring thirty others. Trump was assailed for his comments in reaction to the incident saying that there were "very fine people on both sides" (Gray 2017). James Fields, twenty-one years old pleaded guilty to twenty-nine charges in March 2019, one of which was counted as a hate crime, or "domestic terrorism" that resulted in the death of activist Heather Heyer who was protesting the white nationalists (Zraick and Jacobs 2019). In his online posts, Fields expressed support for white supremacist and neo-Nazi views and policies, as well as violence against nonwhites.

Another deadly and high-profile hate crime occurred in Pittsburgh at the Tree of Life synagogue on the Jewish Sabbath in October 2018 that left eleven worshipers dead. The shooter, Robert Bowers shouted anti-Semitic slurs during the rampage and claimed that the Hebrew Immigrant Aid Society

(HAIS), which has resettled over 400,000 Jews coming to the United States, was aiding refugees in the caravan coming from Central America (Serwer 2018). The Pittsburgh attack was the deadliest against Jews in U.S. history (Garcia 2018). Misinformation coming from ultraconservative media outlets and social media sites that promote conspiracy theories likely influenced Bowers. For example, his belief that George Soros (a Jewish billionaire donor to the Democratic Party) was funding the caravans and were full of ISIS terrorists may be due to Trump's framing of the situation that the caravans represented an "onslaught," and an "assault" by "unknown Middle Easterners" (Garcia 2018).

Vice President Pence also promoted conspiracy theories. He told Fox News, "what the president of Honduras told me is that the caravan was organized by leftist organizations, political activists within Honduras, and he said it was being funded by outside groups, and even from Venezuela . . . So the American people, I think, see through this, they understand this is not a spontaneous caravan of vulnerable people" (Garcia 2018). Fox News had called the caravan an "invasion" over sixty times in October 2018 (Rozsa 2018). Whether Bowers was a viewer of Fox News we don't know. We do, however, have his digital fingerprints. He was very active on the Gab website which hails itself as a guardian of free speech that does not censor individuals who indulge in hate speech and extremism as other platforms do (Berkowitz 2018). Hours before the attack he posted, "HAIS likes to bring invaders in that kill our people. I can't sit by and watch my people get slaughtered. Screw your optics, I'm going in" (Adone et al. 2018).

In April 2019, a self-professed nineteen-year-old neo-Nazi, after shouting anti-Semitic slurs, used an assault-style weapon and opened fire at worshipers inside the Chabad synagogue in Poway in Southern California, killing one person and injuring three others (Dreier 2020). The attacker, John Earnest, posted on online, "I would die a thousand times over to prevent the doomed fate that the Jews have planned for my race. Every Jew is responsible for the meticulously planned genocide of the European race. They act as a unit, and every Jew plays his part to enslave the other races around him, whether consciously or subconsciously. Their crimes are endless" (Dreir 2019). Later, in December 2019 three people were shot dead at a kosher supermarket in Jersey City, NJ (Knowles et al. 2019). Just a few weeks later in Monsey, NY, a man entered the home of an Orthodox Jewish family and stabbed five worshippers with a machete (Dwyer 2019). The attacker, Grafton Thomas, had searched online many times for "why did Hitler hate the Jews." Below (2019) views these types of examples of what she perceives to be a brewing global "race war." She maintains that white power ideology is the connecting thread of all of these attacks which are planned to incite a much larger slaughter by "awakening" others to join the movement.

In July, a nineteen-year-old male in Gilroy, CA, opened fire at a garlic festival killing three and injuring thirteen before taking his own life (May 2019). He had been using Instagram to promote white supremacy, and minutes before the shooting he posted a picture with a caption that told followers to read a nineteenth-century proto-fascist book, "The Might is Right," which glorifies "Aryan" men and condemns racial intermarriage (Alexander 2019). In another act of domestic terrorism, Patrick Crusius shot and killed twenty-two and injured twenty-four at a shooting in a Walmart store in August 2019 in El Paso, TX. Online he explained that he was "simply defending my country from cultural and ethnic replacement brought on by an invasion" (Arango et al. 2019).

His online manifesto titled, "The inconvenient Truth" was inspired by the mass murder of Muslims at Christchurch in New Zealand in March 2019. It begins, "In general, I support the Christchurch shooter and his manifesto. This attack is a response to the Hispanic invasion of Texas . . . If we can get rid of enough people, then our way of life can be more sustainable" (Arango et al. 2019). It goes on to argue that immigration "can only be detrimental to the future of America" and Hispanics would be "changing policy to suit their needs. . . . I am against race mixing because it destroys generic diversity and creates identity problems . . . the natives (American Indians) didn't take the invasion of Europeans seriously, and now what's left is just a shadow of what was" (Arango et al. 2019). Arguing for the creation of ethno-states for different races he elaborates, "I am honored to head the fight to reclaim my country from destruction."

Another *attempted* hate crime in 2019 by a domestic terrorist and white nationalist, which the FBI successfully interrupted, was a plan intended to attack Trump's opponents to establish a "white homeland" (Conley 2019). FBI officers arrested U.S. Coast Guard Lieutenant Christopher Hasson in Maryland after finding a stockpile of weapons in his home that he planned to use against Trump critics, proclaiming that he wanted to trigger a race war. His list of potential targets was Speaker of the House Nancy Pelosi, Senator Elisabeth Warren, and Congresswoman Alexandria Ocasio-Cortez and high-profile journalist Joe Scarborough.

Hasson professed that he was inspired by a right-wing Norwegian terrorist Anders Breivik, who slaughtered seventy-seven people in 2011 in a crusade to resist multiculturalism and immigration (Cullen 2019). The U.S. government submitted a statement to the courts which proclaimed, "The defendant intended to murder innocent civilians on a scale rarely seen in this country" (Conley 2019). As with many recent domestic terrorist attacks, the internet played a role in finding and sharing information with those of a similar persuasion. One of his internet searches included "civil war if Trump impeached" (Cullen 2019).

The FBI was also able to abort the attempted domestic terror attack by Cesar Sayoc, who is a major supporter of Trump and sent bombs through the mail to Democrats he disliked including Hillary Clinton, former president Obama, former CIA. director John Brennan, former director of national intelligence James Clapper, Democratic donor George Soros, the CNN office, and actor Robert De Niro who has been highly critical of the president (Weiser 2019). On Twitter and Facebook, he chastised former president Obama using racial slurs, and threatened former vice president Joe Biden. Federal prosecutors labeled his actions "a domestic terrorist attack" (Weiser 2019).

This xenophobia and violence have spread to schools across the United States and among young people in general. Following the election of Trump, the SPLC released a report entitled, "The Trump Effect: The Impact of the 2016 Election on Our Nation's Schools" (Southern Poverty League Center 2016). The organization surveyed more than 10,000 educators and their findings revealed an increase of incidents that involved swastikas, Nazi salutes, and Confederate flags on school property. At the university level neo-Nazi groups such as Identity Evropa (which was once one of the largest "alt-right" fascists groups but renamed itself the American Identity Movement after many of its members were doxed), The Right Stuff, and Vanguard America have been very active (Bader 2017).

On and off college campuses Evropa has conducted several banner drops decrying immigration, some reading, "Import the Third World, Become the Third World," "Make America White Again," "Imagine a Muslim-Free America," "Are You Sick of Anti-White Propaganda in College? You not Alone," "Take Your Country Back," and "You Will Not Replace Us" (Posner 2017). The distribution of white supremacist propaganda on college and university campus has nearly doubled between 2018 and 2019 (Hassan 2020).

Other far-right groups such as The Patriot Front, The Right Stuff, and Vanguard America also seek to inspire students to oppose multiculturalism and efforts to promote diversity. The Patriot Front has dropped banners reading, "Americans are White. The rest must go" (Bader 2017). They frame their argument by claiming that "non-privileged" whites are victims of unfair government polies and are frustrated by what they see as the "cultural cleansing of white history." On college campuses fliers have been posted with the message of "Look Around White Man, Your Culture is being Eroded." To appear more mainstream, many of these groups are trying to make inroads into the Republican Party. Additionally, leaders of far-right organizations are articulating to their members that rallies and protests are no longer needed given that many of the policies of the Trump administration are consistent with their worldview in terms of policy and language (Becker 2019; Woods and Hahner 2019). Their advice is to recruit through social media and infiltrate the political system to move the mainstream farther toward the extreme.

The work of these organizations to reach out to and recruit those who feel that they are disenfranchised and are subject to injustice—in this case white males—is a hallmark of social movement theories that focus on the role of collective identity. Gamson (1992), for example, discusses the importance of the intrinsic rewards of being part of a movement or organization for the purposes of self-realization and satisfaction, and a sense of group belonging. Ryan and Gamson (2006) note the significance of "injustice frames" for recruitment purposes which these far-right groups utilize in a very powerful way. Tarrow (1988) find that promoting a sense of urgency to a real or perceived injustice (and many of these are perceived rather than real threats) advocates a sense of worthiness to the cause and provides potential recruits with a sense of agency.

Far-right groups also employ the concept of frame bridging as proposed by Snow et al. (1986). This happens when organizations can reach people who share their beliefs and values through information sharing, consciousness-raising efforts, and organizational outreach. It allows them to expand the boundaries of the initial frame to include issues or social problems of importance to potential participants. In this case, leadership combines issues of injustice against white males with a loss of culture and blaming immigrants for their perceived misfortune.

The dynamics of these groups and their supporters also support social movement theories that focus on the role of digital media as a critical resource. The ability to expand networks and mutate at high rates through weak ties and among people who might not receive information or meet similar-minded people any other way is central to Carty's (2015) and Giunigni's (1993) work. These supporters exist in intermediate public spaces that Melucci (1980) theorizes as being a core component of political and civic discussion and engagement in the digital age.

Critical race theory is also necessary to make sense of these dynamics. The obsession with an "invasion" by foreigners and their perceived attempt to shape policy based on their own demographic interests, the need to build an ethno-state and white homeland, fear of a race-based civil war, and the cleansing of white/European culture and history are at the crux of what Schueths (2014), Selod (2014), and Huber et al. (2008) theorize as the basis of protecting white supremacy, oftentimes under the pretense of fake patriotism. Jardina (2019) and Mutz (2018) view this as rooted in what is felt like a decline in social status, primarily among young white males which lends itself to the appeal of far-right groups who promise to protect and maintain their privileged status. The competition for schools, jobs, political representation, and overall resources further spark the kind of resentment against immigrants that Mutz (2018) and Hutter (2014) include in their analyses.

THE RISE OF IDENTITARIANS,
ILLIBERALISM, AND THE ROLE OF ICTS

As the incidents described above reveal, the internet and social media are powerful tools in the repertoire of alt-right groups to recruit new members, build new organizational structures, and fundraise. Indeed, new ICTs serve as a perfect tool for the spread of racist and otherwise hateful ideas among individuals who take advantage of the anonymity of online tools, social media, and messaging boards. Between 2014 and 2015, for example, the number of "likes" on hate group tweets and comments tripled, and between 2015 and 2016 they once again tripled, demonstrating how they are exponentially gaining traction among supporters, if not membership and participation in public, street-based demonstrations (Eversely 2017). To recruit and organize the alt-right movement uses websites and social media platforms such as Stormfront, 4chan, 8chan, Reddit, and Patron, as well as more mainstream devices that include Twitter and Facebook to radicalize people, and young white males in particular.

These kinds of websites proactively attempt to reach young white males who feel slighted and are looking for a scapegoat to assuage their anger and sense of despair. The design of the various sites, through messages, videos, and chat rooms, is intended to convince or reinforce the feeling that white males are victims in the current cultural environment that embraces diversity, multiculturalism, and gender equality (Kingsbury 2019). A strategy paper released by the DHS reads: "In an age of online radicalization to violent extremism and disparate threats, we must not only counter foreign enemies trying to strike us from abroad, but also those enemies, foreign and domestic, that seek to spur violence our youth and our disaffected—encouraging them to strike in the heart of our nation" (Kingsbury 2019). The DHS is focusing on right-wing terrorism and white supremacist groups in particular.

Andrew Anglin, the founder of the Daily Stormer website has been exploring this strategy. He writes online, "Our target audience is white males between the ages of 10 and 30. I include children as young as 10, because an element of this is that we want to look like superheroes. We want something that boys fantasize about being a part of. That is a core element of this. I don't include men over the age of 30, because after that point you are largely fixed in your thinking" (Berkowitz 2018). In addition to targeting members of the GOP and recruitment efforts on college campuses, think tanks such as Richard Spencer's (who coined the term alt-right) National Policy Institute help legitimize white supremacists and nationalist ideologies, and make it easier for white nationalists to share their messages with a broader audience. He frames racial animosity under the rubric that the problem with whites is that they will not promote their own racial identity, or their "rightful place" while other groups increasingly do so (Berkowitz 2018).

The altright.com website posts,

> "Our movement is almost 90 percent young White men who know they are being screwed if things don't start improving. We are de facto not a White advocacy group as much as we are a Young White Men's Advocacy group . . . Minorities have explicit advocacy groups, Jews have just about everything. Young White Men do not have any money or political power . . . or even deep-pocketed supporters. But then, they never have. Young White Men have always had to make up for this disadvantage through their enthusiasm, energy and ambition. They have always had to rise up and take what was theirs". (Nagle 2017)

In 2013, Spencer further elaborated, "We need an ethno-state so that our people can 'come home again' . . . We must give up the false dreams of equality and democracy. Ethnic cleansing is impossible as long as marginalized people have enough votes to stop it. But this roadblock disappears if you get rid of democracy" (Berkowitz 2018). Spencer also claimed that the United States is a "white country designed for ourselves," and added that "the forty years between the 1924 and 1965 law were the country's best" and that "The age of mass immigration and the age of multiculturalism has been an age of division and fragmentation" (Berkowtitz 2018).

Purposively, representatives of the alt-right, like Spencer, reject the white supremacist label to try to appear mainstream. The SPLC summarizes the new white nationalists this way: "Cultured, intelligent and often possessing impressive degrees from some of America's premier colleges and universities, this new breed of white radical advocate is a far cry from the populist politicians and hooded Klansmen of the Old South." Instead of blatantly promoting white supremacy they emphasize racial self-preservation rooted in the supposed superiority of white culture (i.e., racist nativism). They often describe themselves as *identitarians* and embrace cultural nativism, racial self-preservation, and affirm that culture and race are inextricably bound. Thus, they conclude that the replacement of white culture will diminish civilization as other races and ethnic groups are perceived to be intellectually and morally inferior.

They further assert that Western civilization is being endangered by immigrants from developing countries and undermining "traditional Western values" and feel threatened by what they perceive to be the cosmopolitan establishment in the media, universities, government, and the Democratic Party. Data collected by the SPLC finds that there are over 600 active neo-Nazi and white supremacist groups, in addition to hundreds of anti-government militias that either have a stated intention to overthrow liberal democracy or historically engaged in armed struggle (Southern Poverty Law Center 2019).

The "Base" is one of the most recent neo-Nazi groups espousing white supremacy and call for a race war. Seven members were arrested seven days before a gun rally in Richmond, VA, scheduled for January 20, 2019, after the FBI recorded messages among the seven to infiltrate the rally and "derail some trains, kill some people, and poison some water supplies" (MacFarquhar and Goldman 2019). Similar to Al Qaeda it attempts to radicalize over the internet and social media and create independent cells and/or lone wolves to carry out terrorist attacks to achieve the ultimate goal of creating an ethno-state in the Pacific Northwest. The agenda has evolved from discussions and recruiting online to actual acts of violence and training in military and survival skills (MacFarquhar and Goldman 2019).

In late February 2020, five individuals affiliated with a neo-Nazi group were charged with efforts to intimidate, attack, and harass a variety of people, mainly journalists, media buildings, politicians, and faith-based leaders by federal prosecutors (O'Brian 2020). They had links to the white supremacist group, Atomwaffen Division, which is a violent paramilitary neo-Nazi organization. Their main tactic is swatting (calling authorities alluding to an imminent threat a certain location to which they will respond with excessive force as a precaution).

Law enforcement officers began monitoring the group's activities in 2018 once they became aware that they were participating in military-style training and "hate" camps (Baker et al. 2020). The main intent of the group is to spark a race war which they feel would inevitably lead to the collapse of the United States and thereby allowing it to create a white ethno-state (thus sharing an ideological perspective with the Base). This supports Below's (2019) theory of the emergence and purpose of white supremist groups—creating a global race war.

The call for ethnic cleansing and an end to democracy; the desperate desire for a homogenous, white nation-state; and the preservation of a supposed superior culture and values rooted in Western civilization are key to Higham's (1999) understanding of how religious and political differences, which sometimes intersect with racism, often evolve into the desire for ethno-nationalism.

The Trump administration has played a role in encouraging this ideology. For example, in stark defiance of multiculturalism and global democratic liberalism, in October 2018 at a rally in Houston, TX, President Trump declared, "Really, we're not supposed to use that word. You know what I am, I'm a nationalist, OK? I'm a nationalist. Nationalist! Use that word! Use that word . . . radical Democrats want to turn back the clock, go back to the rule of corrupt, power-hungry globalists. You know what a globalist is right . . . a person

that wants the globe to do well, frankly, not caring about our county so much
. . . We can't have that" (O'Brian 2020).

At the United Nations in September 2019, Trump further stated "The
future does not belong to globalists. The future belongs to patriots. The future
belongs to sovereign and independent nations" (Crowley and Sanger 2019).
He also argued that governments must defend their "history, culture and heritage. . . . The free world must embrace its national foundations. It must not
attempt to erase them or replace them. . . . Many of the countries here today
are coping with the challenges of uncontrolled migration. Each of you has the
absolute right to protect your borders. And so, of course, does our country"
(Crowley and Sanger 2019). Previously, Steve Bannon, who was the former
manager of the Trump campaign told an audience in France in March 2018
that "the central government is debasing your citizenship and the big capital-
ists are debasing your personhood. Let them call you racists. Let them call
you xenophobes. Let them call you nativist. Wear it as a badge of honor"
(Bowden 2018).

ILLIBERALISM ON A GLOBAL SCALE

As I mentioned in chapter 3, Bannon is currently setting up a political foundation in Europe which he refers to as "The Movement" to try to solidify
power across the continent that will support right-leaning nationalist parties
to counter the forces of liberal democracy. Trump has a similar agenda. In
addition to the comments above, he left the Human Rights Council, the Paris
Climate Accord, and the Asia-Pacific Trade Pact; revoked funding for the
UN agency that provides education and health care to Palestinians classified
as refugees; announced a withdrawal of troops from Syria without consulting
his administration or allies; boycotted the Global Compact on Immigration;
called EU members a foe and the World Trade Organization a disaster; and
denigrated Canada and Mexico which are the two other members of NAFTA
(Byas 2016).

When he withdrew the United States from the Iran nuclear deal in May
(which the Obama administration solidified together with France, Britain,
Germany, Russia, and China to have Iran agree to cut its enrichment of
uranium in exchange for lifting economic sanctions) France's ambassador
to the United Nations lamented what he called the coming of "a new world
disorder" (Schiritz 2018).

Trump has also expressed ambitions to withdraw from NATO several
times because he perceives the military obligations to be an economic drain,
and according to Michèle Flournoy, who was his undersecretary of defense
under President Barack Obama, "would be one of the most damaging things

that any president could do to U.S. interests" (Barnes and Cooper 2019). James Stavridis, a former allied commander of NATO said a withdrawal would be "a geological mistake of epic proportions" (Barnes and Hooper 2019). Trump further supported some of the most extreme anti-EU politicians during the Brexit debate.

On other fronts Trump refused to sign the collective agreement at the 2018 G7 summit, which championed a dedication to "shared values of freedom, democracy, the rule of law and respect for human rights and our commitment to promote a rules-based international order" (Schake 2018). By doing so, he disregarded decades of alliance building and the economic and political institutions underlying it. Commenting on this defiance Louis Charbonneau, the United Nations director of Human Rights Watch remarked, "It's not just stepping back, it's an assault on one of the most important institutions we have for accountability and monitoring and exposing abuses" (Schwirtz 2018). German foreign minister, Heiko Maas declared, "nothing can be taken for granted any more in foreign policy . . . the United Sates is becoming a place of increasing nationalism, tribalism and self-interest" (Erlanger 2018b).

The disdain for the American president shared by its former allies came to a crescendo in 2019 at the annual Munich Security Conference in February 2019. This was entitled "Who Will Pick up the Pieces?". The agenda was to address the disturbance of the post–World War II order and the insecurity that European allies have regarding the unpredictable behavior of President Trump (Benhold and Erlanger 2019). At the meeting Chancellor Angela Merkel boldly defended the multilateral institutions in opposition to pressure from the United States on European allies to pull out the Iran nuclear deal. She also criticized unilateral moves that included Trump's decision to pull American troops out of Syria, considering a withdrawal from Afghanistan, and his suspension of the Intermediate Range Missile Treaty with Russia (Vennhold and Erlanger 2019).

While her speech was received with robust applause, Vice President Mike Pence was greeted with silence when he notified the members that he was bringing greetings from President Trump. At the conference Pence denounced some of the closest allies of the United States—Britain, France, and Germany for not challenging "Iran's murderous revolutionary regime" (Mark 2019). The contrast was stark symbolically and substantively. While Merkel emphasized collaboration and shared values, Pence put forth a list of demands for the allies that suited American interests (Benhold and Erlanger 2019).

A few hours later, ironically, former vice president under Barack Obama, Joe Biden received a standing ovation for delivering a rebuttal to the administration's "America First" attitude (Rogers and Sanger 2019). In addition to Trump's denigration of globalism and the institutions of liberal democracy, there has also been plenty of support for this type of nativism and xenophobia rhetoric among far-right political pundits and lawmakers. For example, on "The Laura Ingraham Show" which broadcasts on Fox News, Pat Buchanan warned that "This is the great issue of our time. And the real question is whether Europe has the will and the capacity, and America has the capacity to halt the invasion of the countries until they change the character—political, social, racial, ethnic—character of the country entirely. You cannot stop these sentiments of people who want to live together with their own and they want their borders protected" (Blow 2018).

On his blog, conservative radio host Rush Limbaugh posted, "The existential question, however, thus remains: How does the West, America included, stop the flood tide of migrants before it alters forever the political and demographic character of our nations and our civilization?" (Blow 2018). In the past he had written about white America being an endangered species and committing "Western suicide," claiming, "We are truly dealing here with an ideology of Western suicide . . . but on the mega-issue—the Third World invasion of the West—he (Trump) is riding the great wave of the future, if the West has a future" (Blow 2018). In 2017, Representative King from Iowa tweeted, "diversity is not our strength . . . we can't restore our civilization through someone else's babies" (Serwer 2019).

King, like President Trump and others in government also has ties to autocrats and neo-Nazi groups in Europe (Silva 2018). In 2015, he met with the far-right and anti-Islam Dutch politician Geert Wilders, one of the most anti-Muslim politicians in Europe who calls for the closing of mosques. He endorsed a Toronto mayoral candidate with neo-Nazi ties and met with a member of the far-right Austrian Freedom Party (founded in the 1950s by former Nazis) which has been accused of trivializing the Holocaust. On Twitter he follows an Austrian anti-Semitic activist who promotes hanging a portrait of Hitler "in every classroom" (Walker 2019). He is also in agreement with Hungarian leader Orbán, who declared that "Mixing cultures will not lead to a higher quality of life but a lower one" (Nozicka 2017).

King's xenophobic and nationalist rhetoric eventually caught up with him, however, and he was stripped of his House Committee seats (the Judiciary and Agriculture committees) in January 2019. This happened after an interview with the *New York Times* in which he asked, "White nationalist, white supremacist, Western civilization—how did that language become offensive? Why did I sit in classes teaching me about the merits of our history and our civilization?" (Gabriel 2019). He was also quoted in a statement he made in response to the record number of black Americans and women elected to Congress in 2018 saying (referring to a picture of the incoming freshmen), "you could look over there and think the Democratic Party is no country for white men" (Gabriel 2019).

All of these comments above exhibit racist nativism, the desire for ethno-nationalism, and an undeniable communitarian perspective both globally and domestically. Once again the hyperbolic language about of an invasion, the loss of Western culture and heritage, the longing for different ethnic groups (in this context, that is, whites) to live among their own, and the fear of the "suicide" of Western culture speak to the essence of Bridge's (2019), Van Wormart and Link's (2016), Condenstine and Hampshire's (2013), and Garner's (2014) analyses. The "white" code is being challenged, white people are therefore feeling alienated economically, politically, and socially, their superiority did not guarantee any more, and thus the easy scapegoat is immigrants. Rather than relying on blatant bigotry and racism, the arguments and language are couched in terminology that resonates with a sense of patriotism and loyalty to country, and the victimization of whiteness.

WHITE NATIONALIST GROUPS, ICTS, AND THE HYBRID EFFECT TO CARRY OUT HATE CRIMES

Radicalization toward extremism, when it comes to anti-immigrant, anti-Semitic, and Islamophobia attitudes, occurs almost exclusively online and later has consequences on the streets—the hybrid effect as referred to by social movement theorists including Carty (2015) and Jenkins (2006). Sites like Gab are a welcoming place for members of neo-Nazi groups such as The League that also has an agenda intent on attacking and overthrowing liberal democracy, globalization, and multiculturalism. This far-right organization formed in the mid-1990s and is the largest and oldest neo-Confederate group. It relies heavily on the internet and social media to promote an "Anglo Celtic culture" and advocates for a second Southern secession and a society dominated by European Americans (Wayne 2019).

In 2016, the president of the group, Michael Hill published an open letter to the Russian Federation explaining,

"We traditional Southerners look upon the people of Russia as fellow white Christians who are seeking to protect themselves from the corrupt and diabolical forces of globalism. We want to be part of a war with the Russian Federation instigated by the USA/NATO alliance, the head of the globalist cable . . . For over two decades, The League of the South has opposed the infernal machinations of the American Empire. We still seek our independence from it for the survival and well-being of people—the Southern nation. We encourage the Russian Federation to discern that Washington DC . . . has become more and more disconnected from the people over whom they rule . . . we seek friendship and peace with the Russian people and their leaders in the hopes that the

true interests of both can be served by opposing the immoral globalism order".
(Wayne 2019)

The Proud Boys is another new far-right, white supremacist organization
that formed in 2016 and is classified by the SPLC as a hate group. It views
white men and Western culture under siege (Moynihan 2019). To recruit
members, the organization posts and glorifies political violence that it has
engaged in against progressive activists. In 2017, the leader of the group,
Gavin McInnes gave a talk at New York University which several Proud Boys
attended. A fight broke out between protesters of the event and the Proud
Boys and eleven people were arrested by the New York Police Department;
two Proud Boys members were convicted on charges of attempted assault and
riot (Moynihan 2019).

In 2017, at a Trump rally in Berkeley, CA, a supporter of the alt-right was
caught on tape hitting a counterprotester over the head with a shovel. The
image went viral and the Proud Boys organized a crowdfunding campaign
for the attacker's bail, who later became a Proud Boy (Wilson 2018). In
October 2018, McInnes gave a talk at the Metropolitan Republican Club in
Manhattan, NY. Antifascist activist had been protesting outside before the
event and once again a violent struggle broke out and videos showed that the
Proud Boys were the instigator (Shallwant and Weill 2018).

"Roadshow" protests are another outgrowth of online recruitment and
organizational strategies in the white supremacist movement. These events
are planned online in an attempt to bring outside agitators to support white
nationalist rallies in local communities, while making sure there is a clear
strategy and script to follow (Geha 2020). For example, on the website
Occidental Dissent organizers give specific recommendations of what to wear
(khakis and polo shirts so as to look respectable), chants, and symbolical
imagery to use.

Through the spillover effect, which Carty (2015) and Jenkins (2006) view
as an integral part of social movement activity—organizing online and using
public spaces to demonstrate in large numbers—a united and committed
gathering of white nationalists may be perceived by the larger community as
a legitimate social movement. Also, the role of outsiders can provide cover
for locals who support the cause, but do not want to be seen at these kinds of
protest activities in their own communities for fear of reprisal.

The Rise Above Movement is also a very active neo-Nazi group which
promotes violence. The leader of the organization has been involved in
twenty-eight violent incidents in thirteen different states (Sidner 2018). It
distributes videos of members training and spreading graffiti and, similar to
the Proud Boys, shares clips of their members engaged in acts of violence at
rallies against counterprotesters. The founder and leader, Robert Rundo was

arrested in California in October 2018 on charges of organizing riots, federal conspiracy, and inciting violence over the internet, including the events that unfolded at the Unite the Right rally in Charlottesville (Sidner 2018). Four others were indicted on conspiracy to riot and attacking counterprotesters. They have traveled to several countries in Europe to meet and collaborate with other neo-Nazi groups in an attempt to make this an international movement against multiculturalism and democratic liberalism.

One of the most recent and deadliest attacks carried out by an individual in the name of hatred toward immigrants and liberal democracy took place in New Zealand in 2019. The massacre, conducted by Brenton Tarrant, resulted in the death of fifty people and injured dozens more (Hassan 2019). In his seventy-four-page manifesto, entitled "The Great Replacement" and which he posted online minutes before his attack he wrote, "Even if we were to deport all Non-Europeans from our lands tomorrow, the European people would still be spiraling into decay and eventual death. In the end we must return replacement fertility levels, or it will kill us" (Hasan 2019). The manifesto mentions self-proclaimed white supremist Dylan Roof who killed nine African Americans attending a church service in South Carolina in 2015 as a source of inspiration. Tarrant called Trump "a symbol of renewed white identity and common purpose" (Benhold and Eddy 2019).

The New Zealand atrocity demonstrates the contagion of extreme right-wing ideology and violence, and the vital role that the internet and social media play in spreading hate and white supremacist ideology. It was his obsession with online white nationalist message boards and internet sites that at least in part spurred Tarrant's ambitions (Kirkpatrick 2019). He is the first accused mass murderer who plotted a mass killing as itself a meme. He wrote in his manifesto that "Memes have done more for the ethnonationalist movement than any manifesto" (Kirkpatrick 2019). While carrying out the massacre he wore a head camera that allowed him to live stream the attack on Facebook (Graham-McLay et al. 2019). Though Facebook tried to immediately delete the video and canceled his Facebook and Instagram accounts it was distributed on YouTube, Twitter, and Reddit on a massive scale (Stack 2019).

These organizing activities and strategies are representative of Fufekci's (2012) contention that ICTs facilitate community in spite of physical distance through virtual public spheres and can enable new organizational infrastructures and networks of coordinated action that are loosely articulated and decentralized. They further illustrate Juris' (2014) emphasis on aggregation among activists through online tools. These dynamics also highlight the nuanced way that activists are creating a sense of agency and assuring potential recruits that alternatives are possible to the status quo, an essential component of social movement activity that Tilly (2006) gives credence to.

VIOLENCE-FUELED NATIVISM IN THE EU

The ramification of these political trends has real meanings for the lives of immigrants in Europe as well. Critical race theory, the communitarian perspective, and concepts of framing and collective identity provide a useful lens through which to try to comprehend the rising right-wing populism, neofascism, and violence in Europe against minority groups, and the trending toward extreme right-wing nationalism.

The increasing anti-immigrant sentiment across the Atlantic is prevalent. The drain on social and financial resources that Juris (2018) and Van Dyke and Soule (20002) refer to and forms of racism, nativism, and ethno-nationalism as connected to particular historical, cultural, geographic, and political contexts amid the threat of reduced social status among white citizens as pointed out by Jardina (2019) and Mutz (2018) are all relevant. Nativism, justifying and rewarding the superiority of the "native," and racism, reinforcing "White's superiority" often go hand in hand as Bridges (2019) and Herber et al. (2008) argue.

For example, according to the European Union Agency for Fundamental Rights, in 2016 "Asylum seekers and migrants face various forms of violence and harassment across the European Union. These include attacks undertaken by individuals, vigilante groups, and state authorities and crisis of violence, harassment, threats and xenophobic speech" (EUAFR 2016). The majority of these are against immigrants. Statistics from a Greek police report confirms that hate crimes more than doubled in 2017 as compared to 2016 (Kitsantonis 2018). According to a report by France's National Human Rights Advisory Committee, in 2018 anti-Semitic acts in France increased more than 70 percent from the previous year, and the government reported a 74 percent increase in offenses against Jews (Kitsantonis 2018).

Britain has also experienced a rise in anti-immigrant sentiment, and in particular against members of certain religions. The British government reported that between 2013 and 2017 hate crimes against immigrants almost doubled in England and Wales, and those motivated by religious hatred nearly quadrupled (Kirk 2018). The highest number of hate crimes in history was recorded by the police in England and Wales in 2017–2018; most of them undertaken as hate-based crimes on the basis of race and religion (Kirk 2018).

The alt-right group British First, mentioned in chapter 3, is the organizer and mobilizer of many of these incidents. It is a Christian, far-right, nationalist, antimulticulturalism, organization that encourages the undertaking of aggressive acts/hate crimes toward minorities. These include confronting Muslims in public places with a message that Islam is destroying the country and British culture (Camus and Leburg 2017). It has encouraged what it calls the "mosque invasion"—a disruption of Islamic services to intimidate and threaten Muslims and has organized dozens of demonstrations across Britain in opposition to Muslim immigrants. In March 2018, an anonymous letter was sent to people in six communities in England with a message stating that April 3 would be "Punish a Muslim Day" (Joseph 2018). The author of the letter promised to reward points for acts of violence targeting Muslims, which included pulling off a woman's head scarf, killing a Muslim, or bombing a mosque.

One of the leaders of Britain First summarized, "We want Islam banned in the UK. We don't see why we should have to implement sharia courts and have people wearing burkas, Islamic schools, mosques, everywhere in our Christian country" (Glenday 2017). Many are assuming that a holy war will take place in the UK in the near future and the white people will be a minority. Online, the group has 1.6 million followers and has a very global appeal.

The UK-watchdog group, Community Security Trust, found that in 2018 the country surpassed its record of anti-Semitic incidents by over 200 incidents—the most recorded in a single year. It concludes that this trend has been accelerating for years across Great Britain due to the refugee crisis and recent arrival of Muslim immigrants from the Middle East and Africa (Haverluck 2019). The leaders of Britain First, and the ex-leader of the English Defense League, all used social media to spread third divisive narrative before they were banned from most platforms.

Germany has also witnessed a drastic increase in hate crimes against immigrants over the past few years. The AfD Party has been broadly accused of encouraging discrimination and violence against refugees, Muslims, and Jews (Rees et al. 2019). They and other militant right-wing extremist groups have advocated for the desecration of Jewish intuitions and attacks against Jews. In 2016, Germany experienced almost ten attacks against immigrants on a daily basis, and according to the Interior Ministry, three-quarters of the attacks targeted migrants in public places (Carless 2018). Distrust in institutions and the rise of AfD have fractured the usually consensus-driven politics. Authorities say there are now more than 12,000 in Germany who have far-right views and are potentially violent, and Christine Lambrecht, the justice minister said "Far-right terror is the biggest threat to our democracy right now" (Benhold and Eddy 2018).

In 2018, Germany anti-Semitic crimes rose by 20 percent according to government data reported by Germany's domestic intelligence agency and the Federal Office for the Protection of the Constitution has placed the youth wing of the AfD under surveillance and labeled it as an "extremist group" (Bennhold 2019). This organization was established after World War II to protect the country from the rise of any extremist group that may threaten democracy. This is the first time since World War II that any party has been scrutinized to this extent. The main things that caught the agency's attention are widespread physical attacks on immigrants, the free press, and the values and institutions of liberal democracy (Bennhold 2019). On May 26, 2018, Germany's government warned Jewish men to not wear the kippah in public given the rise of attacks against Jews.

In September 2018, in the city of Chemnitz, the worst rioting in Germany in thirty years took place as far-right activists beat those suspected of being foreigners and flashed Nazi salutes, yelling "foreigners out!" (Bredemier 2018). The demonstrations were a reaction to the stabbing of a thirty-five-year-old German man by a Syrian asylum seeker. The police were overwhelmed by their aggressiveness and acts of violence. Counterprotesters challenged them by mobilizing in proximity to them and chanted "Refugees welcome!" (Bredemier 2018).

In June 2019, Walter Lubcke, a conservative politician, who defended refugee policies was fatally shot in his home by a neo-Nazi shot and killed in Hesse (McHugh and Jordans 2020). In October 2019, in Halle there was an attack on a synagogue by someone radicalized online who, after failing to be able to enter a synagogue, killed two passersby. Twelve men were arrested in February 2020 on charges of forming and supporting a far-right terrorist network. They had planned several attacks on politicians, asylum seekers, mosques, and Muslims. In February, a right-wing extremist tried to carry out a large-scale attack on mosques throughout Germany to start a civil war, but their efforts were thwarted by authorities (Ewing and Eddy 2020).

In another affront against immigrants, nine people were killed in February 2020 by Tobias Rathjen in the city of Hanau who opened fire in two shishas that are frequented mainly by Kurdish and Turkish communities. The authorities note that he was self-radicalized online, and he left a video and twenty-four-page manifesto on social media declaring that all races should be eliminated and foreigners who could not be deported should be destroyed. Prime Minister Angela Merkel stated that evidence showed the shooter acted out of "right-wing extremist, racist motives. Out of the hatred against people of other origins, other beliefs or other outward appearances" (Ewing and Eddy 2020).

Bridges (2019) and Garner (2009) argue that racialization is a process that tends to attribute innate characteristics and cultural values to a certain group—a difference between in-groups (shared cultural norms, beliefs, and behaviors) and out-groups (that don't share these) and which exists within the dynamic of a power relationship. Currently a quarter of the population in Germany is immigrants or descendants of immigrants (Ewing and Eddy 2019). The "victimization of whiteness," which intersects with racialization, as contended by Garner (2014), is a reaction to ethnic minorities being granted rights and privileges previously exclusive to the whites who no longer get to determine the boundaries of "belongingness." This is a growing trend in the EU as the above incidents give credence to.

Higham's (1999) reference to how religious and political differences, as well as racism and the perception of a lost cultural heritage historiccally as proven to be persuasive in Europe and the United States. Huber et al. (2008) combine racialization and anti-immigrant sentiment with the manifestation of this ideology within institutions and practices to sustain white privilege which is on full display across both the United States and the EU. The increase of hate crimes and growing xenophobia also support Schueths's (2014) and Lippard's (2011) identification of racist nativism as a way to justify the superiority of the (white) native versus non-native (perceived to be immigrants and/or people of color) who do not fit the Anglo-European heritage, religious traditions, and other values and beliefs deemed dominant. Dietrich's (2014) and Hutter's research demonstrates that when globalization is accompanied by ethnic and racial diversification, membership in far-right groups increases.

CONCLUSION

Domestic terrorism is rising in the United States and in the EU, and according to authorities, much more pernicious than outside threats. Most of the radicalization to commit domestic terrorism is happening online. Social movement theories, theories of immigration, and most importantly critical race theory provide a lens through which we can analyze the developments described in this chapter. Conflict resolution experts who have worked for decades in other countries are now shifting their focus toward the United States for the first time (Tavernise 2019). Their concern is the inflamed rhetoric that politicians have normalized, the amount of misinformation and conspiracy theories that lead to violence.

Both mainstream and social media are being used to fuel this misinformation and conspiracy theories about immigrants, exploiting white anxiety across the dimensions of both class and race. The digital revolution has in particular made it easier and faster for hate groups to share information, organize, and mobilize. The rise of anti-immigrant sentiment, Islamophobia, and anti-Semitism has led to a resurgence of nativist feelings and hate crimes on both sides of the Atlantic. Mainstream news outlets, and specifically Fox News, decry multiculturalism and perpetuate stereotypes about immigrants, opining that immigrants are an "invasion" which is destroying American culture and are to be blamed for the struggles of working-class Americans.

The Trump administration has also (falsely) meddled in the EU's struggle with the immigration crisis, stating that migrants are making their countries unrecognizable, bringing in crime, and making their countries disorderly, which on many occasions has baffled the leaders of the countries he is referring to.

In most of these cases, which is now a global phenomenon, there is an intent to inspire a global "race war"—awakening other potential young people who may become radicalized to join the movement. The word invasion is constant not only on Fox News but also in the online and social media posts that the perpetrators use sometimes minutes before attacking their victims. Much of this, in additional to the broader phenomenon of the surge of hate groups, is accredited to "Trumpism." However, there are global connections between leaders of countries, and grassroots organizations promoting neo-Nazism and white supremacy that adhere to the Great Replacement theory.

Chapter 5

Contentions Politics and Advocacy Work to Support Immigrant Rights

I begin this chapter with a glimpse into some of the more popular waves of protest and other forms of contentious politics (actors working outside of the formal political system and institutional processes to affect social change) that surround the issue of immigration over the past few decades. The main focus is on the events in the United States, though some of the more noteworthy and recent protest activity that has occurred in certain EU countries is also addressed at end of the chapter.

In both the United States and parts of the EU, pro-immigration rights activists have engaged in marches, demonstrations, and rallies. In the United States some businesses activists have also participated in boycotts. A variety of activities are organized to resist pending legislation that was still being debated in Congress, or upcoming elections. Others are in opposition to laws and policies that had already been approved.

In the United States, protest activity increased significantly once Donald Trump was elected president, as well as in Italy and Germany (and other countries in Europe) in light of the emergence and/or resurgence of alt-right groups. Many Italians and Germans also felt that anti-immigrant rhetoric had become too extreme, which has resulted in a steady uptick of protest activity. Across the globe, in fact, there is an increasing fear of the popularity of autocratic leaders, far right-wing extremist groups, and the rise of anti-Semitisms and Islamophobia.

For example, there were large and widespread demonstrations when President Trump introduced the Muslim ban and the zero-tolerance policy that led to the separation of Latinx families and threats to phase out DACA. Thus, this chapter also includes mobilization efforts by the DREAMers— young people brought to the United States at a young age and are without documents but seeking citizenship. There has also been a strong reaction among citizens to detention centers that house children and minors as a result of the zero-tolerance policy, and defiance of the policies that ICE practices which are rooted in the harassment of noncriminal immigrants. Migrants, with the support of others, have also protested against the inhumane conditions in some EU detention camps that are sheltering migrants. The analyses note that it is a combination of citizens, businesses, faith-based groups, and politicians who have joined forces in a call for more humane policies toward immigrants and a pathway to citizenship.

I end the chapter with a discussion of how advocacy work at the grassroots level, with a focus on human rights groups working to reunite separated families and others that are committed to preventing deaths of migrants crossing the U.S.-Mexico border and traversing the Mediterranean Sea, are approaching the crisis of immigration from a slightly different angle through the sponsorship of relief efforts, acts of civil disobedience, and advocacy work.

MARCHES, DEMONSTRATIONS, AND BOYCOTTS TO PROTEST IMMIGRATION POLICY IN THE UNITED STATES

In 1994, Mexican Americans, together with many other groups and individuals, vigorously demonstrated against California Proposition 187 which was proposed by Republican governor Peter Wilson (Arellano 2019). The so-called Save our State legislation sought to limit social welfare benefits to children of parents or legal guardians who were residing in the United States without appropriate documents, including public education and health care (Lopez 1994). Wilson justified the bill on the basis that undocumented immigrants were costing the state of California billions of dollars for services provided to them that should be going to legal residents, and that the state was rewarding immigrants for breaking the law (Davis 1994).

Midgley's (2017), Van Wormart and Lippard's (2011), and Garner's (2014) explanations of how certain variables can explain the "victimization of whiteness" underlie Wilson's logic in appealing to white resentment of foreigners. Even more so, the analyses of Judis (2018) and Higham (1999), which illustrate the intersectionality between nativism and racism and efforts to institutionalize practices that exclude foreigners from benefits enjoyed by citizens are very clear. The "Save our State" rhetoric also resonates with theoretical analyses put forth by Mutz (2018) and Hutter (2014) which illuminate how struggles between immigrants and citizens, as they compete for critical economic and social local resources, often fuel racial tensions and hostility toward immigrants.

In one of the largest protests to ever take place in the city of Los Angeles, CA, an estimated 70,000 demonstrators marched in resistance to Prop 187 (Paret and Aguilar 2016). During the street demonstrations, marchers carried flags from Mexico and other Latin American nations, sending a message of ethnic pride (Lopez 1994). In spite of advice from principals and the super-intendent, on November 2, over 10,000 high school students walked out of their classes in the Los Angeles area protesting the Proposition and marched peacefully in historical numbers (Pyle and Shuster 1999). Though the legisla-tion passed by a slim margin, it was later struck down by the courts. One of its legacies, however, is that it ended the Republican stronghold in California due to the backlash against the legislation (Lopez 1994).

A few years later Proposition 227 was passed by the state legislation in California on June 2, 1998. This required that California public schools teach Limited English Proficiency (LEP), or what was called "transitional bilingual education" in special classes and all other classes were to be taught nearly all in English, thereby eliminating bilingual education (Sifuentes 2008). LEP was seen as the fastest way to assimilate immigrant children for proponents, and racist against immigrant children for those critical of the policy. Though warned by the superintendent to remain in school, once again, high school students walked out of classes to protest outside of City Hall. Despite the resistance to the measure, the Proposition passed with 61 percent of the vote (Green and Johnson 1998). This expression of contentious politics high-lights the necessity of collective identity that social movement theorists like Melucci (2006), Snow et al. (1986), and Benford (1993) highlight. This sense of togetherness can be tangible or intangible in terms of demographics as demonstrated in Jasper and Polleta's (2001) research.

THE SENSENBRENNER BILL

The next large wave of protests took place in 2006 in reaction to other dra-conian legislative measures that were to be passed across the country. H.R. 4437, called the Border Protection, Antiterrorism and Illegal Immigration Control Act, was proposed to classify all undocumented immigrants as crimi-nals, and anyone who helped them enter or remain in the United States would also be charged as criminal felons (American Immigration Council 2018). H.R. 4437 also imposed penalties for anyone hiring undocumented workers and required churches to determine the immigration status of parishioners prior to offering kind assistance. The measure passed in December 2005 in the U.S. House of Representatives (Campbell 2007).

H.R. 4437 did not make it through the Senate, but a number of states soon took matters into their own hands (Campbell 2007). The most widely known was S.B. 1070, the Sensenbrenner bill in Arizona which allowed for racial profiling and allowed police officers to stop anyone suspected of being undocumented during an arrest, detention, and even during routine traffic stops (Greitzer 2010). Entitled the Support Our Law Enforcement and Safe Neighborhoods Act this measure made it a felony to be undocumented in the state unless the individual apprehended could provide "an alien registration document" (Greitzer 2010). In the past this was a civil violation.

Specifically, all individuals over the age of eighteen were required to have on their person proper documents at all times affirming their citizenship status—referred to as the "Show me your Papers" law by critics (Hesson 2013). The bill also included measures for severe penalties for anyone who provided employment or transportation for unauthorized persons. It also criminalized assistance to immigrants in the country illegally who were seeking food, housing, or medical services. The House passed the bill on December 10, resulting in the largest Latinx demonstrations and supporters in the community as the Senate debated the policy (Nowicki 2010). Between March and May 2006, nearly 5 million people protested the proposed legislation in more than 160 cities. Banners and chants consisted of "We come to this country not to take from America, but to make America strong," and "Today we march, tomorrow we vote" (Chavez 2008).

On May 1, thousands gathered in over eighty cities to protests using forms of civil disobedience, including a sit-in at the governor's mansion in Arizona (Hesson 2013). Thousands of activists held a vigil in 2010 outside of the Arizona state Capitol in prayer that Governor Jan Brewer would not sign the bill after it was passed by the state legislature (Rau 2010). Hundreds of students walked out of classes to show their support (Greitzer 2010). One of the main motivations for the protest activity was the prospect of shifting immigration enforcement from federal to state and local authorities.

There were massive protests once the policy passed that lasted for several weeks (Navarrette 2019). The series of demonstrations began in Chicago and continued for eight weeks; the largest nationwide day of protest took place on April 10, 2006, in 102 cities (Hing 2012). The largest *single* protest occurred on March 25, 2006, in downtown Los Angeles when nearly a million marched in what was called "La Gran Marcha." The events caught the authorities and most Angeleans by surprise as it was advertised almost exclusively through Spanish-language media outlets (Navarette 2019). These included Univision, Telemundo, and *La Opinion* (the largest Spanish newspaper in Los Angeles). *La Opinion* and other Spanish newspapers advertised on front pages La "Mega Marcha" (Hing 2012). MMEX—a leading Spanish television outlet in Los Angeles, owned by Univision, called the protests "Pisando Firme," with messages of stepping strong and reminding protesters to march "with pride, with dignity, with order, for you children, for your people and for your community."

These demonstrations culminated on May 1 during the "May Day" demonstrations, also framed as a "Day without Immigrants" and the "Great American Boycott" (Navarrette 2019). Immigrants and their supporters across the country also boycotted the U.S. economy to demonstrate their collective economic clout and to draw awareness to the contribution Latinx workers make to the U.S. economy and society in general and demand a pathway to citizenship. Thousands of protesters marched and boycotted going to work, kept children from going to school, and closed businesses in solidarity with immigrant workers (Stanglin 2017).

Dozens of other May Day, or "Day Without Immigrants" marches in cities throughout the United States caught mainstream media attention. Activists demonstrated in more than 140 cities in 39 states (Yan and Williams 2017). An estimated 100,000 protested on the streets of Chicago and 500,000 in Los Angeles. Framing the agenda as a call for inclusion and a willingness to assimilate marchers chanted "we are American," and unlike the marchers who were protesting Prop 187 they carried mainly American flags.

This is a great example of collective identity being central to protest activity, and illustrative of the need for proper framing to increase awareness about a cause and to try to sway public opinion. By claiming their "Americanness" Latinx marchers were able to challenge the myth that they do not want to assimilate and become part of the fabric of U.S. culture. They also disrupt the assumption that immigrants do not want to integrate nor fit into the "code of belonging" as an American. This is the basis of the work of Garner's (2014), Huber et al.'s (2008), and Higham's (1999) critical race theory. It further validates the work of Bridges (2019), Van Wormart and Link (2014), Conderstine and Hampshire (2013), and Miller (2005).

The Sensenbrenner bill was eventually overturned as being unconstitutional in large part because, according to the constitution, immigration policy is under the realm of the federal government, not of states or local authorities. This was one of the main concerns of the demonstrators. Authorities were allowed/required to use racial profiling as a means to carry out the policy (Gessen 2020). This would impact both citizens and noncitizens, but not whites—the same methods were applicable to Prop 187. This is what Huber et al. (2008) contend to be "racist nativism." They illustrate how rhetoric about undocumented is both nativist and racist because it labels being "brown" and "alien" as a problem no matter how long one may have lived in the country.

THE DREAMERS

Another substantial wave of demonstrations took place in the mid-2000s when young people (mostly high school and college students) and their allies protested to secure the DREAM Act that sought to provide legal status for young immigrants who were brought into the country illegally as children. Breaking the silence imposed on them by their undocumented status, they organized marches, occupied city officials' and college administrators' offices, petitioned politicians, shared their stories through social media and public testimonies, and blocked traffic in busy intersections (Goodman 2012).

They also held prayer vigils, fasted outside of the White House and their congressional representatives' offices, blocked buses that attempted to deport undocumented persons, held sit-ins in congressional offices, protested in front of the Alabama Capitol, outside of the home of Arizona sheriff Joe Arpaio (notorious for his anti-immigration stance and aggressive tactics to apprehend migrants), in front of federal immigration courts, and inside of ICE offices, processing centers, and detention centers (Goodman 2012). Through these tactics they transformed the discussion of immigration reform based on policy changes into a formidable social movement. This represents the fortitude of collective identity that Benford (1993) and Snow et al. (1986) view as critical to the success of contentious politics.

The DREAMers emerged as a subset of the broader mobilization for widespread immigration reform in their support for the DREAM Act. The proposal was first introduced in the Senate in the summer of 2001 and was designed to provide conditional permanent residency to "illegal aliens" of "good moral character" under the age of thirty-five who arrived as minors (before the age of sixteen), do not have proper visa/immigration documentation, attended school on a regular basis, graduated from an American high school, meet in-state tuition and GPA requirements, and have lived in the United States for at least five consecutive years (Goodman 2012). Other options for qualifying were having completed serving two years in the military or attending two years at a four-year institution of higher learning. If the qualifications were met these individuals would have an opportunity to obtain a temporary six-year residency. During this conditional period, however, they would not be eligible for higher education grants, nor would they be able to apply for student loans (Goodman 2012).

Though the proposal did not make it through Congress, in its wake students pivoted and began to mobilize at the state level. In California, students petitioned state legislators in 2006 to introduce the California DREAM Act. This mandated that all students who had completed high school in the state, regardless of immigration status, would be eligible for in-state tuition and have access to all financial assistance for higher education at California state colleges and universities. There were similar mobilizations in New York, Maryland, and Rhode Island, which were successful in the latter two states (Hing 2012).

The frame, "Undocumented, Unafraid and Unapologetic" put immediate and direct pressure on authorities. On March 10, 2010, they held their first "National Coming out Day of Action" as part of their newly organized "Coming out of the Shadows" campaign (Hesson 2013). Student activists held civil disobedience events in many major cities including Chicago, Los Angeles, Phoenix, Miami, New York, and Washington, DC, most taking place in front of federal buildings and consisting of teach-ins, sit-ins, marches, rallies, demonstrations, and hunger strikes (Hing 2012).

DREAMers activists also relied heavily on social media to pressure Congress to pass the proposed bill. They posted videos online with their personal stories and used YouTube to promote a video in which students stated their names and held signs revealing that they were undocumented (Escalona 2011). The United We Dream campaign was also organized online in 2008 with a list of individuals interested in taking action to support immigration reform (United We Dream 2017).

On June 15, 2012, President Obama enacted new guidelines that enabled those who met certain criteria to live and work in the United States without fear of deportation. This was called DACA. However, this has been challenged under President Trump who is trying to phase out the program. Four DREAMers successfully stopped the annual Macy's Thanksgiving Day Parade in New York City in 2017 by sitting down on one of the main parade routes in protest of his efforts in 2017 (Gallagher 2017). They were taken away by the authorities but not arrested.

The DACA legislation is indicative of the communitarian perspective on immigration and global welfare theory that stresses the importance of influencing public opinion through fears of national security and the loss of national identity, which for some time were relatively fixed ethnic and cultural identities. Amstutz (2015), Marin (2015), and Payne (2012) all theorize that these are important to refining competing views on immigration.

Theories pertaining to the regulation of immigration, such as those proposed by Laden and Owen (2007) are also applicable. These theories embrace a moral dimension to migration rooted in a premise that immigrants deserve the same basic human and civil rights in the country they migrated to (Hoffman and Graham 2015; Cole 2011). The protests are thus an expression of the cosmopolitan-oriented approach that views diversity as strength and something to be celebrated.

RESISTANCE TO THE TRUMP ADMINISTRATION'S IMMIGRATION POLICIES

On January 21, 2017, following the election of Donald Trump to the presidency of the United States, and again on inauguration day, millions of people globally took to the streets in support of the Women's Marches. These were organized via social media and took place in every state across the United States in over 650 cities, the day after Trump was elected president (McKane and McCammon 2018). This was the largest single-day demonstration in all of U.S. history as an estimated 5.2 million people joined the mobilization (Chenoweth and Pressman 2017). Protestors shared many grievances, the primary ones rooted in the anti-immigrant rhetoric and misogyny as expressed by Trump. Two years into the Trump presidency, protesters remained active as the Women's Marches evolved into a broader movement labeled "The Resistance" (Kauffman 2017). This elucidates the importance of frame amplification and frame bridging that Snow et al. (1986) find integral to successful mobilization campaigns.

Later, when Trump introduced an order to curtail or freeze refugee admissions and implement the "Muslim Ban," which would bar individuals from several Muslim-majority countries entry into the United States, thousands marched in cities and airports in opposition (Gambino et al. 2017). Due to the ban, dozens of immigrants were held in detention in airports following the decree until a federal judge ruled that all of them must be released (Flores 2017). This is exemplary of Jasper and Polleta's (2001) acknowledgment that a sense of collective identity can be real or perceived on the grounds of empathy and compassion for those other than in one's own "in group." Additionally, tens of thousands of activists gathered in Lower Manhattan, NY, in early January 2020 in reaction to a number of anti-Semitic attacks that had occurred in the surrounding area (Goldbaum and Sedacca 2020).

On June 29, 2018, protesters held marches in dozens of cities throughout the United States to express their opposition to President Trump's zero-tolerance policy that targeted Latinx asylum seekers (Pitosfsy and Nzanga 2018). The outrage about families being torn apart gained steady media coverage and put pressure on legislatures to address the issue. Globally, tens of thousands of demonstrators turned out in the streets in London to protest Trump's visit with a particular focus on the zero-tolerance and family separation policy (Yeginsu and Magra 2018). "Stop Trump" protests featured a giant orange balloon of Trump depicted as a pouting baby in a diaper and holding a smart phone. Protesters also banged pots and pans and played recordings of crying children being separated from their parents at the Mexican border outside of the American ambassador's residence in London where Trump was staying.

This is another good example of Polleta and Jasper's (2001) recognition of the significance of perceived rather than concrete forms of collective identity through the lens of emotion and compassion. These mobilizations also elucidate the cosmopolitan or liberal political theory perspective that adopts a compassionate approach toward immigrants and a respect for their dignity and universal human rights as acclaimed by Hoffman and Graham (2015), Condenstine and Hampshire (2013), and Cole (2011).

In other efforts, which again demonstrate the importance of collective identity (Jenkins 2006; Benford 1993; and Snow et al. 1986) and liberal political theory (Hoffman and Graham 2015; Laden and Owen 2007), protesters showed up in large numbers outside and inside of La Guardia Airport in New York in support of children who had been separated from their parents and flown from Texas to New York due to the zero-policy measure that Trump mandated (Johnson 2018). On July 2, 2018, hundreds gathered in San Diego, CA, for a rally and march, organized by Mijente (a national Latinx organization) and other interfaith and civil rights organizations throughout the downtown area calling for an end to the family separations, ICE, and Operation Streamline (Strickrasha 2019).

Operation Streamline, which was introduced in 2005 by the DHS and employed in Texas and Arizona as a method to fast-track deportations of individuals intercepted while crossing the border without proper documentation, faced severe criticism (Castellans 2018). Protesters descended on the federal court building in Tucson, AZ, and locked arms to block the entrance into the ICE facility. Their main grievance was that Operation Streamline negates immigrants' individual due process and defendants' rights, pointing out that in Tucson, for a period of time, approximately seventy people a day were being prosecuted at the same time and convicted within a few hours (Strickrasha 2019).

In June 2018 in Rio Grande Valley, TX, protestors from around the country descended on the detention centers where child refugees who were separated from their parents were being housed (Rocha et al. 2018). That same month in San Diego, CA, twenty-three religious leaders marched to the Otay Mesa Detention Center chanting, "You are not alone!" and in Portland, OR, protesters blockaded the local ICE headquarters and established an occupation outside of it over the next ten days which morphed into a center to attend to the needs of children and families. In addition to gathering at Lafayette Square across from the White House and other parks and plazas, demonstrations also took place outside of statehouses and ICE buildings (Chasmar 2018).

ICE has long been a central point of contention among immigration activists and especially the agency's targeting of immigrants in hospitals and outside churches, schools, and courthouses which are illegal (Earnshaw and Carlson 2018). The current backlash is due to the fact that ICE has become increasingly more aggressive at Trump's urging. For example, it has been criticized for arresting parents as they dropped off their children at school and for randomly raiding businesses, including a nationwide sweep of 7-Eleven stores across the country in 2018 (Doubeck 2018).

In January 2018, ICE conducted a total of ninety-eight sweeps targeting stores in seventeen states and Washington, DC, arresting twenty-one people who were assumed to be in the country illegally (Spagat and Nooman 2018). Between January and August 2017 overall arrests by ICE rose by over 43 percent from the same time period in 2016 (Spagat and Nooman 2018). These efforts represent what Garner (2009, 2014) refers to as protecting the "White/ Anglo code" which delineates who belongs and who does not which is rooted in nativists' and racists' assessments. They are also indicative of critical race theory that Mutz (2018) and Lippard (2011) acknowledge.

To protect undocumented citizens, many communities have organized Raid Rapid Response Networks. These include measures such as making sure that if one is deported, medications for elderly parents or others in the household are in supply, memorizing at least one phone number, and signing caregiver affidavits so children will have legal guardians (Martinez 2019). Some lawmakers have also aggressively tried to inform immigrants of their rights. For example, Governor Newsom in California distributed a video informing immigrant of their rights and what to do if they see ICE activity in their neighborhood or workplace (Lyster 2019).

The American Civil Liberties Union (ACLU) uses social media platforms to inform immigrants of their rights, translated into fourteen different languages (Jordan and Dickerson 2019). They provide practical responses to hypothetical situations with appropriate answers such as "police are at my home" or "Law enforcement asks about my immigration status." United We Dream, which is a grassroots organization is also using social media in creative ways. It created an app called Notica, which enables undocumented immigrants, if approached by ICE, to immediately notify family and friends (Jordan and Dickerson 2019). The device also provides location data so that those whom they notify can quickly get to the site.

In February 2020, President Trump ramped up his affront on undocumented immigrants by declaring that he was sending law enforcement tactical units from the southern border of the United States to assist ICE agents with arrests in sanctuary cities including Chicago, New York, San Francisco, Los Angeles, Atlanta, Houston, Boston, New Orleans, Detroit, and Newark (Dickerson et al. 2020). Thus, he is fulfilling his promise to punish sanctuary states and cities that refuse to cooperate with ICE. The main unit being deployed is an agency called Border Patrol Tactical Units (BORTAC) which serves as a Special Weapons and Tactics (SWAT) team to assist with Border Patrol. Their main mission is to target known violent individuals and those with long criminal records. Their deployment into major nonborder cities will clearly raise fears in immigrant communities which is another intention of the Trump administration (Dickerson et al. 2020).

Many are critical of this new approach, including the former commissioner of CBP, Gil Kerlikowske, who had overseen tactical units on the border for years. He called it a "significant mistake" (Dickerson and Kanno-Youngs 2020). The former chief of police in Seattle elaborated, "If you were a police chief and you were going to make an apprehension for a relatively minor offence, you don't send in the SWAT team. And BORTAC is a SWAT team . . . They're trained for much more hazardous missions than this" (Dickerson and Kanno-Youngs 2020).

A few successful Democrat candidates, such as Alexandria Ocasio-Cortez in New York and Deb Haaland in New Mexico ran on a platform of defunding or abolishing ICE during the 2018 midterm elections (Yoon-Hendricks and Greenberg 2018). This strategy is acknowledged by political process/political opportunity theory (see Tarrow 2015 and 2012; Meyer 2004) as significant in affecting social change because it can create a division among elites, primarily those working in the formal political system. This gives leverage to activist in their attempt to influence public opinion. These theorists also recognize that often legislation is passed, and policy is established because activists outside of the formal institutional political systems use contentions politics to raise awareness and influence public opinion.

OTHER BOYCOTTS

Earlier in the chapter I mentioned the May Day marches and boycotts. There were several other innovative types of boycotts as well. Governors in several cities, including San Francisco, Los Angeles, Oakland, Minneapolis, Denver, Seattle, and others responded to S.B. 1070 by banning some city employees from work-related travel to Arizona and also minimized city business done with companies which had their headquarters in Arizona (Goth 2017). *La Opinion*, the largest Spanish-language newspaper in the United States, followed lead of Arizona congressman Raul Grijalva to call for an economic boycott by industries in a variety of sectors in Arizona, including tourism (Goth 2017).

Many cities, including Austin, West Hollywood, and El Paso banned travel to Arizona for work-related purposes after S.B. 1070 was signed into law (Goth 2017). There were also boycotts against products, conventions, and even music concerts. The "Sound Strike" coalition was put together by various artists who refused to play concerts until the bill was repealed (Gehr 2017). The boycott cost Arizona around $140 million in lost tourism and business revenue (Vallet 2011). Additionally, sixty CEOs signed a letter to the state legislature that successfully prompted bipartisan opposition to five anti-immigration bills that would have mandated hospitals and schools to check for documents (Vallet 2011).

Activists also shut down businesses across the United States during the "Day Without Immigrants" strike and boycotts that took place in 2017 in reaction to many of Trump's new immigration policies (Stanglin 2017). The goal was to expose the inability of restaurants, construction companies, and other businesses to function without an immigrant workforce and highlight the fact that the U.S. economy would collapse without Mexican and other Latinx workers.

The centrality of immigrant labor in the United States cannot be overstated. For example, the world renowned and legendary chef Anthony Bourdain highlighted the importance of Mexican labor in his statement that read:

> Despite our ridiculously hypocritical attitudes towards immigration, we demand that Mexicans cook a large percentage of the food we eat, grow the ingredients we need to make that food, clean our houses, mow our laws, wash our dishes, look after our children. As any chef will tell you our entire service economy—the restaurant business as we know it—in most American cities, would collapse overnight without Mexican workers. Some of course, like to claim that Mexicans are "stealing American jobs." But in two decades as a chef and employer, I never had ONE American kid walk in my door and apply for a dishwashing job, a porter's position—or even a job as prep cook. (Carrasquillo 2014)

In support of this summary, in 2017 the Pew Research Center estimated that 11 percent of workers in restaurants and bars, 19 percent of the nation's dishwashers, and 17 percent of its bussers are undocumented (Passel and Cohen 2016). Also noting the importance of undocumented labor which benefits the U.S. economy, a study by the Federation for American Immigration Reform concluded that "over the past several decades, the farming sector has grown increasingly dependent on a steady supply of workers who have entered the country illegally, despite the unlimited availability of visas for foreign agricultural guest workers. The agribusiness sector has consistently opposed an immigration policy that would result in a legal workforce. Their position is that current hiring practices are crucial for the survival of the industry, as Americans are not willing to do agricultural work and increasing wages to attract native-born workers would result in significantly higher food prices or a decline in American food production" (Kitroeff and Mohan 2017).

A few theories can be applied to these events. World systems theory as utilized by Silver (2003) and Sassen (1988), in addition to dual labor market theories that Haas et al. (2020), Miller (2009), and Castles et al. (2009) incorporate in their work to argue that structural dynamics in the economic realm, and especially the demand for labor in more developed countries that rely on workers from less developed countries, serve as push and pull factors for immigration. Simply put, migrants coming from poor countries are willing to fulfill labor needs that citizens in the host country are unwilling to do because of low pay and status attached to certain jobs, and oftentimes unsafe working conditions. According to neoclassical economics theory that the above theorists utilize migrants make a cost/benefit calculation to migrate in the hopes of job opportunities and higher wages than they would make in their country of origin.

NONCOMPLIANCE

In defiance of Trump's orders, governors of eight states refused to send or recalled National Guard troops from the border with Mexico that Trump had ordered. New York, North Carolina, Virginia, Maryland, and Massachusetts all reversed their initial agreement (Haag and Bidgood 2018). Many local officials have canceled deals (some of which include several million dollars) to cooperate with ICE and detain immigrants either as they await trial or are put in detention centers (Romero 2019).

Airlines, beginning with American which is the world's largest airline, contested the zero-tolerance policy (Matousek 2018). It requested that the U.S. government not use their flights to assist in the deportations in any manner that would facilitate the deportations of immigrants (Fausett 2018). They were particularly adamant about transporting children who were potentially being separated from their families. In a formal statement which was posted online, the CEO of American Airlines declared, "we have therefore requested the federal government to immediately refrain from using American for the purpose of transporting children who have been separated from their families due to the current immigration policy. We have no desire to be associated with separating families, or worse, to profit from it" (Fausett 2018).

After American posted this announcement on its website, other airlines followed suit in their rejection of the policy. Frontier Airlines sent out a tweet informing the public that it would "not knowingly allow our flights to be used to transport migrant children away from their families" (Fausett 2018). United and Southwest Airlines also sent out public messages declaring that they did not want to cooperate with the separation of families. Some flight attendants posted eyewitness accounts in public and private media outlets documenting groups of Latino children on domestic flights who were accompanied by federal agents rather than their parents (Matousek 2018).

In February 2020, Greyhound Bus, the largest transportation server of inner-city buses in the United States, declared that without warrants, Border Patrol agents would not be able to stop and board buses to check riders' immigration papers (Diaz 2020). In 2018, Greyhound sent out a statement saying, "C.B.P. searches have negatively impacted both our customers and our operations. Greyhound does not coordinate with C.B.P., nor do we support these actions." In 2018, the ACLU circulated a petition that garnered over 200,000 signatures calling on Greyhound to not allow Border Patrol on its buses without a warrant and/or probably cause (Diaz 2020).

HUMAN RIGHTS AND ADVOCACY EFFORTS

Faith-based groups have also played a prominent role in contesting what they perceived to be unjust and draconian immigration policies. In 2005, when the Sensenbrenner bill was introduced Cardinal Mahoney of Los Angeles called on all Catholics to continue to minister to undocumented persons whether it was illegal, asking them to risk their own personal safety to stand with the immigrants (Ponnuro 2016). In July 2019, holding pictures of migrant children who had died in U.S. custody in detention camps, members and nonmembers of religious life formed a cross with their bodies on the floor of the Russell Senate Office Building in Washington, DC, resulting in a total of seventy Catholics being arrested for obstructing a public place. The image of elderly nuns and priests who were videoed as they were escorted out of the building in handcuffs helped to frame the narrative in humanistic terms.

In 2018, former attorney general under President Trump, Jeff Sessions, who is a member of the United Methodist Church received a formal written complaint from over 600 fellow Methodists that was sent to his pastors in Alabama and Virginia regarding his policy of separating families, stating that it was "child abuse" under church law (Zaveri 2018). Sessions had used a Bible passage to defend the zero-tolerance policy in a speech to law enforcers.

The complaint sought a "reconciling process" to urge Sessions to "step back from his harmful actions and work to repair the damage he is currently causing to immigrants, particularly children and families" (Zaveri 2018). In addition to child abuse, the complaint also sought charges of "immorality" for the separations, and "racial discrimination and dissemination of doctrines contrary to the standards of the doctrine of the United Methodist Church" (Zaveri 2018). This is once again a good example of a powerful tactic that activists have in their tool kit—shaming the target of their dissatisfaction.

Pope Francis has been one of the strongest voices pleading for empathy toward immigrants either fleeing horrific conditions in their home countries or seeking a better life for themselves and their families (Yardley and Ahmed 2016). He has shown concern for both the crisis on the U.S.–Mexico border and the travails migrants face trying to make it to Europe. On February 16,

2016, during a visit to Mexico he prayed for compassion toward immigrants while saying mass on the border of the Rio Grande, from the Mexican side in Ciudad Juárez (Yardely and Ahmed 2016). Attendees of the mass, in El Paso, on the other side of the river in the United States also witnessed his message.

The pope stated, "The flow of capital cannot decide the flow of and life of people . . . we cannot deny the humanitarian crisis which in recent years has meant the migration of thousands of people. The human tragedy that is forced migration is a global phenomenon today. The crisis which can be measured in numbers and statistics, we want instead to measure with names, stories, families" (Yardley and Ahmed 2016). In May 2016, he held up a life jacket used by a young Syrian boy who died at sea trying to migrate to Europe with his family. The pope clarified his message by stating, "Migrants are not a danger, they are in danger" (Yardley and Pianigiani 2016).

As ICE detention centers continue to overflow due to the crisis on both sides of the U.S.-Mexico border and now interior cities, charities, churches, and NGOs have filled the void to provide basic necessities and help to reunify families (Del Real and Fernandez 2019). Unannounced mass releases of immigrants by ICE in border cities at bus stations, as they wait for their asylum claims to be heard, have become common place and city resources cannot keep up with the demand as they are beyond capacity. ICE used to provide certain key services under its "Safe Release" policy, which offered financial assistance for transportation and help in contacting family members, but it is now too overwhelmed by the sheer number of immigrants staying in border cities to continue to do so (Doubek 2018). Thus, these groups are now playing a critical role in addressing the humanitarian crisis.

Other activists try to reduce the amount of deaths and hardships immigrants face crossing the desert or sea by assisting them with basic necessities for their journey and immediate arrival in their destination country. The United Nation's International Organization for Migration reported in January 2019 that for the fifth year in a row more than 4,500 people were assumed to have died or gone missing on migration routes around the globe in 2018. The U.S.-Mexico border is one of the deadliest borderlands (Machi 2019). Some of the most active groups assisting migrants on this border are Desert Samaritans, No More Deaths, and Border Angels.

These NGOs leave blankets, food, and jugs of water in the desert for migrants to help them survive the challenges of the journey. They also provide migrants with cellphones so that they can reach out to relatives or friends who they are trying to reach in the United States (Stelloh 2019). The phones are critical as immigrants are easy prey for those who to seek to take advantage of them by offering them an opportunity to use their cell phone, only to use the phone number for extortion purposes.

To undermine these grassroots efforts, the Trump administration has criminalized humanitarian aid on the border. For instance, in Tucson, AZ, activists that are volunteers with No More Deaths went to trial facing charges for several federal crimes in their efforts to leave food and water in the Sonoran Desert and to provide shelter for migrants (Ortega 2019). This happened after the group published a report that accused Border Patrol agents of vandalizing or confiscating food and other types of aid (Stelloh 2019). The actions were recorded and the images of the agents kicking over and pouring out jugs of water spread widely on social media, thus gaining support for the No More Deaths efforts and embarrassing Border Patrol.

More specifically, Scott Warren, a member of No More Deaths, was charged with three felonies after being arrested in January 2018 in Ajo, AZ, for assisting two undocumented young male migrants who needed medical attention and food (Goodman 2019). He had brought them to the shelter that No More Deaths runs in Ajo for medical treatment and food assistance. Facing up to twenty years in prison, he pleaded not guilty to one count of conspiracy to transport and harbor the two men and two counts of harboring undocumented immigrants (Ortega 2019). He is currently facing a retrial.

ADVOCACY EFFORTS AND PROTESTS IN THE EU

Many activists in the EU also work to save the lives of migrants making the treacherous journey to reach Europe. The United Nations' 2018 Report verified that about half of all immigrants who died trying to make it to Europe did so in an attempt to cross the Mediterranean Sea (Horowitz 2018b). Those attempting to cross in 2018 were twice as likely to perish as those in 2017. Most of the loss of life is due to the fact that smugglers take advantage of desperate immigrants and charge exorbitant fees for the journey. To enhance their profits, they use cheap and flimsy vessels and board immigrants at levels that far exceed maximum capacity protocols. Many of the makeshift boats, which are not seaworthy, capsize or become shipwrecked. The lack of adequate sea patrol, and in many cases resistance to it by Mediterranean countries (as discussed in chapter 3), has compounded the crisis (IOM UN Migration 2019).

Another issue is the refusal of certain European countries to accept refuges due to the rise of nativism and anti-immigrant feelings. Playing on these fears some politicians emphasize the economics of cost of helping migrants who are peril in the sea. For example, in a statement released in January 2019, the crew of Sea-Watch 3 (an NGO rescue team) demanded coordinated and humane response by EU states—offering safe routes and sharing the resettlement burden. It read:

The calls of countries such as Italy, Malta and Greece on other EU states for
the reception and resettlement of refugees are justified . . . so it is high time that
Europe make new arrangements for the reception and resettlement of people
who are simply seeking a safe haven. There must come an end to the pushing
to and from of exhausted and often traumatized human beings . . . where again
and again decisions are made on an ad hoc basis, apparently with the greatest
difficulty about which European country will admit a handful of people to their
asylum procedure. (UNHRC 2019)

Other global humanitarian advocacy work across Europe in response to
the immigration crisis and in an attempt to combat the reemergence of nativism activists has been creative in nature. For example, globally recognized
director Steven Spielberg brought his blockbuster movie, "Schindler's List"
to movie theaters in Europe hoping to create dialogue amid what he referred
to as a "renewed cycle of hate" (Eddy 2019). In fact, a survey from 2018
revealed that less than half of people aged 18–34 said they know "very little"
about the Holocaust (Eddy 2019). For Spielberg this was worrisome as he
noted the rise of anti-Semitism in many of the EU countries, and in Germany
especially. An independent theater, Cinnexx, offered free tickets to members
of AfD (the ultraconservative and anti-immigrant Alternative for Germany
Party) to its screening on January 27 which is Holocaust Remembrance Day
(Eddy 2019).

As previously noted, faith-based groups and clergy have been outspoken
and active in advocacy work. In the Netherlands, in order to protect migrants
from immigration authorities, pastors held an ongoing church service at
Bethel Church, taking advantage of Dutch law which does not allow police
to disrupt a church service to make an arrest (Kingsley 2018). The holding
of continual masses was done to protect a refugee family from Armenia who
were given a deportation order. The service led to a national movement across
the Netherlands with more than 550 pastors from about twenty denominations
rotating through the church to maintain the ongoing service (Kingsley 2018).
In Italy, several Italian clergy members, including cardinals and bishops,
have pleaded with authorities to allow migrant rescue ships to dock in Italy,
offering to take responsibly for the migrants (Marcheti 2017). This was in
reaction to the decision by the leader of Italy, Matteo Salvini, to stop accepting the ships as a deterrent strategy to immigration.

Street protests, rallies, and demonstrations are other tactics that pro-immigration activists have been engaging in across Europe. For example, when
European far-right leaders met in Prague in December 2017 for a conference
hosted by the anti-Islam and anti-immigration Freedom and Direct Democracy
Party in 2018 to unify their stance on immigration, they were met with large
protests rejecting their alt-right populism and xenophobia (Heijmans and de

Goeij 2019). More than 200,000 marched in Berlin protesting against xeno-phobia and the rise of the AfD Party. This was nearly ten times the number that attended the weekly anti-immigrant marches in Dresden at the climax of the popularity of AfD in 2015 (Behhold and Eddy 2018).

In Austria, a group called the "Grannies" are also critical of the rise of far-right groups who they see as undermining the advances of the post–World War II order. Through rallies and demonstrations, they challenge the growing nativist ideology and neofascist tendencies in an attempt to preserve liberal democracy and civil rights (Eddy 2019). To expand on this, they have started to work with similar groups in Germany and have a large following on social media (Eddy 2019).

In December 2019, the Sardines Protest Movement in Italy gained traction against Salvini's leadership as tens of thousands gathered in Rome to hold its first national rally (Horowitz 2019). The name of the movement signifies its ability to pack citizens into public plazas "like sardines." The incentives for the massive demonstrations are a rejection of the antimigrant policies and uncivil language, as well as the anti-EU, antiglobalist rhetoric (Carbonaro 2019). Moreover, they also demand respect for the constitution and institutions that they feel are being abused by Salvini.

In Britain, there were dozens of large protests, some of the largest the country has ever experienced, in reaction to Brexit (Santora and Schaverien 2019). The most notable one was the First People's Vote March, which convinced hundreds of thousands of British citizens on the eve of the vote to make their voice heard through contentious politics on the streets (Santora and Schaverien 2019). The protest against President Trump's visit to the country was referenced earlier in the chapter. Although Trump claimed that there were "tremendous crowds of well-wishers" during his visit to London, a YouGov poll revealed that two-thirds of British citizens had a negative opinion of him, and the speaker of the House of Commons refused him to address Parliament.

CONCLUSION

This chapter has provided an overview of some of the recent and popular waves of protest and other forms of contentious politics regarding immigration and government policies that both immigrants and citizens in the United States and the EU find controversial and unjust. The Trump presidency and leaders in certain European countries have fueled the resistance to anti-immigration rhetoric and legislation against Muslims, Jews, and Latinx immigrants.

In addition to contentious politics, other grassroots organizations participate in advocacy work with a focus on the human rights of immigrants, and
in particular trying to save lives of migrants crossing the U.S.-Mexico border
and the Mediterranean Sea. Social movement theories, especially those that
highlight the importance of collective identity to help groups mobilize, framing which assists in influencing public opinion, and political process theory to
have influence over the formal political sphere, are useful in giving us a lens
through which to analyze these dynamics. Immigration theories and theories
such as world systems, global welfare theory, and the divergent perspectives
of the cosmopolitan versus communitarianism approach to the regulation of
immigration are also helpful, as is critical race theory.

Conclusion

People are still being displaced at a very high rate across the globe for a variety of reasons, and the anti-immigrant sentiment has been rising in synch. The original welcoming tone has changed, and the United States and member countries of the EU are still grappling with the 1948 Declaration of Human Rights mandate of how to balance universal rights versus the sovereignty of nation-states.

Within the broad framework of immigration theories, the communitarian versus cosmopolitan approaches are on opposite ends of the spectrum in terms of how to accommodate refugees and asylum seekers. This is especially true during times when there are high volumes of immigrants arriving or attempting to arrive at countries' borders. Of course, under these very broad lenses we have distinct theories that focus on the particulars of each as discussed in chapter 1. While some leaders want to make their countries and citizens "first," and are downplaying or rejecting a sense of the global post–World War II order, others are seeking to retain a common global community rooted in multiculturalism and paths of integration for immigrants.

What makes the situation particularly difficult is that in the EU there is no centralized control over immigration or institutions in place to deal with immigration even during regular times, let alone a crisis, making it that much more of a challenge to regulate borders and policies. There is also a growing sense among large segments of the population across Europe that elites and bureaucrats in Brussels do not understand the average European citizen and that there is a lack of democracy and transparency. This has resulted in high levels of distrust of the EU idea and practices. Exploiting this, as well as anti-immigrant posturing, populist leaders have been campaigning on the basis of restoring economic prosperity for working-class citizens, national sovereignty, Christian identity, and Western cultural values.

In fact, while promising more transparency, economic equality, and a political voice for regular citizens, both the United States and several EU countries are experiencing a surge of strongman politics as leaders centralize their power to subvert constitutional checks and balances. This is accompanied by the rise of extreme right-wing groups that, influenced by their leaders, scapegoat immigrants for many of the current problems, be they economic, political, or social. These anti-immigrant and racists perspectives are often contingent on certain historical trends and a questioning of national identity.

Loyalists are replacing competent politicians and lawmakers and long-standing democratic norms are increasingly threatened. In the United States this is referred to as "Trumpism," in the EU this falls under the label of "Euroskepticism." There is also a clear attack on the media—the fourth pillar of democracy. Many right-wing populist leaders regularly refer to the media as "fake news" and the "lying press."

A REVIEW OF IMMIGRATION PATTERNS IN THE UNITED STATES AND NEW UPDATES

I argue in chapter 2 that U.S. foreign policy has had a huge impact on immigration flows and therefore understanding the geopolitical context is crucial. As I have shown, the United States has experienced multiple waves of migration in response to fluctuating demands for labor, nationalist goals of land settlement, and racialized policies. Manifest Destiny was replaced by policies of outward conquest and economic and political domination to fuel the U.S. economy and keep U.S. business interests safe in Mexico, Central America, and other parts of Latin America and the Caribbean.

The Monroe Doctrine in the early 1800s, for example, extended Manifest Destiny externally to south of the border. This was followed by interventionist policies by financially and militarily supporting coups throughout Latin America, with the U.S. Marines invading several Latin American countries on numerous occasions under the guise of national security. As a result, there was a huge immigration flow to the United States as many of these countries were gutted of their natural resources, workers were not making high enough wages to support themselves and their families, and there was constant political instability amid gross human rights violations.

Also portrayed in chapter 4, the Bracero (guest worker program) in the mid-1900s allowed for seasonal work for Mexicans and allowed for circular migration patterns on the U.S.-Mexico border. However, as the need for labor in the United States shifted once U.S. citizens returned from serving in World War II, immigration policy was modified, resulting in Operation Wetback which deported most of the Mexican laborers as well as Mexican Americans who were indeed American citizens. Thus, this was the beginning of the racialization of immigrants from south of the border.

Later, during the BIP program in the 1980s and under the paradigm of neoliberalism, which led to the creation of the maquila industry, Mexican labor was once again exploited though this time within the country of Mexico itself. Other international agreements such as NAFTA and the War on Drugs to combat narco-trafficking, which wreaked economic, political, and social havoc in the lives of many Mexicans, led to further waves of migration.

The United States also altered immigration laws to accommodate "deserving" as opposed to "undeserving" immigrants, usually depending on the type of the political system in place in their country of origin. This was of prominence during the Cold War and its aftermath. For example, there was a major distinction between refugees from Central America seeking asylum as compared to those fleeing Cuba. While the United States was propping up and supporting dictators in Central America in return for keeping the countries safe for U.S. businesses, Cubans were given preferential treatment because they were fleeing a communist government.

While peace accords were signed in El Salvador and Guatemala after years of civil war with the U.S. government supporting ruthless authoritarian dictators as opposed to the citizens fighting for democracy, human rights, and overall justice, they did not address the root causes of the civil wars and injustices. Thus, in both of these countries, in addition to Honduras—the Northern Triangle—violence continues to ravage societies, drug cartels operate with impunity, human rights are routinely ignored, economic inequality is at all-time highs, and there is little hope for legitimate democracy among most of the population. The destabilization opened a vacuum that has been filled by nonstate actors such the drug cartels and corrupt politicians and police officers, once again leading to massive waves of migrants trying to escape the country.

Another recent development has been the creation of informal border patrol units, militias and vigilantes, in addition to formal border control efforts on the U.S.-Mexico border. Additionally, Prevention through deterrence measures have included Operation Hold the Line and Operation Gatekeeper among several others. This militarization of the border has made the journey much more treacherous, forcing immigrants to pay exorbitant fees to smugglers for their assistance. It has also led to an explosion of deaths in desert and river crossings.

Furthermore, new agencies were created post 9/11 to bolster deterrence efforts, externalization policies, and create fear in migrant communities. The DHS, for example, created after 9/11 instituted the ICE agency which apprehends migrants in the interior of the country, and the government has not only increased the number of Border Patrol agents but has also deployed the

National Guard to hinder the caravans from Central America from entering into the United States.

NEW POLICIES UNDER PRESIDENT TRUMP

Following the election of President Trump there has been a steep rise in white supremacy groups and dialogue in support of ethno-nationalism, though Trump did not *create* this dynamic. Indeed, the U.S. willingness to settle refugees and welcome them is part reality and part of idealizing a mythic past. While the United States did accept more refugees than any other country following the atrocities of World War II and the Holocaust, we can go back to the 1700s and document Benjamin Franklin's public statements about the threat of Germans overrunning America culture. There was also the Chinese Exclusion Act in the late 1800s, and the 1924 quota system that all but barred any group allowed asylum or citizenship other than Western Europeans.

Also, under Trump the government implemented the Muslim ban, which resonates with 1924 policy. It has also ended the Central America Minors Program which attempts to reunite families, is trying to phase out the DACA program, has referred to refugees fleeing countries with few whites as "shit-hole" countries, and has publicly stated the desire for white, highly skilled workers, for example, from Norway. This again highlights the racist nativism as embedded in the history and contemporary era of the United States.

Even more recently in early March 2020, ICE began 24-hour surveillance operations around homes and workplaces of immigrants suspected of being undocumented (Dickerson et al. 2020). Hundreds of officers, in unmarked cars, are being deployed to increase arrests. These special agents typically conduct long-term investigations into dangerous criminals and traffickers. The agenda is to "flood the streets" and arrest as many undocumented persons as possible. Other recent measures are that detained migrants have 24, rather than 28 hours (which was the case in the past) to consult with lawyers before their interview with an asylum officer (Kanno-Youngs 2020).

As discussed earlier, the United States changes its immigration laws based on the need for labor of immigrants south of the border. Challenging Trump's increasingly aggressive attempts to keep out, and deport those who are living in the United States without authorization, acting chief of staff Mick Mulvaney has made it clear in public statements that the United States needs more immigrants in order to sustain economic growth (Smialek andKanno-Youngs 2020). He references that the native work force is slowing at a rapid pace as the current generation is having fewer children, and that immigrants account for about half of the labor force's expansion over the past two decades. Yet, the United States added only 505,000 immigrants in

2019 which is the fewest since the 1980s (Center for Migration Studies 2019). There is also a major Mexican exodos—a reverse migration pattern (Jordan 2020). For example, in 2010 there were approximately 11.75 million people with undocumented status in the United States; this dropped to 10.6 million in 2018 (Center for Migration Studies 2019). This is due to more aggressive deportation tactics put into place by the Trump administration and a strong Mexican economy which is influencing many immigrants to return to their home country.

THE RISE AND DECLINE OF LIBERAL DEMOCRACY IN EUROPE

In many EU countries, as illustrated in chapter 3, there is a divisive tension between those who live in the countryside and smaller cities and those in metropolitan areas. Many of the latter feel disdain toward the urban elites running the country, whom they feel do not understand the struggles of the working class. The 2008 crisis played a major factor leading to the rising hostility toward immigrants and distrust of government, leaving an opening for autocratic leaders who have exploited fear and the victimization of whiteness that many Europeans feel, and which is related to what is perceived to be the loss of national identity, Christianity, culture, and heritage.

Additionally, throughout the EU there are strong efforts in place to keep immigrants out, and those who have been able to enter Europe are charged with not wanting to assimilate. Like the United States, the EU has been using externalized policies to stem the tide of immigrants by paying some countries to keep asylum seekers from reaching Europe. As noted, Brussels funds the Libyan Coast Guard to intercept migrant boats before they reach international waters, Spain pays Morocco, and other countries such as Italy and France have curtailed or outright abolished search-and-rescue missions, restricted aid groups, and closed ports to emergency rescue vessels. Italy has also enlisted Libyan militias to stifle migration across the Mediterranean and Greece has built borders with Turkey, Spain with Morocco, and Hungary with Serbia.

While overall immigrants were welcomed following World War II, by 2018, according to the Pew Global Attitudes Survey, citizens in many EU countries currently feel that the influx of refugees will "increase terrorism and take jobs and social benefits away from residents" (Amaral et al. 2018). This is accompanied by a rise of populist leaders who are suspect of the EU, migrants, and Islam and run on campaigns that promise a new era of far-right nationalism. Leaders have also blamed the increasing rates of economic inequality, which has steadily been expanding across Europe, on immigrants and globalism, and prey on young white working-class men who are struggling economically and feel culturally alienated through misinformation campaigns and fear tactics such as the promotion of the Great Replacement ideology that leaders of far-right parties and coalitions easily manipulate to scapegoat immigrants. This is leading to a dramatic rise of white supremacy, anti-Semitisms, and Islamophobia, which in many cases is being repackaged as identitarianism to have a more patriotic appeal.

Thus, Europe has taken a surprising turn from the post–World War II era toward far-right nationalism. Leaders of this movement have gained power in Hungary and Poland and are part of coalition governments in Austria and Italy, and have seats in parliaments in Germany, the Netherlands, Spain, and France. Much of this is a result of the growing Islamophobia and white anxiety. In Spain, for example, the leader of the Vox Party has warned of an "Islamist invasion" and in France the National Front Party proclaims that the French will be outnumbered by Muslim immigrants and the country will be dictated by Sharia law.

Immigration has served as catalyst to Euroskepticism, and as a consequence, the Schengen zone, which was created to facilitate global integration is in jeopardy mainly because it does not include a common external border. This has caused problems for much of the area since once inside, there is little to deter refugees from traveling to their preferred destination. Under the law, the EU country where immigrants first arrive is responsible for registering them and determining whether they are refugees and stipulates that other countries could return any migrants who crossed into them from the country of first arrival.

However, during the immigration influx following Arab Spring and other crises, most countries did not register immigrants and allowed them to cross borders, and they could not be returned if they were not tracked. Some countries have had to bear the brunt of the immigration more than others, mainly those that are easiest to reach by land or sea. Thus, the Dublin Agreement, which demarcated which EU member state would be responsible for the asylum application process and typically the responsible member was the state through which the refugee first entered in the EU was canceled.

HOW EU COUNTRIES HAVE RESPONDED TO THE IMMIGRATION CRISIS

As I reiterate throughout the manuscript, theories of immigration and critical race theory can help us understand the contemporary anti-immigrant and ethno-nationalism sentiments on both sides of the Atlantic. I also maintain that social movement theories assist in clarifying the trajectory of Europe's stance toward immigration. Leaders' condemnation of undocumented immigrants and blaming them for economic difficulties is indicative of strain theory—citizens being deprived of jobs, better wages, and social services due to the influx of immigrants. Reference to immigrants bringing chaos, drugs, crime, and violence was a successful use of framing that influenced public opinion toward a rejection of immigrants. This highlights the significance of framing, and of collective identity, as it manifests itself as an "us vs. them" mentality.

The snapshot below of how EU countries have responded to the massive wave of migrants over the past few years embodies the predictions of certain theories of immigration, social movements, and critical race theory and the conditions under which ethno-nationalism emerges and thrives.

During the reconstruction period following World War II, the Wind Rush generation was welcomed in Britain on the basis of the immigrant labor they provided. However, these migrants were not accepted or acknowledged as citizens, and when the economy soured, they were no longer welcomed. In the contemporary era, children of this generation have faced strong regulations in terms of receiving government benefits unless they can validate their immigration status. Part of this is due to the 2008 economic crisis, which fueled nativism and the Brexit vote as many citizens wanted sovereignty to control their borders.

In Italy, Salvini ran on a platform of expelling all undocumented immigrants for economic reasons and put forth a hard-line communitarian perspective, complaining about the economic distress migrants put on the economy, thus appealing to sense of injustice for Italian citizens. His message was that national identity must be protected from foreigners and one way to manifest this is by invoking the ideology of communitarianism into the institutions and legal workings of society.

The main frustrations in France are broader and more embedded in Euroskepticism, though like Salvini, Macron boasted about how many immigrants the government had expelled or refused entry into the country. France is currently trying to attract skilled immigrants while closing the door on others, and implemented a policy under which immigrants would have to wait three months before qualifying for nonurgent health care, similar to the measures taken in Britain and in the United States under the "public charge" policy.

On a campaign slogan of "Poland for Poles" the far-right Law and Justice Party, represented by Kaczynski came to power in 2015 with a message of national pride, ethno-nationalism, and an anti-immigrant posturing. He warned voters that migrants are bringing "dangerous diseases" and "various types of parasites" to Europe though now he is welcoming Christian migrants from Ukraine. This parallels Trump's desire for highly skilled, white immigrants.

In Spain, the ultranationalist Vox Party, which promotes nationalism, traditional values and Catholicism made it into Parliament for the first time. Its slogan was to "make Spain great again" and called for the abolition of the 2007 "law of historical memory" which mandated the removal of General Franco's symbols from public places, and for building walls around two of the Spanish enclaves in North Africa to exclude immigrants from entering Spain.

In Turkey, following the failed military coup in 2016, Erdogan declared a three-month state of emergency and purged and arrested tens of thousands of citizens. He shut down 131 media originations and issued warrants for the arrest of approximately ninety journalists who he charged with being implicated in the coup and has imprisoned more journalists than any other country.

When running for a fourth time in Hungary, Orbán promised to protect Hungarian culture from outsiders proclaiming, "Hungary First," warning that Hungary was losing its sovereignty in an attempt to instill fear among Hungarian citizens. He further claimed that Brussels was paying activists, bureaucrats, and politicians to argue that immigration should be considered a human right, thus robbing Hungary of its sovereignty.

In Germany, the Premier of Bavaria warned that Germans must prioritize their own citizens and ran on a platform of "Germany for Germans," border security, law and order, and a rejection of liberal democracy, declaring that his concern is for Germans, not all European citizens. In Sweden, the Swedish Democrats Party has called for the preservation of Swedish DNA" and ethnic purity. In 2018, Denmark created new laws for low-income, Muslim "ghetto children" requiring them to be separated from their families for at least 25 hours a week for mandatory instruction in "Danish values," or forced assimilation.

THE USE OF MAINSTREAM AND SOCIAL MEDIA TO FUEL ANTI-IMMIGRANT PERSPECTIVES

The rise of Islamophobia, anti-Semitic positions, and white supremacy is a global phenomenon and has resulted in extreme sensibilities embracing nativism and a dramatic increase in hate crimes, mainly committed by individuals who fear the destruction of Western civilization. As I illustrate in chapter 4, the Trump administration uses both mainstream and social media to engage in misinformation campaigns and purposeful falsehoods to exploit the anxiety that many members of the white working class feel by scapegoating Muslim and Latinx immigrants. Media pundits also play a role in setting immigration policy through their close relationship with, and influence over, the Trump administration.

I also reference in chapter 4 that because of the rhetoric and narratives about Muslims, and especially post 9/11 that centered on fear mongering many in the United States, there are exaggerated perceptions of Muslims' presence and power. There is a similar phenomenon taking place in France, Germany, and other regions in the EU, much of it due to the highly negative claims in the media regarding immigrants. For example, Brian Kilmeade on Fox News went so far as to say that "all terrorists are Muslims." He also intuited that since Americans marry "other species" they wind up in violent gangs. Others in the media have claimed that immigrants threaten the electoral system; a plot by Democrats to get more votes and to change the culture, constantly referring to the caravans from Central America as an "invasion."

In a similar vein, conservative political pundit, Rush Limbaugh on his radio show explained that (regarding the caravans) "the objective is to dilute and eventually eliminate or erase what is known as the distinct or unique American culture. This is why people call it an invasion. There's something behind this, folks, all these caravans amassing. This just doesn't happen organically. This is part of a targeted political project to flood this country and to paralyze the Trump administration."

In 2018, Fox News host, Tucker Carlson opined, "This is really destroying one culture and replacing it with the new foreign culture." Trump extended his anti-Muslim perspective in comments he has made about Muslim refugees in Europe implying that they are responsible for terrorism, high crime rates, the breakdown of law and order in Europe, and immigrants are destroying its culture.

Much of this rhetoric is most likely playing a role in the troubling increase of hate crimes and domestic terrorism. White supremacy and ultranationalism are currently among the greatest domestic security threats in the United States and the EU with immigrants, Jews, and Muslims being the main targets. As I report in chapter 4, in 2018 anti-Semitic attacks killed more Jews around the world than in any year in decades. There was a 600 percent increase in the followership of American white nationalist accounts on Twitter between 2012 and 2016. The Anti-Defamation League confirms that 71 percent of the extremist-related fatalities in the United States between 2008 and 2019 were committed by members of far-right or white supremacist movements.

According to the European Union Agency for Fundamental Rights, in 2016 "Asylum seekers and migrants face various forms of violence and harassment across the EU. These include attacks undertaken by individuals, vigilante groups, and state authorities and crisis of violence, harassment, threats and xenophobic speech" (The European Agency for Fundamental Rights). The majority of these are against immigrants. Statistics from a Greek police report confirms that hate crimes more than doubled in 2017 as compared to 2016, and according to a report by France's National Human Rights Advisory

Committee, in 2018 anti-Semitic acts in France increased more than 70 percent from the previous year, and the government reported a 74 percent increase in offenses against Jews.

Britain has also experienced a rise in anti-immigrant sentiment, and in particular against members of certain religions, reporting that between 2013 and 2017 hate crimes against immigrants almost doubled in England and Wales, and those motivated by religious hatred nearly quadruple. In 2018, the UK surpassed its record of anti-Semitic incidents by over 200 incidents: the most recorded in a single year, much of it the repercussion of the refugee crisis and recent arrival of Muslim immigrants from the Middle East and Africa. Germany has also witnessed a drastic increase in hate crimes against immigrants over the past few years. The AfD Party has been broadly accused of encouraging discrimination and violence against refugees, Muslims, and Jews.

Conflict resolution experts who have worked for decades in other countries are now shifting their focus toward the United States for the first time (Tavernise 2019). Their concern is the inflamed rhetoric that politicians have normalized, the amount of misinformation and conspiracy theories that lead to violence. Given the racist rhetoric used by Trump—calling Mexicans "rapists" and "criminals," and his attempt to ban immigrants from Muslim-majority countries it is not unreasonable to surmise that this may be emboldening groups and individuals to engage in hate crimes. At his rallies Trump emphatically self-identifies as a nationalist and encourages his supporters to wear this—a badge of honor.

In fact, the director of the SPLC's Intelligence Project, Heidi Beirich stated, "This president is not simply a polarizing figure but a radicalizing one. Rather than trying to defuse hate encourage unity, as presidents of both parties have done, President Trump elevates it—with both his rhetoric and his policies. In doing so, he's given people across America the go-ahead to act on their worst instincts" (Conley 2019).

There is a copycat approach to domestic terrorism that has a global reach, from the New Zealand shooter to the one in El Paso and everywhere in between. Domestic terrorism has been rising in the United States and in the EU, and according to authorities, this is much more pernicious than outside threats. There is an intent to inspire a global "race war"—awakening other potential young people who may become radicalized to join the movement and embrace the Great Replacement ideology.

The perpetrators of mass shooters targeting immigrants and religious groups site their fears of minorities having political power, the "invasion" of immigrants, the need for an ethno-state and fear of the "great replacement" by immigrants. They, and neo-Nazi groups in general, perceive themselves to be an endangered species and the only path forward, for survival, is a global race war, ethnic cleansing, and an end to democracy to preserve the superior, Aryan culture.

RESISTANCE

In chapter 5, I cover a variety of efforts undertaken by human rights activists, NGOs, faith-based groups, lawmakers, and certain industries to promote respect and protection for immigrants. For example, there were large and widespread demonstrations when President Trump introduced the Muslim ban and the zero-tolerance policy that led to the separation of Latinx families and threats to phase out DACA and to protect the DREAMers. Cities across the United States witnessed some of the largest protest ever against attempts to pass anti-immigrant laws at the federal and state levels. The largest in one location took place after the inauguration of President Trump.

Activists have also protested against policies such as Operation Streamline and the aggressive tactics of ICE. Other NGOs have organized awareness campaigns using social media to let undocumented immigrants know their rights. Human rights groups have also mobilized to reunite separated families, and others are committed to preventing deaths of migrants crossing the U.S.-Mexico border and traversing the Mediterranean Sea.

In addition to relief efforts, there have been numerous acts of civil disobedience, noncompliance by lawmakers and certain industries. NGOs continue their rescue missions in the Mediterranean, despite attempts by governments to thwart their efforts. Advocacy groups have risked criminal prosecution to save lives of migrants crossing the deserts and seas and assisting in migrants in other humane ways. In a number of EU countries, faith-based groups practice civil disobedience, activists hold street protests and rallies against xenophobia and illiberalism and the rise of neofascism. Thus, for those of concerned that nations uphold the rights of migrants and respect their dignity, though the last several years have been bleak, there is a significant push-back effort to support and assist them.

References

Abramsky, Sasha. 2019. "Trump Threatens to Unleash Paramilitary Violence in the US." *Truthout,* March 21, 2019. https://truthout.org/articles/trump-threatens-to-u nleash-paramilitary-violence-in-the-us.

Aceedo, Nicole. "Who's Pueblo Sin Fronteras, The Group Behind the Migrant Caravan that Drew Trump's Ire?" *ABC News*, April 24, 2018. https://www.influenc ewatch.org/non-profit/centro-sin-fronteras.

Acuna, Rodolfo. 1972. "Treaty of Guadalupe Hidalgo." In *Occupied America: The Chicano Struggle,* edited by Rodolfo Acuna, 27–31. Harper & Row Publishers.

Adams, David. 2019. "Guatemala's 'Embryonic' Asylum System Lacks Capacity to Serve as Safe U.S. Partner, Experts Say." *Univision*, August 19. https://www.uni vision.com/univision-news/immigration/guatemalas-embryonic-asylum-system-la cks-capacity-to-serve-as-safe-u-s-partner-experts-say.

Adone, Dakin, Jason Hanna, Joe Sterling and Paul Murphy. 2018. "Hate Crime Charges Filed in Pittsburgh Synagogue Shooting that Left 11 Dead." *CNN*, October 29, 2018. https://www.cnn.com/2018/10/27/us/pittsburgh-synagogue-active-shoo ter/index.html.

Ahmed, Azam, Miriam Jordan and Elisabeth Malkin. 2019. "Mexico Protests U.S. Decision to Return Asylum Seekers." *The New York Times*, January 25, 2019. https ://www.nytimes.com/2019/01/25/world/americas/mexico-asylum-seekers.html.

Alba, Richard and Nancy Foner, 2014. "Comparative Immigrant Immigration in North Africa and Western Europe: How Much Do the Grand Narratives Tell Us?" *International Migration Review*, September 29, 2014. https://onlinelibrary.wiley .com/doi/full/10.1111/imre.12134.

Albright, Madeleine. 2018. *Fascism: A Warning*. New York: Harper Collins.

Al Jazeeera. 2017. "Turkey's Failed Coup: All You Need to Know." *Al Jazeera*, July 5, 2017. https://www.aljazeera.com/news/2016/12/turkey-failed-coup-attempt -161217032345594.html.

Allison, Erica and Diane Taylor. 2019. "Home Office Abandons Six-Month Target for Asylum Decisions." *The Guardian*, May 7, 2019. https://www.theguardian.

com/uk-news/2019/may/07/home-office-abandons-six-month-target-for-asylum
-claim-decisions.

Alvarez, Michael and John Brehm. 1997. "Are Americans Ambivalent Towards Racial Policies?" *American Journal of Political Science* 41 (2): 345–374.

Amaral, Ernesto, Mahiet Woldetsadik and Gabriela Armenta. 2018. "Challenges to the Integration of Syrian Refugees." *International Journal of Population Studies* 4 (1): 39–56.

American Immigration Council. 2020. "Policies Affecting Asylum Seekers at the Border." January 20, 2020. https://www.americanimmigrationcouncil.org/research /policies-affecting-asylum-seekers-border.

American Progress Organization, 2017. https://www.americanprogress.org/.

Amnesty International. 2017. "The Human Rights Risks of External Migration Policies." https://www.refworld.org/pdfid/593fecfe4.pdf.

Amstutz, Mark. 2015. "Two Theories of Immigration." *First Things*, December 15, 2015. https://www.firstthings.com/article/2015/12/two-theories-of-immigration.

Anderson, Christina and Steven Erlanger. 2018. "Sweden's Centrists Prevail Even as Far Right Has its Best Showing Ever." *The New York Times*, September 9, 2018. https://www.nytimes.com/2018/09/09/world/europe/sweden-elections.html.

Anti-Defamation League. 2020. "Online Hate and Harassment Report: The American Experience." https://www.adl.org/online-hate-2020.

Applebaum, Anne. 2017. "Britain After Brexit: A Transformed Political Landscape." *Journal of Democracy* 28 (1): 53–58.

Appleby, Kevin. 2020. "Implementation of the Global Compact on Safe, Orderly and Regular Migration: a Whole-of-Society Approach." *Journal on Migration and Human Security* 8 (2): 214–229.

Apuzzo, Matt and Milan Schreuer. 2018. "Belgium's Prime Minister Resigns After Revolt Over Migration." *The New York Times*, December 18, 2018. https://www.nyt imes.com/2018/12/18/world/europe/right-wing-migration-belgium-collapse.html.

Arango, Tim, Nicholas Bogel-Burroghs and Katie Benner. "Minutes Before El Paso Shooting Hate-Filled Manifesto Appears Online." 2019. *The New York Times*, April 3, 2019. https://www.nytimes.com/2019/08/03/us/patrick-crusius-el-paso -shooter-manifesto.html.

Bache, Ian, Simon Blumer, Stephen George and Own Parker. 2015. *Politics in the European Union*. London: Oxford University Press.

Bacon, David. 2015. "The Maquiladora Workers of Juarez Find Their Voice." *The Nation*, November 20, 2015. https://www.thenation.com/article/archive/the-maqu iladora-workers-of-juarez-find-their-voice.

Bacon, David. 2018. "Counties Cancel ICE Detention Contracts." *The American Prospect*, July 18, 2018. https://prospect.org/civil-rights/counties-cancel-ice-detent ion-contracts.

Baczynska, Gabriela and Sara Ledwith. 2016. "The Walls Go Up in Europe." *Reuters* April 4, 2016. https://www.reuters.com/investigates/special-report/europe-migran ts-fences.

Bader, Eleanor. 2017. "Neo-Nazis Target College Campuses in Recruitment Drive." *Truthout* October 28, 2017. https://truthout.org/articles/neo-nazis-target-college-campuses-in-recruitment-drive.

Bahceli, Yoruk. 2015. "Dutch Plan Tougher Asylum Policy as Migrants Flock to Europe." August 30, 2015. https://www.reuters.com/article/us-europe-mig rants-netherlands/dutch-plan-tougher-asylum-policy-as-migrants-flock-to-europe-i dUSKCN0QZ09C20150830.

Baker, Peter. 2018. "'Use That Word!': Trump Embraces the 'Nationalist' Label." *The New York Times*, October 23, 2018. https://www.nytimes.com/2018/10/23/us/ politics/nationalist-president-trump.html.

Baker, Peter. 2019. "Trump Declares a National Emergency and Provokes a Constitutional Clash." *The New York Times*, February 15, 2019. https://www.nyt imes.com/2019/02/15/us/politics/national-emergency-trump.html.

Barker, Kim and Nicholas Kulish. 2019. "Inquiry into Migrant Shelter Poses Dilemma: What Happens to the Children?" *The New York Times*, January 5, 2019. https://www.nytimes.com/2019/01/05/us/southwest-key-migrant-shelters.html.

Barnes, Julian and Helene Cooper. 2019. "Trump Discussed Pulling U.S. From NATO, Aids Say Amid New Concerns Over Russia." *The New York Times*, January 14, 2019. https://www.nytimes.com/2019/01/14/us/politics/nato-presiden t-trump.html.

Barreto, Matt, Sylvia Manzano, Ricardo Ramirez and Kathy Rim. 2009. "Mobilization, Participation and Solidaridad." *Urban Affairs Review* 44 (5): 736–764.

Barry, Ellen and Martin Selsoe Sorensen. 2018. "In Denmark, Harsh New Laws for Immigrant 'Ghettos.'" *The New York Times*, July 1, 2018. https://www.nytimes. com/2018/07/01/world/europe/denmark-immigrant-ghettos.html.

Bauman, Zygmunt. 2014. "An Adorno 'Liquid Modern 'Times?" *The Sociological Review* 62 (4): 908–917.

Baur, Thomas and Klaus Zimmerman. 1999. "Occupational Mobility of Ethnic Migration." https://www.econstor.eu/handle/10419/20893.

Beck, Ulrich. 2011. "Cosmopolitanism as Imagined Communities of Global Risk." *American Behavioral Scientist* 55 (10): 1346–1361.

Becker, Joe. 2019. "The Global Machine Behind the Rise of Far-Right Nationalism." *The New York Times*, August 10, 2019. https://www.nytimes.com/2019/08/10/ world/europe/sweden-immigration-nationalism.html.

Beech, Eric. 2018. "Trump Signs Memo Ending 'Catch and Release' Immigration Policy. *Reuters*, April 6, 2018. https://journals.sagepub.com/doi/full/10.1111/1467 -954X.12214.

Beirch, Heidi. 2019. "The Year in Hate: Rage Against Change." *Southern Poverty Law Center*, February 20, 2019. https://www.splcenter.org/fighting-hate/intelligen ce-report/2019/year-hate-rage-against-change.

Beitz, Charles. 2005. "Cosmopolitanism and Global Justice." In *Current Debates in Global Justice*, edited by Gillian Block and Darrell Moelldorf, 11–27. Dordrecht: Springer.

Belew, Kathleen. 2019. *Bring the War Home*. Cambridge: Harvard University Press.

Beltran, Adriana. 2017. "United States Assistance for Central America." May 23, 2017. https://www.appropriations.senate.gov/imo/media/doc/052317-Beltran-Tes timony.pdf.

Benford, Robert. 1993. "Frame Disputes within the Nuclear Disarmament Movement." *Social Forces* 71 (3): 677–702.

Benford, Robert and David Snow. 2000. "Framing Processes and Social Movements: An Overview and Assessment." *Annual Review of Sociology* 26: 611–639.

Bennett, Clifford and Helen Powell. 2019. "Encrypted Extremism: Inside the English-Speaking Islamic State Ecosystem on Telegram." *George Washington Program*, June, 2019. https://extremism.gwu.edu/isis-online-reports.

Bennhold, Katrin. 2019. "Germany Intelligence Agency Puts Far-Right Party on Warning." *The New York Times*, January 15, 2019. https://www.nytimes.com/2019 /01/15/world/europe/alternative-for-germany-investigation.html.

Bennhold, Kartin and Melissa Eddy. 2018. "As Voters on Left and Right Rebel, Glimpse of a Post-Merkel Germany." *The New York Times*, October 15. https:// www.nytimes.com/2018/10/15/world/europe/merkel-germany-bavaria-vote.html.

Bennhold, Katrin and Melissa Eddy. 2019. "Hitler or Hocke? Germany's Far-Right Party Radicalizes." *The New York Times*, October 26, 2019. https://www.nytimes. com/2019/10/26/world/europe/afd-election-east-germany-hoecke.html.

Bennhold, Katrin and Steven Erlanger. 2019. "Merkel Rejects US. Demands That Europe Pull Out of Iran Nuclear Deal." *The New York Times*, February 16, 2019. https://www.nytimes.com/2019/02/16/world/europe/merkel-speech-munich.html.

Berberoglu, Berch. 2019. *Nationalism and Nationalist Movements in the Age of Neoliberal Globalization*. New York: Rowman and Littlefield Press.

Berendt, Joanna. 2018. "Poland Elections Reveal a Deeply Divided Nation." *The New York Times*, November 5, 2018. https://www.nytimes.com/2018/11/05/world/euro pe/poland-elections-law-and-justice.html.

Berg, Rebecca. 2015. "Cuban and Haitian Refugees at GTMO." https://gtmoinnola.w ordpress.com/portfolio/116.

Berkowitz, Bill. 2018. "Trump's Border Crisis Is Rooted in Fears of White Dispossession?" Buzzflash, June 28, 2018. http://legacy.buzzflash.com/comment ary/trump-s-border-crisis-weaponizes-birth-dearthers.

Berman, Sheri. 2019. *Democracy and Dictatorship in Europe: From the Ancien Regime to the Present Day*. London: Oxford University Press.

Bernstein, Hamutal and Nicole DuBouis. 2018. "Bringing Evidence to the Refugee Integration Debate." *Urban Institute*, April. https://www.urban.org/sites/default/ files/publication/97771/bringing_evidence_to_the_refugee_integration_debate_0 .pdf.

Berver, Lindsay. 2019. "Fox News Condemns Host Jeanine Pirro's Remarks About Representative Ilhan Omar's Hijab." *The Washington Post*, March 11, 2019. https:/ /www.washingtonpost.com/arts-entertainment/2019/03/11/fox-news-condemns-h ost-jeanine-pirros-remarks-about-rep-ilhan-omars-hijab.

Beyerlein, Kraig, Peter Ryan, Aliyah Abu-Hazeem and Amity Pauley. 2018. "The 2017 Women's March: A National Study of Solidarity Events." *Mobilization: An International Quarterly* 23 (4): 425–449.

Bier, David. 2016. "No One Knows how Long Legal Immigrants will have to Wait." *Cato at Liberty*, June 28, 2016. https://www.cato.org/blog/no-one-knows-how-lo ng-legal-immigrants-will-have-wait.

Bittner, Jochen. 2018. "How the Far-Right Conquered Sweden." *The New York Times*, September 6, 2018. https://www.nytimes.com/2018/09/06/opinion/how-the -far-right-conquered-sweden.html.

Blinder, Scott and Lindsay Richards. 2020. "UK Opinion Toward Immigration: Overall Attitudes and Level of Concerns." *The Immigration Observatory*, January 20, 2020. https://migrationobservatory.ox.ac.uk/resources/briefings/uk-public-op inion-toward-immigration-overall-attitudes-and-level-of-concern.

Blizzard, Brittany and Jeanne Batalova. 2020. "Cuban Immigrants in the United States in 2018." *Immigration Policy Institute*, June 11, 2020. https://www.migratio npolicy.org/article/cuban-immigrants-united-states-2018.

Blow, Charles. 2018. "White Extinction Anxiety." *New York Times*, June 24, 2018. https://www.nytimes.com/2018/06/24/opinion/america-white-extinction.html

Boffey, Daniele and Christian Davis. 2017. "Poland May be Stripped of EU Voting Rights Over Judicial Independence." *The Guardian*, July 19, 2017. https://www .theguardian.com/world/2017/jul/19/poland-may-lose-eu-voting-rights-over-judici al-independence.

Boffey, Danielle and Lorenso Tondo. 2018. "Italy's Call for France and Spain to Open Ports to Migrants is Rejected." *The Guardian*, August 30, 2018. https:// www.theguardian.com/world/2018/aug/30/italy-call-france-spain-open-ports-migr ants-rejected-eu.

Bonner, Raymond. 2016. *Weakness and Deceit: America and El Salvador's Dirty War*. New York: OR Books.

Bonner, Robert. 2012. "The Cartel Crackdown." *Foreign Affairs* 91 (5): 12–15.

Boulainne, Shelley. 2009. "Does Internet Use Affect Engagement: A Meta-Analysis of Research." *Political Communication* 26 (2): 193–211.

Bowden, John. 2018. "Bannon Says He Will Set Up Group in Europe to Boost Far-Right Figures." *The Hill*, July 21, 2018. https://thehill.com/blogs/blog-briefing-room/news/398171-bannon-says-he-will-set-up-group-in-europe-to-boost-far-right.

Bowles, Nellie. 2019. "'Replacement Theory,' a Racist, Sexist Doctrine, Spreads in Far-Right Circles." *The New York Times,* March 18, 2019. https://www.nytimes. com/2019/03/18/technology/replacement-theory.html.

Brack, Nathalie and Olivier Costa. 2019. *Euroscepticism within the EU Institutions: Diverging Views of Europe*. New York: Routledge.

Bredemier, Jamie. 2018. "German Officials: 'Fake News' Helped Stoke Anti-Migrant Protests." *VOA News*, August 29, 2018. https://www.voanews.com/europe/german -officials-fake-news-helped-stoke-anti-migrant-riot.

Bremmer, Ian. 2018. *Us vs. Them: The Failure of Globalism*. New York: Penguin Press.

Bridges, Khiara. 2019. *Critical Race Theory: A Primer*. St. Paul, MN: Foundations Press.

Brigida, Anna-Catherine. 2018. "Salvadorian Await Justice in Civil War Killings as One of Its First Victims Sainted." *The Guardian,* October 14, 2018. https://www .theguardian.com/world/2018/oct/14/el-salvador-oscar-romero-civil-war-

Brookings Institute. 2018. "Non-Hispanic Members of Race Source: U.S. Decennial Census and Census Population Estimates." *Metropolitan Policy Program*, June 21, 2018. https://www.brookings.edu/wp-content/uploads/2018/01/2018-jan_brooking s-metro_millennials-a-demographic-bridge-to-americas-diverse-future.pdf.

Brooks, Brad. 2019. "Victims of Anti-Latino Hate Crimes Soar in the U.S: FBI Report." *Reuters*, November 12, 2019. https://www.reuters.com/article/us-hatec

rimes-report/victims-of-anti-latino-hate-crimes-soar-in-us-fbi-report-idUSK
BN1XM2OQ.

Brubaker, Rogers. 2017. "Why Populism?" *Theory and Society* (46): 357–385.

Buchanan, Patrick. 2014. "Will the U.S. Become Balkanized?" *The American Conservative*, July 15, 2014. https://www.theamericanconservative.com/will-the-u-s-become-balkanized.

Burley, Shane. 2018. "The Fall of the 'Alt-Right' Came from Anti-Fascism." *Truthout*, April 5, 2018. https://truthout.org/articles/the-fall-of-the-alt-right-came-from-anti-fascism.

Byas, Steve. 2016. "Trump Threatens to Leave World Trade Organization." *The New American*, August 2, 2016. https://www.thenewamerican.com/usnews/politics/item/23777-trump-threatens-to-leave-world-trade-organization.

Campbell, Jason. 2007. *The Politics of Discrimination: A Philosophical Investigation of House Resolution 4437*. Priori Press.

Camus, Jean-Yves and Nicolas Lebourg. 2017. *Far-Right Politics in Europe*. London: Belknap Press.

Canas, Jesus and Eva Saiz. 2018. "Migrant Arrivals Push Shelter to Breaking Point in Southern Spain." *Immigration Newsletter*, July 26, 2018. https://english.elpais.com/elpais/2018/07/26/inenglish/1532595385_902317.html.

Cantu, Francisco. 2018. "Cages Are Cruel. The Desert is, Too." *The New York Times*, June 30, 2018. https://www.nytimes.com/2018/06/30/opinion/sunday/cages-are-cruel-the-desert-is-too.html.

CAP Immigration Team and Michael Nicolson. 2017. "The Facts on Immigration Today." *Center for American Progress*, April 20, 2017. https://www.american progress.org/issues/immigration/reports/2017/04/20/430736/facts-immigration-today-2017-edition.

Capo, Julio. 2017. "The White House Used This Moment as Proof the United States Should Cut Immigration." *Time*. https://time.com/4888381/immigration-act-mariel-boatlift-history.

Caporros, Martin. 2019. "Vox and the Rise of the Extreme Right in Spain." *The New York Times*, November 13, 2019. https://www.nytimes.com/2019/11/13/opinion/spain-election-vox.html.

Carbonero, Giulia. 2019. "Anti-Salvini 'Sardines' Movement Spreads Across Italy." *CGTN*, November 24, 2019. https://newseu.cgtn.com/news/2019-11-24/Anti-Salvini-sardines-movement-spreads-across-Italy-LRpOe7zSwg/index.html.

Carpenter, Galen. 2019. *Gullible Superpower: Unite States Supports Bogus Foreign Democratic Movements*. Washington, D.C.: Cato Institution.

Carrasaquillo, Adrian. 2014. "Relationships with Mexico and Its People." *BuzzFeed News*, May 4, 2014. https://www.buzzfeednews.com/article/adriancarrasquillo/anthony-bourdain-perfectly-captures-americas-hypocritical-re.

Carty, C Victoria and Karina Masias. 2014 "Immigration on the U.S.-Mexican Border: The of Neoliberal Policies and U.S. Foreign Policy on Migration Forces." In *Scholars and Southern California Immigrants in Dialogue: New Conversations in Dialogue*, edited by Victoria Carty, Tekle Woldemikael and Rafael Luevano, 3–20. Boston, MA: Brill Publishers.

Carty, Victoria. 2015. *Social Movements and New Technology*. New York: Lexington Press.

Castellans, Marielana. 2018. "Hundreds Call for ICE to be Abolished and Protest Operation Streamline." *Popular Restance.org*, July 5, 2018.

Castillo, Maria. 2004. *Land Privatization in Mexico: Urbanization, Formation of Regions, and Globalization in Regions*. New York: Taylor and Francis.

Castle, Stephen. 2020. "Will Big Ben Chime for Brexit?" *The New York Times*, January 15, 2020. https://www.nytimes.com/2020/01/15/world/europe/brexit-big -ben.html.

Castles, Stephen and Mark Miller. 2009. *The Rise of Migration*. New York: Palgrave Press.

Cendrowicz, Leo. 2015. "Refugee Crisis: EU Pays Three Billion to Turkey in Exchange for help on Dealing with European Migration." *Independent*, November 20. https://www.independent.co.uk/news/world/europe/refugee-crisis-eu-pays -3bn-to-turkey-in-exchange-for-help-on-dealing-with-european-migration-a675 3861.html.

Chasmar, Jessica. 2018. "Ann Coulter Calls Weeping Immigrant Children 'Actors': 'These Kids Are Being Coached.'" *The Washington Times*, June 18, 2018. https:// www.washingtontimes.com/news/2018/jun/18/ann-coulter-calls-children-weeping -border-child-ac.

Chavez, Leo. 2008. *The Latino Threat: Constructing Immigrants, Citizens, and the Nation*. Palo Alto, CA: Stanford University Press.

Chokshi, Niraj. 2019. "PewDiePie put in Spotlight After New Zealand Shooting." *The New York Times,* March 15, 2019. https://www.nytimes.com/2019/03/15/techn ology/pewdiepie-new-zealand-shooting.html.

Chomsky, Noam. 2015. "Greece Faces 'Savage Response' for Taking on Austerity 'Class War.'" *Democracy Now!* July 1, 2015. https://www.democracynow.org/2 015/7/1/chomsky_greece_s_syriza_spain_s.

Chrishti, Mazaffar and Claire Bergeron. 2011. "Post 9-11 Policies Dramatically Alter the U.S. Immigration Landscape." *Migration Policy Institute*, September 8, 2011. https://www.migrationpolicy.org/article/post-911-policies-dramatically-alter -us-immigration-landscape.

Churchill, David. 2019. "Europe's Child Migrant Shame." *Daily Mail*, December 28, 2019. https://www.dailymail.co.uk/news/article-7831587/Europes-child-migrant -shame-Greek-camp-Lesbos.html.

Clark, Simon. 2020. "How White Supremacy Returned to Mainstream Politics." *Center for American Politics*, July 1, 2020. https://www.americanprogress.org/ issues/security/reports/2020/07/01/482414/white-supremacy-returned-mainstream -politics/

Clarke, Kevin. 2019. "While U.S. Fixates on the Border Wall, Populist World Leaders Still Turn Migrants Away." *America Magazine*, January 11, 2019. https:// www.americamagazine.org/politics-society/2019/01/11/while-us-fixates-border-w all-populist-world-leaders-still-turn-migrants.

Cobb, Russel and Paul Knight. 2008. "Immigration: Cubans Enter U.S. at Texas-Mexico Border." *Houston Press*, June 9, 2008. https://www.houstonpress.com/n ews/immigration-cubans-enter-us-at-texas-mexico-border-6575312.

Cohen, Ben. 2019." One in Four Germans Believe 'Jews Have Too Much Power' Study Reveals." *The Algemeiner*, October 24. https://www.algemeiner.com/2019/10/24/one-in-four-germans-believe-jews-have-too-much-power-new-survey-reveals/.

Cohen, D'Vera, Jeffery Passel and Ana Gonzalez-Barrera. 2017. "Recent Trends in Northern Triangle Immigration." *Pew Research Center: Hispanic Trends*, December 7, 2017. https://www.pewresearch.org/hispanic/2017/12/07/recent-trends-in-northern-triangle-immigration.

Cohen, Roger. 2018. "How Democracy Became the Enemy." *The New York Times*, April 6, 2018. https://www.nytimes.com/2018/04/06/opinion/sunday/orban-hungary-kaczynski-poland.html.

Cole, Teju. 2011. "Cosmopolitan Dissociation." In *Contemporary Literature and the End of the* Novel, edited by Pieter Vermeulen, 81–104. London: Palgrave Macmillan.

Collinson, Sarah. 2009. "The Political Economy of Migration Processes: An Agenda for Research and Analysis." Working Paper Series. *International Migration Institute.* https://www.migrationinstitute.org/publications/wp-12-09

Conley, Julia. 2019. "As Racist Attacks Soar Under Trump, White Nationalist Plotted Massacre." *Common Dreams*, February 21, 2019. https://truthout.org/articles/as-hate-crimes-soar-under-trump-white-nationalist-had-domestic-terror-plan.

Connoly, Kae and Jose Le Blond. 2018. "Bavaria Election: Merkel's Conservative Allies Humiliated." *The Guardian*, October 14. https://www.theguardian.com/world/2018/oct/14/bavaria-poll-humiliation-for-angela-merkel-conservative-allies.

Conrneilius, Wayne. 2004. "Evaluating Enhanced U.S. Border Enforcement." *Migration Policy Institute*, May 1, 2004. http://publications.unidosus.org/handle/123456789/1074.

Considerdine, Erica and James Hampshire. 2013. "Immigration Policy Under New Labour: Europe at a Critical Juncture." *British Politics* 9: 275–296.

Cosse, Eve. 2019. "The Alarming Rise of Anti-Semitism in Europe." *Human Rights Watch*, June 4, 2019. https://www.hrw.org/news/2019/06/04/alarming-rise-anti-semitism-europe.

Cottam, Martha and Otwin Marenin. 2005. "The Management of Border Security in NAFTA: Imagery, Nationalism, and the War on Drugs" *International Criminal Justice Review* 15 (5): 5–377.

Crisp, James. 2018. "Dutch Police Foil Major Terror Plot in Raids." *The Telegraph*, September 27, 2018. https://www.telegraph.co.uk/news/2018/09/27/dutch-police-foil-major-terror-plot-raids.

Crouch, David. 2014. "Anti-immigrant Party Pushes Sweden to Brink of Political Chaos." *The Guardian*, December 3, 2014. https://www.theguardian.com/world/2014/dec/03/sweden-coalition-far-right-threatens-block-budget-immigration.

Crowley, Michael. 2017. "The Man Who Wants to Unmake the West." *Politico Magazine*, March/April, 2017. https://www.politico.com/magazine/story/2017/03/trump-steve-bannon-destroy-eu-european-union-214889.

Crowley, Michael and David Sanger. 2019. "Trump Celebrates Nationalism in U.N. Speech and Plays Down Iran Crisis." *The New York Times*, September 24. https://www.nytimes.com/2019/09/24/us/politics/trump-nationalism-united-nations.

Cullen, Thomas T. 2019 "The Grave Threats of White Supremacy and Far-Right Extremism." *The New York Times*, February 22, 2019. https://www.nytimes.com/2 019/02/22/opinion/christopher-hasson-extremism.html.

Cunha, Alice, Marta Silva and Rui Frederico. 2015. *The Borders of Schengen*. Brussels: Peter Lang.

Council of Europe. 2020. https://www.coe.int/en/web/portal.

Da Silva, Chantal. 2018. "Why is the Trump Administration So Against the U.N.'s Global Migration Pact?" *Newsweek*, December 10, 2018. https://www.new sweek.com/why-trump-administration-so-against-uns-global-migration-pact-125 2215.

Davidson, Thomas and Mabel Berezin. 2018. "Britain First and The UK Independence Party: Social Media and Movement-Party Dynamics." *Mobilization: An International Quarterly* 23 (4): 485–510.

Davis, Jack. 2019. "Normally Pro-Trump Lou Dobbs Says White House Has Lost Its Way." *The Western Journal,* March 7, 2019. https://www.westernjournal.com/ normally-pro-trump-lou-dobbs-says-white-house-lost-way.

Davis, Mais. 1994. "1,500 Students Leave Schools Over Prop. 187: Protests: Youths Walk Out of Classes at 11 Campuses in Oxnard and Camarillo; March Through Oxnard." *Los Angeles Times*, October 29, 1994. https://www.latimes.com/archives /la-xpm-1994-10-29-mn-55952-story.html.

Davis, Mike and Justin Chacan. 2006. *No One is Illegal*. London: Haymarket Press.

Del Real, Jose. 2019. "California Governor Announce Withdrawal of National Guard Troops from Border Duty." *The New York Times,* February 11, 2019. https://www .nytimes.com/2019/02/11/us/california-border-troops.html.

Delgado-Wise, Raul and Covarrubias Marquez. 2007. "The Reshaping of Mexican Labor Exports Under NAFTA: Paradoxes and Challenges." *International Migration Review* 41 (3): 656–679.

Democracy Now! 2019. "Activist Scott Warren, Facing Federal Charges for Aiding Migrants Says He Won't Be Deterred." *Democracy Now!* August 19, 2019. https:/ /www.democracynow.org/2019/8/19/no_more_deaths_scott_warren.

DenUyl, Sophia. 2018. "Los Angeles's "Counter-Terrorism" Program Could Sweep 10 Million into Dragnet." *Truthout*, July 20, 2018. https://truthout.org/articles/los-a ngeless-counter-terrorism-program-could-sweep-10-million-into-dragnet.

Diamond, Larry. 2019. Ill Winds: *Saving Democracy from Russian Rage, Chinese Ambition and American Complacency*. London: Penguin Press.

Diamond, Larry and Richard Gunther. 2001. *Political Parties and Democracy*. Baltimore, MD: Johns Hopkins University Press.

Diaz, Johnny. 2020. "Greyhound to Stop Allowing Border Patrol Agents on Its Buses Without Warrants." *The New York Times*, February 22, 2020. https://www.nytimes. com/2020/02/22/us/greyhound-border-patrol.html.

Dickerson, Caitlin. 2018. "Detention of Migrant Children Has Skyrocketed to Highest Levels Ever." *The New York Times*, September 12, 2018. https://www.nytimes.com /2018/09/12/us/migrant-children-detention.html.

Dickerson, Catilin. 2020. "Confusion on the Border as Appeals Court Rules Against Trump's 'Remain in Mexico' Policy." *New York Times*, February 28, 2020. https

://www.nytimes.com/2020/02/28/us/migrants-court-remain-in-mexico-mpp-injunc tion.html.

Dickerson, Caitlin, Ron Nixon, Helene Cooper and Elisabeth Malkin. 2018. "Migrants at the Border: Here's Why There's No Clear End to Chaos." *The New York Times*, November 26, 2018. https://www.nytimes.com/2018/11/26/us/politics /migrants-border-trump-.html.

Dickerson, Caitlin, Zolan Kanno-Youngs and Annie Correal. 2020. "Flood the Streets': ICE Targets Sanctuary Cities with Increased Surveillance." *The New York Times*, March 6, 2020. https://www.nytimes.com/2020/03/05/us/ICE-BORTAC-s anctuary-cities.html.

Dietrich, David. 2014. *Rebellious Conservatives: Social Movements in Defense of Privilege*. London: Palgrave Macmillan.

Dinan, Stephen. 2018. "Judge Rules Trump's DACA Phaseout Legal." *The Washington Times*, March 5, 2018. https://www.washingtontimes.com/news/2018/ mar/5/trump-daca-phaseout-legal-judge-rules.

Domonsoske, Camala and Richard Gonzalez. 2018. "What We Know: Family Separation and 'Zero Tolerance' at the Border." *NPR*, June 10. https://www.npr .org/2018/06/19/621065383/what-we-know-family-separation-and-zero-tolerance -at-the-border.

Dorling, Danny. 2016. *Peak Inequality: Britain's Ticking Time Bomb*. Chicago: The University of Chicago Press.

Doubek, James. 2018. "ICE Targets 7-Eleven Stores in Nationwide Immigration Raids." *NPR*, January 11, 2018. https://www.npr.org/sections/thetwo-way/2018/01 /11/577271488/ice-targets-7-eleven-stores-in-nationwide-immigration-raids.

Drake, Bruce and Jacob Poushter. 2016. "In Views of Diversity, Many Europeans are Less Positive Than Americans." *Pew Research Center*, July 12, 2016. https://www .pewresearch.org/fact-tank/2016/07/12/in-views-of-diversity-many-europeans-are- less-positive-than-americans/.

Drier, Peter. 2020. "Why Anti-Semitism Is on the Rise in the United States." *Portside*, January 17, 2020. https://portside.org/2020-01-22/why-anti-semitism- rise-united-states.

Drucker, David. 2018. "Heidi Heitkamp Challenges Trump on Border Security Plan." *Washington Examiner*, August 10, 2018. https://www.washingtonexaminer.com/ news/campaigns/heidi-heitkamp-challenges-trump-on-border-security-plan-wher e-is-it

Dunai, Marton. 2018. "Soros University Promises No Exodus from Hungary Despite Orban Law." *US News*, May 1, 2018. https://www.usnews.com/news/world/articl es/2018-05-01/soros-university-promises-no-exodus-from-hungary-despite-orban -law.

Dunn, Tom. 2018. "Donald Trump Told Teresa May How To Do Brexit But 'She Wrecked It." *The Sun*, July 13, 2018. https://www.thesun.co.uk/news/6766531/tr ump-may-brexit-us-deal-off.

Durkin, Erin. 2018. "Laura Ingraham Condemned After Saying Immigrants Destroy 'The American We Love.'" *The Guardian*, August 9, 2018. https://www.theguard ian.com/media/2018/aug/09/laura-ingraham-fox-news-attacks-immigrants.

Dustmann, Christian and Albrecht Glitz. 2015. "How Do Industries and Firms Respond to Changes in Local Labor Supply?" *Journal of Labor Economics* 33 (3): 711–750.

Dwyer, Colin. 2019. "Jersey City Shooting Was a Targeted Attack on the Jewish Kosher Deli." *NPR*, December 11, 2019. https://www.npr.org/2019/12/11/7870 29133/jersey-city-shooting-was-a-targeted-attack-on-the-jewish-kosher-deli.

Earnshaw, Rob and Carole Carlson. 2018. "Dozens Rally Outside Portage Restaurant After Workers Detained in ICE Raid." *Post-Tribune*, December 19, 2018. https://www.chicagotribune.com/suburbs/post-tribune/ct-ptb-ice-protest-portage-st-1220-story.html.

Eddy, Melissa. 2018. "German Far Right and Counter Protesters Clash in Chemnitz." *The New York Times*, August 28, 2018. https://www.nytimes.com/2018/08/28/world/europe/chemnitz-protest-germany.html.

Eddy, Melissa. 2019. "Offered Free Tickets for 'Schindler's List,' Germany's Far Right Sees Provocation." *The New York Times*, January 3, 2019. https://www.nytimes.com/2019/01/03/world/europe/schindlers-list-afd-germany.html.

Edwards, Jim. 2017. "It's Funny to Think That Brexit Might Kill Pret a Manger." *Business Insider*, March 11. https://www.businessinsider.com/brexit-might-kill-pret-a-manger-2017-3.

Edwards, Jim. 2019. "The European Union's Subversion of Democracy Contributed to the Recession in Italy." *Business Insider*, February 2, 2017. https://www.businessinsider.com/democracy-in-eu-and-recession-in-italy-2019-1.

Egan, Timothy. 2019. "How Words Became Weapons, and Wimps." *Times Free Press*, February16, 2019. https://www.timesfreepress.com/news/opinion/times-commentary/story/2019/feb/16/how-words-become-weapons-and-wimps/488821.

Eljechtimi, Ahmed. 2018. "Morocco Plays Cat an Mouse With Africans Headed to Europe." *Reuters* September 18, 2018. https://www.reuters.com/article/us-europe-migrants-morocco/morocco-plays-cat-and-mouse-with-africans-headed-to-europe-idUSKCN1LZ0MD.

Ellion, Larry and Dan Atkinson. 2016. *Europe Isn't Working*. New Haven: Yale University Press.

Elliot, Larry. 2018. "Italy's Policies Make Sense-It's Eurozone Rules That are Absurd." *The Guardian*, May 20, 2018. https://www.theguardian.com/business/2018/may/20/italys-policies-make-sense-its-eurozone-rules-that-are-absurd.

Ellyatt, Holly. 2018. "'Pack Your Bags' Italy's New Leaders Tell 500,000 Illegal Migrants – But It Will Cost Them." *CBSN NEWS*, June 5, 2018. https://www.cnbc.com/2018/06/04/pack-your-bags-italys-new-leaders-tell-500000-illegal-migrants--but-itll-cost-them.html.

Embury-Dennis, Tom. 2018. "Italy's Deputy PM Salvini Called for 'Mass Cleansing, Street by Street, Quarter by Quarter', Newly Resurfaced Footage Reveals." *The Independent*, June 21, 2018. https://www.independent.co.uk/news/world/europe/italy-matteo-salvini-video-immigration-mass-cleansing-roma-travellers-far-right-league-party-a8409506.html.

Emerson-Smith, Joshua. 2018. "Hundred protest Outside of Otay Mesa Detention Center Calling for Release of Asylum Seekers." *The San Diego Tribune*, June

10, 2018. https://www.sandiegouniontribune.com/news/immigration/sd-me-asylu
m-protesters-20180610-story.html.

Erlanger, Steven. 2018a. "Sweden Was Long Seen as a 'Moral Superpower.' That
May Be Changing." *The New York Times*, September 8, 2018. https://www.nyt
imes.com/2018/09/07/world/europe/sweden-election-far-right.html.

Erlanger, Steven. 2018b. "Migration to Europe Is Slowing, but the Political Issue
Is as Toxic as Ever." *The New York Times,* June 22, 2018. https://www.nyt
imes.com/2018/06/22/world/europe/migration-europe-merkel-seehofer-germany
.html.

Esses, Victoria, Leaha Hamilton and Danielle Gaucher. 2017. "The Global Refugee
Crisis: Empirical Evidence and Public Implications for Improving Public Attitudes
and Facilitating Refugee Resettlement." *Society for the Psychological Stud of
Social Issues* 11 (1): 78–123.

EUAFR. European Commission Against Racism and Intolerance. https://www.coe
.int/en/web/european-commission-against-racism-and-intolerance/about.

European Network Against Racism. 2014. https://www.socialplatform.org/events/eu
ropean-network-against-racism-eu-anti-racism-days.

European Think Tank. 2011. https://www.europarl.europa.eu/thinktank/en/document
.html?reference=IPOL-LIBE_ET(2011)453167.

European Union Agency for Fundamental Rights. 2020. https://europa.eu/european
-union/about-eu/agencies/fra_en.

Evans, Geoffrey, Noah Carl and James Dennison. 2017. "Brexit: The Causes and
Consequences of the UK's Decision to Leave the EU." *European University
Institute*. https://cadmus.eui.eu/handle/1814/50544?show=ful.l.

Eversley, Melanie.2017. "Study: 'Hate' Groups Explode on Social Media." *USA
Today*, February 23, 2017. https://www.usatoday.com/story/news/2017/02/23/hate
-groups-explode-social-media/98284662/.

Ewing, Jack and Melissa Eddy. 2020. "Germany Shooting is Deadliest Yet in Upsurge
of Far-Right Attacks." *European World News*, February 20, 2020. https://dnyuz.c
om/2020/02/20/germany-shooting-is-deadliest-yet-in-upsurge-of-far-right-attacks.

Faber, Sebastian and Becquer Seguin. 2019. "Spain's Radical Right is Here to Stay-
but Did it Ever Leave?" *The Nation*, January 10, 2019. https://www.thenation.com
/authors/becquer-seguin.

Fausset, Richard. 2018. "Airlines Ask Government Not to Use Their Flights to Carry
Children Separated at the Border." *The New York Times*, June 20, 2018. https://ww
w.nytimes.com/2018/06/20/us/airlines-transport-immigrant-children.html.

Favell, Adrian. 1999. "To Belong or Not to Belong: The Postcolonial Question."
In *the Politics of Belonging: Migrants and Minorities in Contemporary Europe*,
edited by Adrian Favell and Andrew Geedes, 1–22. New York: Routledge.

Felix, Hoffman. 2019. Police Brutality Against Yellow Vests Protests Risks More
Than an Eye For an Eye." *The Global Post*, March 13, 2019. https://theglobepost
.com/2019/03/13/france-police-yellow-vests.

Fernandez, Itziar, Juan-Jose Igartua, Felix Moral, Elena Palacios, Tania Acosta and
Dolores Munoz. 2012. "Language Use Depending on News Frame and Immigrant
Origin." *International Journal of Psychology* 48 (5): 772–784.

Fernandez, Kelly. 2006. "The Crimes and Consequences of Illegal Immigration: A Cross Border Examination of Operation Wetback 1943–1954." *Western Historical Quarterly* 27 (4): 421–444.

Fikes, Bradley. 2018. "Gathering Aims to Relaunch Minuteman Project, Fortify Border in Response to Central American Caravan." *Los Angeles Times*, May 5, 2018. https://www.latimes.com/local/lanow/la-me-ln-sd-minutemen-20180505-story.html.

Fioretti, Julia. 2014. "EU Sea Rescue Mission Off Italy Extended Until at Least End-2015." *Reuters*, February 10, 2014. https://news.trust.org/item/20150219133550-fpbel.

Fisher, Dana, Lorien Jasny and Dawn M. Dow. 2018. "Why Are We Here? Patterns of Intersectional Motivations Across the Resistance." *Mobilization: An International Quarterly* 23 (4): 451–468.

Fisher, Max. 2019. "Brexit Mess Reflects Democracy's New Era of Tear-It-All Down." *The New York Times*, March 29, 2019. https://www.nytimes.com/2019/03/29/world/europe/brexit-theresa-may-democracy-chaos.html.

Folkenflik, David. "Univision Anchor Jorge Ramos Removed From Trump Press Conference." *NPR*, August 25, 2019. https://www.wnyc.org/story/univision-anchor-jorge-ramos-removed-from-trump-press-conference.

Freeze, Melanie, Mary Baugartner, Peter Bruono, Jacob Gunderson, Joshua Olin, Morgan Ross and Justine Szafran. 2020. "Fake Claims of Fake News: Politics, Misinformation, Warnings, and the Tainted Truth Effect." *Political Behavior*. https://link.springer.com/article/10.1007/s11109-020-09597-3.

Frelick, Bill. 2007. "Haitians At Sea: Asylum Denies." *NACLA*, September 25, 2007. https://nacla.org/article/haitians-sea-asylum-denied.

Frelick, Bill, Ian Kysel and Jennifer Podkul. 2016. "The Impact of Externalization of Migration Controls on the Rights of Asylum Seekers and other Migrants." *Journal on Migration and Human Security* 4 (4): 190–220.

Friedman, George. 2013. "Beyond the Post-Cold War World." *On Geopolitics*, April 2, 2013. https://worldview.stratfor.com/article/beyond-post-cold-war-world.

Friedman, Thomas. 2018. "Can I Ruin Your Party? One of Two Pillars in the West is in Jeopardy." *The New York Times*, August, 7. https://www.nytimes.com/2018/08/07/opinion/can-i-ruin-your-dinner-party.html.

Friedman, Thomas. 2019. "The Trump Musical: 'Anything Goes.' Leaders Around The World Have Learned that they Can Do as They Wish Without the U.S. Calling Them Out." *The New York Times*, March 5, 2019. https://www.nytimes.com/2019/03/05/opinion/trump-netanyahu.html.

Fry, Wendy. 2019. "Mexico, U.S. Will Attempt to 'Freeze' Arms Trafficking at San Diego-Tijuana Border Crossing." *The San Diego Tribune*, October 22, 2019. https://www.sandiegouniontribune.com/news/border-baja-california/story/2019-10-22/mexico-us-operation-frozen-gun-trafficking-san-diego-tijuana.

Fukuyama, Francis. 1992. *The End of History and the Last Man*. New York: Free Press.

Gabey, Sarah and Neil Caren. 2016. "The Rise of Inequality: How Social Movements Shape Discursive Fields." *Mobilization: An International Quarterly* 21 (4): 413–429.

Gabriel, Trip. 2019. "A Timeline of Steve King's Racist Remarks and Divisive Actions." *The New York Times*, January 15, 2019. https://www.nytimes.com/2019/01/15/us/politics/steve-king-offensive-quotes.html.

Gallindo, Rene and Jami Vigil. 2006. "Are Anti-Immigrant Statements Racist or Nativist? What Difference Does it Make?" *Latino Studies* (4): 419–447.

Gallaher, J.J. 2017. "Dreamers Stage Protest During Macy's Thanksgiving Day Parade." *ABC* News, November 23, 2017. https://abcnews.go.com/US/dreamers-stage-protest-macys-thanksgiving-day-parade/story?id=51352646.

Galston, William. 2018. *Anti-Pluralism-The Populist Threat to Liberal Democracy.* New Haven: Yale University Press.

Gambino, Lauren, Sabrina Siddiqui, Paul Owen and Edward Helmore. 2017. "Thousands Protest Against Trump's Travel Ban in Cites and Airports Nationwide." *The Guardian*, January 20, 2017. https://www.theguardian.com/us-news/2017/jan/29/protest-trump-travel-ban-muslims-airports.

Gamson, William. 1990. *The Strategy of Social Protest.* Belmont, CA: Wadsworth.

Garcia, Carlos. 2018. "Mike Pence says the President of Honduras Told Him Who is Really Funding the Caravan." *The Blaze*, October 23, 2018. https://www.theblaze.com/news/2018/10/23/mike-pence-says-the-president-of-honduras-told-him-who-is-really-funding-the-migrant-caravan.

Garcia, Juan. 2008. *Mexicans in the Midwest, 1900–1932.* Tucson: University of Arizona Press.

Garcia, Juan Romero. 1980. *Operation Wetback: The Mass Deportation of Mexican Undocumented Workers in 1954.* Westport, CN: Praeger.

Garcia-Long, J.D. 2018. "What Life is Like on The U.S. Mexico Border." *America Magazine*, April 4, 2018. https://www.americamagazine.org/politics-society/2018/04/04/what-life-us-mexico-border.

Garner, Steven. 2009. "Empirical Research into White Racialized Identities in Britain." *Sociology Compass* 3 (5): 789–802.

Garner, Steven and Saher Selod 2014. The Racialization of Muslims: Empirical Studies of Islamophobia." *Critical Theory* 41 (1): 9–19.

Gathmann, Sandra. 2019. "Politics of Fear in the Spanish Elections." *Aljazeera*, May 2, 2019. https://www.aljazeera.com/blogs/europe/2019/05/politics-fear-spanish-elections-190502160025813.html.

Gauthier, Brendan. 2018. "Study: No Relation Between Immigration and Crime." *AlterNet*, April 6, 2018. https://www.alternet.org/2018/04/study-no-relation-immigration-crime/

Geha, Joseph. 2020. "Silicon Valley Pain Index Shows 'White Supremacy' Prevalent Across Institutions." *Mercury News*, June 23, 2020. https://www.mercurynews.com/2020/06/23/silicon-valley-pain-index-shows-white-supremacy-prevalent-across-institutions/

Gehr, Richard. 2017. "Trump's Overturned Travel Ban is Still Causing Chaos for Musicians." *Rolling Stone*, February 7, 2017. https://www.rollingstone.com/music/music-news/trumps-overturned-travel-ban-is-still-causing-chaos-for-musicians-127371/.

Gelatt, Julia. 2005. "Schengen and the Free Movement of People Across Europe." *MPI*, October 1, 2005. https://www.migrationpolicy.org/article/schengen-and-free-movement-people-across-europe.

Gessen, Masha. 2020. "Trump's Immigration Rule is Cruel and Racist- But It's Nothing New." *New Yorker*, January 29, 2020. https://www.newyorker.com/news /our-columnists/trumps-immigration-rule-is-cruel-and-racistbut-its-nothing-new.

Gest, Justin. 2016. *The New Minority: White Working-Class Politics in an Age of Immigration and Inequality*. London: Oxford University Press.

Gest, Justin, Tyler Renny and Jeremy Mayer. 2018. "Roots of the Radical Right: Nostalgic Deprivation in the United States and Britain." *Comparative Political Studies* 51 (13): 1694–1719.

Giungi, Marco. 1999. *How Social Movements Matter: Past Research, Present Problems, Future Developments*. Minneapolis: University of Minnesota Press.

Glass, Andrew. 2009. "Castro Launches Mariel Boatlift, April 20, 1980. *POLITICO,* April 20, 2019. https://www.politico.com/story/2009/04/castro-launches-mariel -boatlift-april-20-1980-021421.

Gleijeses, Piero. 1991. *Shattered Hope: The Guatemalan Revolution and the United States, 1944–1954*. Princeton, NJ: Princeton University Press.

Glenday, James. 2017. "Britain First: A Day with the UK's Anti-Islam Alt-Right Group." *ABC News*, November 29, 2017. https://www.abc.net.au/news/2017-03-05 /a-day-with-alt-right-britain-first/8324680.

Gluffrida, Angela and Joh Henley. 2019. "France Condemns Italy's Meeting with Gilets Jaunes Leader." *The Guardian*, February 6, 2019. https://www.theguardian.c om/world/2019/feb/06/italys-deputy-pm-luigi-di-maio-meets-senior-gilets-jaunes -figure.

Goldbaum, Christina and Mathew Sedacca. 2020. "Solidarity March Against Anti-Semitism: Thousands Rally After Attacks." *The New York Times*, January 5, 2020. https://www.nytimes.com/2020/01/05/nyregion/anti-semitism-solidarity-m arch-nyc.html.

Goldbereg, Michelle. 2019. "Stephen Miller is a White Nationalist. Does it Matter?" *The New York Times*, November 20, 2019. https://www.nytimes.com/2019/11/18/ opinion/stephen-miller-white-nationalism.html.

Gomez, Alan. 2017a. "Obama Ends 'Wet Foot, Dry Foot' Policy for Cubans." *USA Today*, January 12, 2017. https://www.usatoday.com/story/news/world/2017/01/12 /obama-ends-wet-foot-dry-foot-policy-cubans/96505172.

Gomez, Alan. 2017b. "What President Trump Has Said About the Travel Ban." *USA Today,* June 11, 2017. https://www.usatoday.com/story/news/politics/2017/06/11/ what-president-trump-has-said-about-muslims-travel-ban/102565166.

Gomez, Melissa. 2018. "Congressman Steve King Retweets a Nazi Sympathizer." *The New York Times*, June 13, 2018. https://www.nytimes.com/2018/06/13/us/po litics/steve-king-collett-nazi.html.

Gonyea, Don. 2017. "Majority of White Americans Say They Believe Whites Face Discrimination." *NPR* October 12, 2017. https://www.npr.org/2017/10/24/5596 04836/majority-of-white-americans-think-theyre-discriminated-against.

Gonzalez, Juan. 2011. *Harvest of Empire: A History of Latinos in America*. New York: Penguin Press.

Gonzalez-Barrera, Anna and Phillip Connor. 2019. "Around the World, More People Say Immigrants a Strength Than a Burden." *Pews Research Center*, March 4, 2019. https://www.pewresearch.org/global/wp-content/uploads/sites/2/2019/05/

Pew-Research-Center_Global-Views-of-Immigrants_2019-03-14_Updated-2019 -05-02.pdf.

Goodman, Adam. 2012. "Undocumented and Unafraid." *Salon*, March 29, 2012. https://www.salon.com/2012/03/29/immigration_activists_announce_theyre_undo cumented_and_unafraid.

Goodman, Amy. 2019. "Activists Face Jail Time for Providing Aid to Migrants Crossing Desert." *Truthout*, January 15, 2019. https://truthout.org/video/activists -face-jail-time-for-providing-aid-to-migrants-crossing-desert.

Goodman, Peter. 2018. "The Post World War II Order Is Under Assault From the Powers That Built It." *The New York Times*, March 26, 2018. https://www.nytimes. com/2018/03/26/business/nato-european-union.html.

Goodwin, Mathew and Oliver Heath 2016. "The 2016 Referendum, Brexit and the Left Behind: An Aggregate-level Analysis of the Result." *The Political Quarterly* 87(3): 323–332.

Gorondi, Pablo. 2017. "Hungary's Leader calls Migration 'Trojan Horse' of Terrorism." *Associated Press*, March 7, 2017. https://www.businessinsider.com/ ap-hungarys-leader-calls-migration-trojan-horse-of-terrorism-2017-3.

Goth, Brenna. 2017. "Years Later, Some Cities Ban Employees from Traveling to Arizona Over SB 1070." *The Republic*, May 30, 2017. https://www.azcentral.com /story/news/local/phoenix/2017/05/30/arizona-sb-1070-boycott-travel-ban-cities/3 12893001.

Gould, Roger V. 1991. "Collective Action and Network Structure." *American Sociological Review* 58: 182–196.

Graham, David. 2018. "Trump Says Democrats Want Immigrants to 'Infest' the U.S." *The Atlantic*, June 10, 2018. https://www.theatlantic.com/politics/archive/2018/06/ trump-immigrants-infest/563159.

Graham-McLay, Charlotte, Austin Ramzy and Daniel Victor. 2019. "Christchurch Mosque Shootings Were Partly Streamed on Facebook." *The New York Times*, March 14, 2019. https://www.nytimes.com/2019/03/14/world/asia/christchurch-s hooting-new-zealand.html.

Grant, Harriet and John Domokos. 2011. "Dublin Regulation Leaves Asylum Seekers with Their Fingers Burnt." *The Guardian*, October 7, 2011. https://www.theguard ian.com/world/2011/oct/07/dublin-regulation-european-asylum-seekers.

Gray, Rosie. 2017. "Trump Defends White-Nationalist Protesters: 'Some Very Fine People on Both Sides." *The Atlantic*, August 15, 2017. https://www.theatlan tic.com/politics/archive/2017/08/trump-defends-white-nationalist-protesters-some -very-fine-people-on-both-sides/537012.

Grayson, George. 2014. *The Cartels: The Story of Mexico's Most Dangerous Criminal Organizations and Their Impact on U.S. Security*. Santa Barbara, CA: Praeger.

Green, Nick and Pamela Johnson. 1998. "Students at Three High Schools Stage Prop. 227 Protests." *Los Angeles Times*, June 6, 1998. https://www.latimes.com/archives /la-xpm-1998-jun-06-me-57165-story.html.

Grietzer, Nicholas. 2010. "Arizona's New Law, SB1070, Prompts Protests." *Daily Bruin*, April 28, 2010. https://dailybruin.com/2010/04/28/arizonas-new-law-sb-1 070-prompts-protests.

Grossman, Matt and David Hopkins. 2016. *Asymmetric Politics: Ideological Republicans and Group Interest Democrats*. New York: Oxford University Press.

Grynbaum, Michael. 2018. "'Fake News' Goes Global as Trump, in Britain, Rips the Press." *The New York Times*, July 13, 2018. https://www.nytimes.com/2018/07/13/business/media/trump-cnn-london.html.

Grynbaum, Michael. 2019. "Jeanine Pirro's Show Is Bumped by Fix to the President's Chagrin." *The New York Times*, March 16, 2019. https://www.nytimes.com/2019/03/16/business/media/jeanine-pirro-fox-news-muslim.html.

Grynbaum, Michael and Eileen Sullivan. 2019. "Trump Attacks the Times, in a Week of Unease for the American Press." *The New York Times*, February 20, 2019. https://www.nytimes.com/2019/02/20/us/politics/new-york-times-trump.html.

Grynbaum, Michael and Katie Rogers. 2019. "White House Bars 4 U.S. Journalists from Trump's Dinner with Kim in Hanoi." *The New York Times*, February 27, 2019. https://www.nytimes.com/2019/02/27/business/media/reporters-banned-trump-hanoi.html.

Haag, Matthew and Jess Bidgood. 2018. "Governors Refuse to Send National Guard to Border, Citing Child Separation Practice." *The New York Times*, June 19, 2018. https://www.nytimes.com/2018/06/19/us/national-guard-trump-children-immigration.html.

Haas, Ernst. 2018. *Nationalism, Liberalism and Progress: The Rise and Fall of Nationalism*. Ithica: Cornell University Press.

Haas, Hein de, Mathes Czaika, Marie-Larence Flahaaus, Edo Mahendra, Katherina Natter, Simoona Vezzoli and Maria Viares-Varela. 2019, "International Migration: Trends, Deterrents and Policy Effects." *Population and Development Review* 45 (4): 885–922.

Haberman, Maggie and Katie Benner. 2019. "Trump Lashes Out at Fox News Poll as Barr Meets with Murdock." *New York Times*, October 11, 2019. https://www.nytimes.com/2019/10/10/us/politics/fox-news-poll-trump-impeachment.html.

Habermas, Jurgen. 2013. "Democracy, Solidarity, and European Crisis." In *Road Map to a Social Europe,* edited by Anne-Marie Grozeher, Bjorn Hacker, Wolfgang Kowalsky, Jan Machnig, Henning Meyer and Brigette Unger, 4–13. London: Social Europe.

Habermas, Jurgen. 2018. *The New Conservatism*. Cambridge: Polity Press.

Harding, Luke. 2015. "Angela Merkel: Plan to Share 160,000 Refugees Across EU May Not Be Enough." *The Guardian*, September 8, 2015. https://www.theguardian.com/world/2015/sep/08/angela-merkel-eu-refugee-sharing-plan-may-not-be-enough-germany-europe.

Harris, Gardiner and Azam Ahmed. 2018. "U.S., Supporting Mexico's Plan, Will Invest $5.8 Billion in Central America." *The New York Times*, December18, 2018. https://www.nytimes.com/2018/12/18/us/politics/united-states-mexico-central-america-investment.html.

Harvey, Neil. 1998. *The Chiapas Rebellion: The Struggle for Land and Democracy*. Durham: Duke University Press.

Hassana, Adeel. 2019. "Hate-Crime Violence Hits 16-Year High, F.B.I. Reports." *The New York Times,* November 12, 2019. https://www.nytimes.com/2019/11/12/us/hate-crimes-fbi-report.html.

Haverluck, Michael. 2019. "Anti-Semitism Hits Record High in Europe." *One News Now* February 8, 2019. https://onenewsnow.com/culture/2019/02/08/anti-semitism -hits-record-high-in-europe.

Heijmans, Philip. 2018. "Hungary Set to Criminalize Aiding Migrants with 'Stop Soros' Bill." *Aljazeera*, June 20, 2018. https://www.aljazeera.com/news/2018/06/h ungary-criminalises-aiding-migrants-stop-soros-bill-180620133647787.html.

Held, David. 1995. *Democracy and Global Order.* Cambridge: Polity Press.

Hendow, Maegan. 2017. "Tunisian Migrant Journeys: Human Right Concerns for Tunisians Arriving by Sea." *Migration and Human Rights* 2 (3): 187–209.

Herber, Joanna, Jon Mae and Jane Wills. 2008. "Multicultural Living?: Experiences of Everyday Racism Among Ghanaian Immigrants in London." *European Urban and Regional Studies* 15 (2): 103–117.

Hernandez, Kelly. 2006. "The Crimes and Consequences of Illegal Immigration: A Cross Border Examination of Operation Wetback 1943–1954." *Western Historical Quarterly* 37 (4): 421–443.

Hesson, Ted. 2013. "9 DREAMeR Actions That Advanced Immigration Reform." *ABC News*, August 10, 2013. https://abcnews.go.com/ABC_Univision/dreamer- protests-advanced-immigration-reform/story?id=19915997.

Higgins, Tucker. 2020. "The Supreme Court Rules Against Trump's Bid to End Program Shielding 'Dreamer' Immigrants." *MNBC*, June 18, 2020. https://ww w.cnbc.com/2020/06/18/supreme-court-rules-against-trump-in-bid-to-end-obama -era-immigration-program-shielding-dreamers.html.

Higham, John. 1999. "Instead of a Sequel, or How I Lost My Subject." In *The Handbook of International Migration: The American Experience*, edited by Charles Hirschman, Philip Kasinitz, and Josh DeWind, 383–389. New York: Russell Sage Foundation.

Hightower, Jim. 2018. "A Wall Won't Fix Immigration." *Buzzflash*, June 20, 2018. http://legacy.buzzflash.com/commentary/a-wall-won-t-fix-immigration.

Hing, Bill. 2102. "Beyond DACA- Deifying Employer Sanctions Through Civil Disobedience." *Law Review* 52(1): 301–341.

Hinkley, Story. 2016. "Cuban Migrants." *The Christian Science Monitor*, January 13. https://www.csmonitor.com/USA/Foreign-Policy/2017/0113/Why-Obama-shut- the-open-door-to-US-for-Cuban-migrants.

Hirschfeld Davis, Julie and Michael Shear. 2019. *Border Wars: Inside Trump's Assault On Immigration.* New York: Simon & Shuster.

Hobolt, Sarah and James Tilly. 2014. *Blaming Europe: Responsibility Without Accountability in the European Union.* Oxford: Oxford University Press.

Hochschild, Arlie. 2016. *Strangers in Their Own Land.* New York: New Press.

Hodges, Dan. 2018. "The Entire Nation is Hiding Behind Amber Rudd Over the Windrush Outrage." *Daily Mail*, April 28, 2018. https://www.dailymail.co.uk/ne ws/article-5670067/DAN-HODGES-entire-nation-hiding-Amber-Rudd-Windrush -outrage.html.

Hoffmann, Abraham. 1972. "Mexican Repatriation Statistics: Some Suggested Alternatives to Carey McWillimas." *Western Quarterly Review* 3 (4): 391–404.

Hoffman, John and Paul Graham. 2015. *Introduction to Political Theory.* New York: Routledge Press.

Holthouse, David. 2005. "Minutemen, Other Anti-Immigrant Groups Stake Out the Arizona Border." *Intelligence Report*, June 27, 2005. https://www.splcenter.org /fighting-hate/intelligence-report/2005/minutemen-other-anti-immigrant-militia-g roups-stake-out-arizona-border.

Hooper, John. 2013. "Pope Attacks 'Globalization of Indifference' in Lampedusa Visit." *The Guardian*, July 8, 2013. https://www.theguardian.com/world/2013/jul /08/pope-globalisation-of-indifference-lampedusa.

Horowitz, Jason. 2018a. "This Italian Town Once Welcomed Migrants. Now, It's a Symbol for Right- Wing Politics." *The New York Times*, July 7, 2018. https://www .nytimes.com/2018/07/07/world/europe/italy-macerata-migrants.html.

Horowitz, Jason. 2018b. "Italy Orders Seizure of Migrant Rescue Ship." *The New York Times*, November 20, 2018. https://www.nytimes.com/2018/11/20/world/ europe/italy-aquarius-seizure-order.html.

Horowitz, Jason and Elizabeth Povoledo. 2020. "Italy Election Deals Blow to Nationalist Leader Salvinin." *The New York Times*, January 26, 2020. https://www .nytimes.com/2020/01/26/world/europe/italy-election-Salvini.html.

Horowitz, Jason, Nick Corasaniti and Ashley Southall. 2015. "Nine Killed in Shooting at Black Church in Charleston." *The New York Times*, June 17, 2015. https:/ /www.nytimes.com/2015/06/18/us/church-attacked-in-charleston-south-carolina .html.

Horton, Alex. 2018. "Tucker Carlson's Suggestions That Immigrants Make the U.S. 'Dirtier' Costs Fox News an Advertiser." *The Washington Post*, December 15, 2018. https://www.washingtonpost.com/business/2018/12/15/tucker-carlson-sugg ested-immigrants-make-us-dirtier-it-cost-fox-news-an-advertiser.

Huber, Lindsay, Corin Lopez, Maria Malagon, Daniel Solorzano and Veronica Velez. 2008. "Getting Beyond the 'Symptom,' Acknowledging the 'Disease': Theories of Racist Nativism." *Contemporary Justice Review* 11 (1): 39–51.

Hughey, Mathew. 2016. "Hegemonic Whiteness: From Structure and Agency to Identity Allegiance." In *The Construction of Whiteness: An Interdisciplinary Analysis of Race Formation and the Meaning of White Identity*, edited by Stephen Middleton, David Roediger and Donald Shaffer, 212–233. University Press of Mississippi.

Human Rights Watch. 2013. "Turning Migrants into Criminals: The Harmful Impact of U.S. Border Prosecutions." *Human Rights Watch*, May 22, 2013. https://www .hrw.org/report/2013/05/22/turning-migrants-criminals/harmful-impact-us-border- prosecutions.

Human Rights Watch. 2019. "Greece Camp Conditions Endanger Women and Girls' Rights." *Human Rights Watch*, December 4, 2019. https://www.hrw.org/news/ 2019/12/04/greece-camp-conditions-endanger-women-girls#.

Human Rights Watch. 2020. "Greece: Island Camps Not Prepared for Covid- 19." https://www.hrw.org/news/2020/04/22/greece-island-camps-not-prepared-c ovid-19#.

Huntington, Samuel. 2009. "The Hispanic Challenge." *Foreign Policy*, October 2009. https://foreignpolicy.com/2009/10/28/the-hispanic-challenge.

Hussain, Murtaza. 20018. "Muslims Accused of Plotting Violence Get Seven Times More Media Attention and Four Times Longer Sentences." *The Intercept*, April

4, 2018. https://theintercept.com/2018/04/05/muslims-violence-media-attention-p rosecution/.

Hutter, Swen. 2014. *Protesting Culture and Economics in Western Europe: New Cleavages in Left and Right Politics.* Minneapolis: University of Minneapolis Press.

Hutton, Will. 2015. "Angela Merkel's Human Stance on Immigration is a Lesson to Us All." *The Guardian*, August 29, 2015. https://www.theguardian.com/comment isfree/2015/aug/30/immigration-asylumseekers-refugees-migrants-angela-merkel.

Iati, Marisa. 2020. "Jewish Solidarity March in New York Draws Thousands in Wake of Anti-Semitic Attack." *The Washington Post*, June 5, 2020. https://www.was hingtonpost.com/religion/2020/01/05/jewish-solidarity-march-new-york-draws-thousands-wake-anti-semitic-attacks.

Immerewahr, Daniel. 2019. *How to Hide an Empire: A History of the Greater United States.* New York: Farrar, Straus and Giroux.

Inghilleri, Moira. 2012. *Interpreting Justice: Ethics, Politics and Language.* New York: Routledge.

Jackson, David. 2017. "Former Intel Chief James Clapper on Trump Speech: 'I Just Find This Extremely Disturbing.'" *The Washington Times*, August 23, 2017. https://www.elpasotimes.com/story/news/politics/2017/08/23/former-intel-chief-jamescl apper-trump-speech-i-just-find-extremely-disturbing/592817001.

Jackson, Fraser. 2019. "Italy's 'Sardines' to Bring Protest Movement Against Far Right to Rome." *France 24*, December 12. https://www.france24.com/en/2019121 4-italy-s-sardines-bring-protest-movement-far-right-rome-matteo-salvini-dem onstrations.

Jamieson, Amber. 2017. "Your Are Fake News: Trump Attacks CNN and Buzzfeed Reporters At News Conference." *The Guardian*, January 11, 2017. https://www.the guardian.com/us-news/2017/jan/11/trump-attacks-cnn-buzzfeed-at-press-conference.

Jardina, Ashley. 2019. *White Identity Politics.* New York: Cambridge University Press.

Jarret, Charles. 1999. "The Importance of Racial-Ethnic Identity and Social Setting for Blacks, Whites and Multiracials." *Sociological Perspectives* 42 (4): 711–737.

Jenkins, Henry. 2006. *Convergence Culture.* New York: New York University Press.

Johnson, Jake. 2018a. "'This is What Solidarity Looks Like': Mass Demonstrations at LaGuardia Airport as Kids Ripped from Parents Arrive in New York." *Portside*, June 21, 2018. https://portside.org/2018-06-21/what-solidarity-looks-mass-demons trations-laguardia-airport-kids-ripped-parents-arrive.

Johnson, Jake. 2018b. "In Affront to Those Fleeing US-Backed Wars, Trump Slams Door on Refugees." *Truthout.* September 18, 2018. https://truthout.org/articles/in -affront-to-those-fleeing-us-backed-wars-trump-slams-door-on-refugees.

Jordan, Miriam. 2019. "Trump Administration to Nearly Double Size of Detention Center for Migrant Teenager." *The New York Times*, January 15, 2019. https://www.nytimes.com/2019/01/15/us/migrant-children-shelter-tent-city-tornillo-hom estead.html.

Jordan, Miriam. 2020. "A Mexican Exodus Is Helping Shrink the Undocumented Population." *The New York Times*, February 26, 2020. https://www.nytimes.com/2 020/02/26/us/undocumented-population-study-mexicans.html.

Jordan, Miriam and Caitlin Dickerson. 2019. "As Trump Threatens Deportations, Immigrant Communities Brace for New Arrests." *The New York Times*, June 18, 2019. https://www.nytimes.com/2019/06/18/us/immigration-raids-fear-families. html.

Joseph, Yonette. 2018. "'Punish a Muslim Day' Rattles UK Communities." *The New York Times*, March 11, 2018. https://www.nytimes.com/2018/03/11/world/europe/ uk-muslims-letters.html.

Judis, John. 2018. *The Nationalist Revival: Trade, Immigration and the Revolt Against Globalization*. New York: Columbia Global Reports.

Jurris, Jeffrey. 2014. "Embodying Protest Cuture and Performance within Social Movements." In *Conceptualizing Culture in Social Movement Research*, edited by Britta Baumgarten, Priska Daphi and Peter Ulrich, 227–246. New York: NY Palgrave Macmillan.

Kagan, Robert. 2018. *The Jungle Grows Back: The Case for American Power*. New York: Alfred A. Knopf.

Kahn, Ricard and Douglas Kellner. 2003. "Internet Subcultures and Oppositional Politics." In *The Post-Subcultures Reader*, edited by D. Muggleton. London: Berg.

Kanno-Youngs, Zolan. 2020. "Trump Administration Adds Six Countries to Travel Ban." *The New York Times*, January 21, 2020. https://www.nytimes.com/2020/0 2/04/learning/lesson-of-the-day-trump-administration-adds-six-countries-to-trave l-ban.html.

Kanno-Youngs, Zolan and Caitlin Dickerson 2019. "The Trump Administration Expands Fast-Tracked Deportations for Undocumented Immigrants." *The New York Times*, July 22, 2019. https://www.nytimes.com/2019/07/22/us/politics/trump -immigration-deportations.html.

Kanno-Youngs, Zolan and Maya Averbunch. 2019. "Waiting for Asylum in the United States, Immigrants Live in Fear in Mexico." *The New York Times*, April 5, 2019. https://www.nytimes.com/2019/04/05/us/politics/asylum-united-states-mi grants-mexico.html.

Kanter, James. 2015. "The EU Asks Member Countries to Accept Quotas of Migrants." *The New York Times*, July 22, 2015. https://www.nytimes.com/2015 /05/28/world/europe/european-union-asks-member-countries-to-accept-quotas-of- migrants.html.

Kaplan, Ivy. 2018. "UN Records Over 3,000 Deaths from Migration in 2018." *The Global Post*, November 2, 2018. https://theglobepost.com/2018/11/02/un-migran ts-deaths.

Karlin, Mark. 2018. "The Nightmare of Neoliberal Fascism." *Truthout*, June10, 2018. https://truthout.org/articles/henry-a-giroux-the-nightmare-of-neoliberal-fascism.

Kauffman, L. A. 2017. "The Trump Resistance can be Best Described in One Adjective: Female." *The Guardian*, July 23, 2014. https://www.theguardian.c om/commentisfree/2017/jul/23/trump-resistance-one-adjective-female-womens-m arch.

Kerwin, Donald. 2018. "The US Refugee Resettlement Program- A Return to First Principles: How Refugees Help to Define, Strengthen, and Revitalize the United States." *CMS Report*, June, 2018. *Journal of Migration and Human Society*. https://

www.researchgate.net/publication/325929380_The_US_Refugee_Resettlement_P rogramA_Return_to_First_Principles_How_Refugees_Help_to_Define_Strengthe n_and_Revitalize_the_United_States.

Kim, Hackwon and Ronald Sundstrom. 2014. "Xenophobia and Racism." *Critical Philosophy of Race* 2 (1): 20–45.

Kimiko, de Freytas-Tamura. 2018. "British Citizen One Day, Illegal Immigrant the Next." *The New York Times*, April 24, 2018. https://www.nytimes.com/2018/04 /24/world/europe/britain-windrush-immigrants.html.

Kingsbury, Alex. 2019. "Rethinking Terrorism: The Department of Homeland Security is Broadening its Focus to Include Battling White Supremist Attacks." *The New York Times.* September 23, 2019. https://www.nytimes.com/2019/09/23/opini on/dhs-domestic-terrorism.html.

Kingsley, Patrick. 2018. "To Protect Migrants from Police, a Dutch Church Service Never Ends." *The New York Times*, December 10, 2018. https://www.nytimes.com /2019/01/30/world/europe/netherlands-church-vigil-refugees.html.

Kingsley, Patrick and Steven Erlanger. 2018. "Hungary's Democracy is in Danger, E.U. Parliament Decides." *The New York Times*, September 12, 2018. https ://www.nytimes.com/2018/09/12/world/europe/hungary-eu-viktor-orban .html.

Kirk, Ashley. 2018. "Hate Crimes Linked to Religion Doubled in Three Years." *The Telegraph*, October 16, 2018. https://www.telegraph.co.uk/news/2018/10/16/hate -crime-linked-religion-doubled-three-years.

Kirkpatrick, David. 2019. "Massacre Suspect Traveled the World but Lived on the Internet." *The New York Times*, March 15, 2019. https://www.nytimes.com/2019/0 3/15/world/asia/new-zealand-shooting-brenton-tarrant.html.

Kitsantonis, Niki. 2020. "Greece's Answer to Migrants, a Floating Barrie, Is Called a 'Disgrace.'" *The New York Times*, February 1, 2020. https://www.nytimes.com/2 020/02/01/world/europe/greece-migrants-floating-barrier.html.

Kitschelt, Henry. 1986. "Political Opportunity Structures and Political Protest: Movements in Four Democracies." *British Journal of Political Science* 16 (1): 57–85.

Kitschelt, Henry. 1995. *The Radical Right in Western Europe: A Comparative Analysis*. Ann Arbor: University of Michigan Press.

Kitroff, Natalie and Geoffrey Mohan. "Wage Rises on California Farms. Americans Still Don't Want the Job." *Los Angeles Times*, March 12, 2017. https://www.lat imes.com/projects/la-fi-farms-immigration.

Kneebone, Susan. 2009. *Refugees, Asylum Seekers and the Rule of Law: Comparative Perspectives*. Cambridge University Press.

Koblin, John. 2019. "Tensions Flare Between Trump and Fox News." *The New York Times*, August 30, 2019. https://www.nytimes.com/2019/08/30/business/media/ trump-fox-news.html.

Koopmans, Ruud and Susan Olzak. 2004. "Discursive Opportunities and the Evolution of Right-Wing Violence in Germany." *American Journal of Sociology* 110 (1): 198–230.

Krajewski, Adrien. 2015. "Poland Says Cannot Take Migrants Under EU Quotas Without Guarantees After Paris Attacks." *Reuters*, November 14, 2015. https://mo bile.reuters.com/article/amp/idUSL8N1390NI20151114.

Kudnani, Hanas. 2019. "We Need to Talk About Germany." *Foreign Affairs,* September/October, 2019. https://www.foreignaffairs.com/articles/germany/2019 -08-15/we-need-talk-about-germany.

Kugle, Andrew. 2018. "Trump: We Can't 'Allow These People to Invade Our Country.'" *Free Beacon*, June 24, 2018. https://freebeacon.com/issues/trump-cant -let-illegal-immigrants-invade-country.

Kundnan. Hans. 2019. "Liberalism's Betrayal of Itself-and the Way Back." *The Economist*, February 14, 2019. https://www.economist.com/open-future/2019/02 /14/liberalisms-betrayal-of-itself-and-the-way-back.

Kurry, Helmut and Slawomir Redo. 2018. *Refugees and Migrants in Law and Policy*. Spring International Publishing. https://www.springer.com/gp/book/97833 19721583.

Lacapria, Kim. 2017. "President Trump and 'What's Happening in Sweden Last Night.'" *Snopes*, February 17. https://www.snopes.com/news/2017/02/20/president -trump-sweden-incident/.

Laden, Anthony and David Owen. 2007. *Multiculturalism and Political Theory*. New York: Cambridge University Press.

Lane, Oliver. 2016. "Hungarian Leader Orban Blames EU for Migrant Crisis, Foresees the 'Destruction of Europe.'" *Breitbart*, March 16, 2016. https://www .breitbart.com/europe/2016/03/16/hungarian-leader-orban-blames-eu-for-migrant -crisis-foresees-the-destruction-of-europe.

Lang, Marissa. 2019. "Dozens Arrested in D.C. in Catholic-led Protest Over Trump's Immigration Policies." *The Washington Post*, July 10, 2019. https://www.hou stonchronicle.com/news/article/Dozens-arrested-in-D-C-in-Catholic-led-protest -14105886.php.

Langsdon, Ian. 2018. "Trump Says Crime in Germany is Way Up. Statistics Show Otherwise." *The Washington Post*, June 18, 2018. https://www.washingtonpost.com.

Larger, Thibault. 2018. "Matteo Salvini: Italian Ports Closed to Migrants." *Politico*, December 23, 2018. https://www.politico.eu/article/matteo-salvini-italian-ports -closed-to-migrant.

Leconte, Cecile. 2010. *Understanding Euroscepticism*. London: Red Globe Press.

Lee, Edmund. 2019. "Trump Sings Praises of Hannity and Limbaugh in Rose Garden." *The New York Times*, February 15, 2019. https://www.nytimes.com/2019 /02/15/business/media/trump-hannity-limbaugh-coulter.html.

Leonhardt, David. 2019. "It Isn't Complicated: Trump Encourages Violence." *The New York Times*, March 17, 2019. https://www.nytimes.com/2019/03/17/opinion /trump-violence.html.

Leutert, Stephanie and Caitlyn Yates. 2018. "A 'Safe Third Country' Agreement with Mexico Won't Fix U.S. Migratory Challenges." *Lawfare*, August 30, 2018. https ://www.lawfareblog.com/safe-third-country-agreement-mexico-wont-fix-us-migr atory-challenges.

Leruth, Benjamine and Simon Usherwood. 2018. *The Routledge Handbook of Euroscepticism*. New York: Rutledge Press.

Levitsky, Steven and Daniel Ziblatt. 2019. "Why Autocrats Love Emergencies." *The New York Times*, January 12, 2019. https://www.nytimes.com/2019/01/12/opinion /sunday/trump-national-emergency-wall.html.

Li, David. 2018. "Trump: Immigration Has 'Changed the Fabric' of Europe." *New York Post*, July 12, 2018. https://nypost.com/2018/07/12/trump-immigration-has-changed-the-fabric-of-europe/.

Lind, 2020. *The New Class War: Saving Democracy from the Managerial Elite*. New York: Penguin Random House.

Lippard, Cameron. 2011. "Racist Nativism in the 21st Century." *Sociology Compass* 5 (7): 591–601.

Long-Garcia, J.D. 2020. "One Year Later, How Has Trump's 'Remain in Mexico' Policy Affected Asylum Seekers?" *American Magazine*, January 30, 2020. https://www.americamagazine.org/politics-society/2020/01/30/one-year-later-how-has-trumps-remain-mexico-policy-affected-asylum.

Lopez, Ian Haney. 2014. *Dog Whistle Politics: How Coded Racial Appeals Have Reinvented Racism and Wrecked Middle Class*. New York: Oxford University Press.

Lopez, Robert. 1994. "L.A. March Against Prop. 187 Draws 70,000: Immigration: Protestors Condemn Wilson for Backing Initiative that they Say Promotes 'Racism, Scapegoating." *Times*, October 17, 1994. https://www.latimes.com/archives/la-xpm-1994-10-17-mn-51339-story.html.

Loucaides, Darren. 2018. "Will Bannonism Play in Spain?" *The World*, July 2, 2018. https://slate.com/news-and-politics/2018/07/vox-party-in-spain-could-bring-right-wing-populist-wave-with-help-from-steve-bannon.html.

Lubbers, Marcel and Peer Scheepers. 2010. "Divergent Trends of Euroscepticism in Countries and Regions in the European Union." *European Journal of Political Research* 49 (6): 787–817.

Lyster, Lauren. 2019. "'You Do Not Have an Open Door;' Governor Newsom Reassures Immigrants of Rights Ahead of Expected ICE Raids." *KTLA News*, June 12, 2019. https://ktla.com/news/local-news/socal-authorities-leaders-in-other-cities-respond-to-ice-raids-expected-on-Sunday.

Macchi, Victoria. 2019. "2019 Among Deadliest Years for Migrants Trekking to US." *VOA News*, September 4, 2019. https://www.voanews.com/usa/2019-among-deadliest-years-migrants-trekking-us.

MacFarquar, Neil and Adam Goldman. 2020. "A New Face of White Supremacy: Plots Expose Danger of the 'Base.'" *The New York Times* January 22, 2020. https://www.nytimes.com/2020/01/22/us/white-supremacy-the-base.html.

Magdy, Samy. 2018. "Rescue Group: Libya Left Migrants to Die in Mediterranean." *America Magazine*, July 17, 2018. https://www.americamagazine.org/politics-society/2018/07/17/rescue-group-libya-left-migrants-die-mediterranean.

Malone, Tim. 2018. "The Proper Response to Trump's UN Speech Isn't Laughter, It's Terror." *Truthout*, September 29, 2018. https://truthout.org/articles/the-proper-response-to-trumps-un-speech-isnt-laughter-its-terror.

Malsin, Jared. 2016. "Turkey's President Is Using the Coup Attempt to Crack Down on the Media." *Time*, July 29, 2016. https://time.com/4429177/turkeys-president-is-using-the-coup-attempt-to-crack-down-on-the-media.

Mansoor, Ali and Bryce Quillin. 2006. "Migration and Remittances: Easter Europe and the Former Soviet Union." *World Bank elibrary*. https://elibrary.worldbank.org/page/copyright.

Marchetti, Silva. 2017. "Italy is Pleading with Europe to Help Deal with a Record Influx of Refugees." *Time*, July 11. https://time.com/4850999/italy-europe-refugees-frontex-boats-rome-ports-ngos/.

Marin, Roxana. 2015. "The Satanic Verses, Multiculturalism, and the Multiplicity of Perspectives in British Literature at the End of the 1980s." In *11th Conference on British and American Studies: Embracing Multitudes of Meaning*, edited by Marinela Burada, Oana Tatu and Raluca Sinu. Cambridge: Cambridge Scholars Publishing. https://trove.nla.gov.au/work/192664509.

Mark, Michelle. 2018. "John Kelly: It's Not 'Cruel' to Separate Families at the Border- Children will be 'Put in Foster Care or Whatever.'" *Business Insider*, May 11, 2018. https://www.businessinsider.com/john-kelly-family-separation-policy-illegal-border-crossing-2018-5.

Marosi, Richard. 2010. "Mexico Arrests Shed Light on Migrant-Kidnapping Outfits." *Los Angeles Times*, July 28, A33.

Martinez, Nuria Marquez. 2019. "'Document, Reassure, Keep Calm': A Behind the Scenes Look at Training Citizens to Respond to ICE." *Mother Jones*, June 28, 2019. https://www.motherjones.com/politics/2019/06/rapid-response-network-santa-clara-training-ice-immigration/.

Massey, Douglas. 1999. "International Migration at the Dawn of the 21st Century: The Role of The State." *Population and Development Review* 25: 303–322.

Massey, Douglas, Joaquin Arango, Graeme Hugo, Ali Kouaouci, Adela Pellrinot and Edward Taylor. 1998. *Worlds in Motion: International Migration at the End of the Millennium*. London: Oxford University Press.

Matousekk, Mark. 2018. "Homeland Security Press Secretary Fired Back at United and American Airlines After They Told the US Government Not to Fly Children Separated from Their Parents on Their Planes." *Finance*, June 20, 2018. https://finance.yahoo.com/news/homeland-security-press-secretary-fired-200200934.html.

May, Patrick. 2019. "Gilroy Garlic Festival Shooting Victims Aged 1, 13 and 25." *Santa Cruz Sentinel*, July 30, 2019. https://www.santacruzsentinel.com/2019/07/29/local-emergency-proclamation-after-3-killed-and-12-wounded-at-gilroy-garlic-festival.

McAdam, Doug. 1982. *Political Process and the Development of Black Insurgency 1930–1970*. Chicago, IL: University of Chicago Press.

McAdam, Doug. 2018. "Putting Donald Trump in Historical Perspective: Racial Politics and Social Movements from the 1960's to Today." *The Resistance: The Dawn of the Anti-Trump Opposition Movement*, 27–53.

McArdle, Mairead. 2018. "Sessions: 'We Never Really Intended to Separate Children.'" *National Review*, June 21, 2018. https://www.nationalreview.com/news/jeff-sessions-separating-children-immigration.

McElwen, Sean. 2018. "The Power of 'Abolish ICE.'" *The New York Times*, August 4, 2018. https://www.nytimes.com/2018/08/04/opinion/sunday/abolish-ice-ocasio-cortez-democrats.html.

McFarlan Miller, Emily. 2018. "Researchers Find Link Between Trump Tweets and Spike in Anti-Muslim Hate." *America Magazine*, July 18, 2018. https://www.ame

ricamagazine.org/politics-society/2018/07/18/researchers-find-link-between-trump-tweets-and-spike-anti-muslim-hate.

McGloghin, Eliott. 2019. "Marines Charged with Smuggling Immigrants into the United States." *CNN,* July 9, 2019. https://www.cnn.com/2019/07/09/us/marines-immigrants-smuggling-charges/index.html.

McHugh, David and Frank Jordans. 2020. "Grief, Anger and Calls for Action After Shooting in Germany." *AP Press*, February 21. https://www.wivb.com/news/germany-to-raise-police-presence-after-racist-shooting.

McKane, Rachel and Holly McCammon. 2018. "Why We March: The Role of Grievances, Threats and Movement Organizational Resources in the 2017 Women's Marches." *Mobilization: An International Quarterly* 23 (4): 401–424.

McVeigh, Rory. 2009. *The Rise of the Ku Klux Klan: Right-Wing Movements and National Politics.* Minneapolis: University of Minneapolis Press.

Media Matters. 2018. "Fox's Pete Hegseth: Caravan 'Looks a Lot More like an Invasion than Anything Else.'" *Media Matters for America*, November 2, 2018. https://www.mediamatters.org/fox-friends/foxs-pete-hegseth-caravan-looks-lot-more-invasion-anything-else.

Media Matters. 2019. "Kilmeade: Americans Don't Have 'Pure Genes' like Swedes because 'We Keep Marrying Other Species and Other Ethnics.'" *Media Matters for America*, July 8, 2019. https://www.mediamatters.org/video/2009/07/08/kilmeade-americans-dont-have-pure-genes-like-sw/151856.

Melucci, Alberto. 1996. *Challenging Codes of Collective Action in the Information Age.* Cambridge, MA: Cambridge University Press.

Menijvar, Cecilia. 2014. "Immigration Law Beyond Borders: Eternalizing and Internalizing Border Controls in an Era of Securitization." *Annual Review of Law and Society*10 (1): 353–369.

Menjivar, Cecilia and Andrea Gomez Cervantes. 2018. "El Salvador: Civil War, Natural Disasters, and Gang Violence Drive Migration." *Migration Information Source,* August 29, 2018. https://www.migrationpolicy.org/article/el-salvador-civil-war-natural-disasters-and-gang-violence-drive-migration.

Mersky, Marcie. 2005. "Human Right in Negotiating Peace Agreements in Guatemala." *TheInternational Council on Human Rights Policy,* March 7–8, 2015. http://www.ichrp.org/files/papers/58/128_-_Guatemala_-_Human_Rights_in_Negotiating_Peace_Agreements_Mersky_Marcie__26_May_2005.pdf.

Mervosh, Sarah. 2018. "Facing Attacks, George Soros's Foundation Will Shut Down in Turkey." *The New York Times*, November 26, 2018. https://www.nytimes.com/2018/11/26/world/europe/george-soros-open-society-turkey-closes.html.

Mervosh, Sarah. 2019. "Immigration Authorities Arrest More Than 280 in Texas in Largest Workplace Raid in Decade." *The New York Times*, April 4, 2019. https://www.nytimes.com/2019/04/04/us/texas-immigration-raid.html.

Meyer, Nhat. 2019. "Gilroy Garlic Festival Shooting Victims Aged 6, 13 and 25." *Bay Area News Group*, July 27, 2019. https://www.santacruzsentinel.com/2019/07/29/local-emergency-proclamation-after-3-killed-and-12-wounded-at-gilroy-garlic-festival.

Michael, Maggie, Lori Hinnant and Renato Brito. 2019. "Making Misery Pay: Libya Militias Take EU Funds from Migrants." *AP Press*, December 30, 2019. https://ap news.com/9d9e8d668ae4b73a336a636a86bdf27f.

Midgley, James. 2017. "Investing in Communities in the United States, Social Capital, Asset Building and Local Enterprise." In *Social Investment and Social Welfare*, edited by James Midgley, Espen Dahlt and Conley Wright. *Elra Online*. https://www.elgaronline.com/view/edcoll/9781785367823/9781785367823.00013 .xml.

Miles, Robert. 1989. "Nationality, Citizenship, and Migration to Britain, 1945-1951." *Journal of Law and Society* 16 (4): 426–442.

Minder, Raphael. 2019. "Spain's Far Right Vox Party See Breakout Moment in New Election." *The New York Times*, February 16, 2019. https://www.nytimes.com/2 019/02/16/world/europe/spain-elections-vox-far-right.htm.l.

Minkin, Steve. 2018. "A Climate of Violence: Refugees and Global Warming." *Common Dreams,* December 5, 2018. https://commons.commondreams.org/t/a-cli mate-of-violence-refugees-and-global-warming/58176.

Miroff, Nick. 2018. "Government: 463 Migrant Parents May Have Been Deported Without Their Children." *The Washington Post*, July 23, 2018. https://www.wash-ingtonpost.com.

Misra, Neil. 2015. "The Relevance of NATO in the Modern World." *The Journal of International Relations*, December 5, 2015. http://www.sirjournal.org/research/ 2015/12/4/the-relevance-of-nato-in-the-modern-world.

Mohammad, Arshad and David Alexander. 2019. "Obama Says Coup in Honduras is Illegal." *Reuters*, June 29, 2019. https://www.reuters.com/article/us-honduras-usa -sb/obama-says-coup-in-honduras-is-illegal-idUKTRE55S5J220090629.

Momigliano, Anna. 2018. "It's Been 25 Years Since Anyone in Italy Trusted the Government." *Foreign Affairs*, September 12, 2018. https://foreignpolicy.com /2018/09/12/its-been-25-years-since-anyone-in-italy-trusted-the-government.

Morin, Chloe. 2018. "Macron's Immigration Policy Offends Pretty Much Everybody." *Bloomberg*, March 13, 2018. https://www.bloomberg.com/opinion/articles/2018 -03-14/emmanuel-macron-s-immigration-policy-offends-all-parties.

Moynihan, Patrick. 2019. "Two Proud Boys Sent to Two Years in Brawl with Anti-FascistsAt Republican Club." *The New York Times*, October 22, 2019. https://ww w.nytimes.com/2019/10/22/nyregion/proud-boys-antifa-sentence.html.

Mutz, Diana. 2018. "Status Threat, Not Economic Hardship, Explains the 2016 Presidential Vote." *PNAS* 115 (9): E4330–E4339.

Nagle, Angela. 2017. "The Lost Boys." *The Atlantic*, December 2018. https://www .theatlantic.com/magazine/archive/2017/12/brotherhood-of-losers/544158.

Nasa, Rahima. 2018. "In New York, Intolerance Has Become Routine." *AlterNet*, July 18, 2018. https://www.alternet.org/2018/07/new-york-intolerance-has-be come-routine.

Navarette, Ruben. 2019. "After El Paso Shooting, Mexican Americans Can No Longer Be Ambivalent Minority." *USA Today,* August 16, 2019. https://www.usa today.com/story/opinion/2019/08/16/mexican-americans-immigration-el-paso-sh ooting-minority-racism-column/2010038001.

Nellas, Detris and Costas Kantouris. 2019. "Migrants in Greece Set Fires at Camp; at Least 1Killed." *AP News,* September 29, 2019. https://apnews.com/92a15950e8f 948ef99ebdbcb5df2f966.

Nelson, Soraya. 2018. "Hungary Reduces Number of Asylum-Seekers It Will Amit to 2Per day." *NPR,* February, 2018. https://www.npr.org/sections/parallels/2018 /02/03/582800740/hungary-reduces-number-of-asylum-seekers-it-will-admit-to-2-per-day.

Nevins, Joseph. 2019. *Operation Gatekeeper and Beyond: The War on Illegals and the Making of the U.S.-Mexico Border.* New York: Routledge Press.

Ngai, May. 2004. *Impossible Subjects: Illegal Aliens and the Making of Modern America.* Princeton, NJ: Princeton University Press.

Nixon, Ron. 2018a. "Migrant Detention Centers Are 'Like a Summer Camp,' Official Says at Hearing." *The New York Times,* July 31, 2018. https://www.nytimes.com/2 018/07/31/us/politics/migrant-detention-centers-trump-senate.html.

Nixon, Ron. 2018b. "Asylum Claims Jump Despite Trump's Attempt to Limit Immigration." *The New York Times,* December 10, 2018. https://www.nytimes. com/2018/12/10/us/politics/trump-asylum-border-.html.

Nossiter, Adam. 2019. "Thousands Rally Against Anti-Semitism in France." *The New York Times,* February 19, 2019. https://www.nytimes.com/2019/02/19/world/euro pe/france-antisemitism-rallies-cemetery.html.

O'Brien, Luke. 2017. "The Making of an American Nazi." *The Atlantic,* December, 2017. https://www.theatlantic.com/magazine/archive/2017/12/the-making-of-an-american-/544119/.

O'Keefe, Ed. and Anne Gearan. 2018. "Trump Condemned for 'shithole' Countries Remark, Denies Comment but Acknowledges 'Tough' Language." *The Washington Post,* January 13, 2018. https://www.washingtonpost.com/politics/trump-ackn owledges-tough-language-but-appears-to-deny-shithole-remark/2018/01/12/c713 1dae-f796-11e7-beb6-c8d48830c54d_story.html.

Olmstead, Molly. 2018. "Trump Explains That 'You Have to Take Children Away' in Unhinged Speech to Small-Business Owners." *The Slate* June 1, 2018. https://sl ate.com/author/molly-olmstead/29.

Onishi, Norimitsu. 2019. "Franc Announces Tough New Measure on Immigration." *The New York Times,* November 6, 2019. https://www.nytimes.com/2019/11/06/ world/europe/france-macron-immigration.html.

O'Toole, Molly. 2016. "Is NATO Still Relevant? Trump's Not the Only One Asking." *Foreign Policy,* April 1, 2016. https://foreignpolicy.com/2016/04/01/is-nato-still-relevant-trumps-not-the-only-one-asking.

Pannetta, Grace. 2019. "Conservative Media Described Immigration as 'Invasion' Hundreds of Times Before the El Paso Shooter Echoed the Same Language." *Business Insider,* August 12, 2019. https://www.businessinsider.in/conservative-m edia-described-immigration-as-an-invasion-hundreds-of-times-before-the-el-paso -shooter-echoed-the-same-language/articleshow/70647057.cms.

Paoli, Giacoma. 2016. "Why Now is the Time for a Unified Response to Europe's Immigration Crisis." *RAND Corporation,* February 27. https://www.rand.org/blog /2016/02/why-now-is-the-time-for-a-unified-response-to-europes.html.

Paret, Marcel and Guadalupe Aguilar. 2016. "Golden State Uprisings: Migration Protests in California, 1990–2010." *Citizenship Studies* 20 (3–4): 359–378.

Paris, Erna. 2018. "Victor Orban's War on George Soros and Hungary's Jews." *The Globe and Mail*, June 1, 2018. https://www.theglobeandmail.com/opinion/article -viktor-orbans-war-on-george-soros-and-hungarys-jews.

Parker, Christopher and Matt Barreto. 2013. *Change They Can't Believe in: The Tea Party and Reactionary Politics in America.* Princeton, NJ: Princeton University Press.

Passel, Jeffrey, D'Vera Cohn and Anna Gonzalez-Barrera. 2012. "Migration Between the U.S. and Mexico." *Hispanic Trends,* April 23, 2012. https://www.pewresearch.o rg/hispanic/2012/04/23/net-migration-from-mexico-falls-to-zero-and-perhaps-less.

Payani, Panikoszo. 2020. *Migrant History: A New History of London.* Great Britain: Gomer Press Ltd.

Payne, Abigail. 2012. "Changing Landscapes for Charities in Canada: Where Should We Go?" *School of Public Policy Publications* Volume 5. University of Calgary. https://journalhosting.ucalgary.ca/index.php/sppp/article/view/42405.

Perenyi, Zsigmond. 2018. "In Defense of Orban." *Atlantic Council*, May 31, 2018. https://www.atlanticcouncil.org/blogs/new-atlanticist/in-defense-of-orban.

PEW Research Center. 2012. "Global Attitudes and Trends." April 20, 2012. https://www.pewresearch.org/global/2012/04/20/spring-2012-survey-data.

PEW Research Center. 2017. "Rise in U.S. Immigrants from El Salvador, Guatemala and Honduras Outpaces Growth from Elsewhere." December 7, 2017. https://www.pewresearch.org/hispanic/2017/12/07/rise-in-u-s-immigrants-from-el-salvador-gu atemala-and-honduras-outpaces-growth-from-elsewhere.

Pew Research Center. 2017. "U.S. Muslims Concerned About their Place in Society But Continue to Believe in the American Dream." June 26, 2017. https://www.pewforum.org/2017/07/26/findings-from-pew-research-centers-2017-survey-of-us -muslims/.

PEW Research Center. 2018. "U.S. Unauthorized Immigrants Total Dips to Lowest Level in a Decade." November 27, 2018. https://www.pewresearch.org/hispani c/2018/11/27/u-s-unauthorized-immigrant-total-dips-to-lowest-level-in-a-decade.

Pianigiani, Gaia. 2018. "Malta Cracks Down on a Humanitarian Ship That Carried Migrants." *The New York Times*, July 2, 2018. https://www.nytimes.com/2018/07 /02/world/europe/malta-migrant-ships-crackdown.html.

Pianigiani, Gaia. 2019. "Pope Francis Appeals to Europe to Show 'Solidarity' with Migrants." *The New York Times*, January 7, 2019. https://www.nytimes.com/2019 /01/07/world/europe/francis-nationalism-immigration.html.

Pitosfsky, Marina and Merdie Nzanga. 2018. "People will March in All 50 States to Protest Trump's 'Zero Tolerance' Immigration Policy." *USA Today*, June 20, 2018. https://www.wkyc.com/article/news/nation-now/hundreds-of-thousands-exp ected-at-immigration-rallies-against-trump-activists-say/465-ef61ae72-30ce-48fd-ab04-74564bd8cf49.

Pitt, William Rivers. 2019. "White Supremacists are Infiltrating the GOP from the Ground Up." *Truthout*, March 9, 2019. https://truthout.org/articles/white-supr emacists-are-infiltrating-the-gop-from-the-ground-up.

Politi, Danie. 2017. "Did Fox News Lead Trump to Believe There was a Terror Attack on Sweden?" *Slate*, February 18, 2017. https://slate.com/news-and-pol itics/2017/02/did-fox-news-segment-lead-trump-to-believe-there-was-a-terror-atta ck-in-sweden.html.

Polletta, Francesca. 2008. "Culture and Movements." *The Annals of the American Academy of Political and Social Science* 6 (1): 78–96.

Polletta, Francesca and James Jasper. 2001. "Collective Identity and Social Movements." *Annual Review of Sociology* 27: 283–305.

Ponnuro, Ramesh. 2016. "Roger Cardinal Mahoney." *National Review*, March 22, 2016. https://www.nationalreview.com/corner/roger-cardinal-mahony-ramesh-pon nuru.

Pop, Vaentina and Giovanni Legorano 2019. "The EU's New Headache: Skeptics are Poised to Gain from Power from Within." *The Wall Street Journal*, May 22, 2019. https://www.wsj.com/articles/the-eus-new-headache-skeptics-are-poised-to -gain-power-from-within-11558537314.

Portes, Alejandro and Reuben Rumbaut. 2014. *Immigrant America: A Portrait*, 4th edition. Los Angeles, CA: University of California Press.

Posner, Sarah. 2017. "How the Conservative Movement Went All in with Trumpism." *Rolling Stone Magazine*, February 27, 2017. https://www.rollingstone.com/politics /politics-features/how-the-conservative-movement-went-all-in-for-trumpism-1249 64.

Povoledo, Elisabetta. 2018. "Rescue Ship Docks in Malta as 8 Nations Agree to Take Its Migrants." *The New York Times*, June 27, 2018. https://www.nytimes.com/2018 /06/27/world/europe/migrants-ship-malta.html.

Putterman, Mark. 2018. "A Century of Intervention Created the Immigration Crisis." *The Medium*, June 20, 2018. https://medium.com/s/story/timeline-us-intervention -central-america-a9bea9ebc148.

Pyle, Jeffery. 1999. "Race, Equality and the Rule of Law: Critical Race Theory's Attack on the Promises of Liberalism." *Boston College Law Review* 40 (3): 787–827.

Quelly, James. 2018. "Hate Crimes Rise in California for Third Straight Year, State Report Says." *Baltimore Sun*, July 18, 2018. https://www.baltimoresun.com/la-me- ln-hate-crimes-surge-california-20180710-story.html.

Quinlan, Robert. 2006. "Gender and Risk in a Matriarchal Caribbean Community: A View from Behavioral Ecology." *American Anthropology* 106 (3): 464–279.

Qiu, Linda. 2018. "Border Crossings Have Been Declining for Years, Despite Claims of a 'Crisis of Illegal Immigration." *The New York Times*, June 20, 2018. https:// www.nytimes.com/2018/06/20/us/politics/fact-check-trump-border-crossings-decl ining-.html.

Qiu, Linda. 2019. "Trump Repeats False Claim About El Paso Crime, This Time in El Paso." *The New York Times*, February 12, 2019. https://www.nytimes.com/2019 /02/12/us/politics/trump-rally-fact-check.html.

Ramos, Jorge. 2019. "Trump: 'I'm Using Mexico.'" *The New York Times,* October 7, 2019. https://www.nytimes.com/2019/10/07/opinion/trump-im-using-mexico. html.

Rees, Jonas, Yann Jens Tellmann and Andreas Zick. 2019. "Climate of Hate: Similar Correlates of Far-Right Electoral Support and Right-Wing Hate Crimes in Herman." *Frontiers in Psychology* 10: 2328. https://www.ncbi.nlm.nih.gov/pmc/ar ticles/PMC6813724/?report=classic.

Rein, Lisa, Abigail Hauslohnert and Sandya Somashekhar. 2017. "Federal Agents Conduct Immigration Raids in at Least Six States." *The Washington Post*, February 11, 2017. https://www.washingtonpost.com/national/federal-agents-conduct-sw eeping-immigration-enforcement-raids-in-at-least-6-states/2017/02/10/4b9f443a -efc8-11e6-b4ff-ac2cf509efe5_story.html.

Reitman, Janet. 2018. "U.S. Law Enforcement Failed to See the Threat of White Nationalism: Now They Don't Know How to Stop It." *The New York Times*, November 3, 2018. https://www.nytimes.com/2018/11/03/magazine/FBI-charlot tesville-white-nationalism-far-right.html.

Rocha, Alana, Jacob Villanueva and John Jordan. 2018. "Chaos at the Texas-Mexico Border: Scenes from Tornillo to the Rio Grande Valley." *The Texas Tribune,* June 24, 2018. https://www.texastribune.org/2018/06/24/photos-texas-mexico-border -shelters-protests-tornillo-el-paso.

Rogers, Katie and David Sanger. 2019. "Among EU Allies, Americans Offer Competing Visions." *The New York Times*, February 16, 2019.

Rogers, Katie and Ron Nixon. 2018. "A Border Patrol Agent (And Frequent Fox News Guest) Has Trump's Ear on Immigration." *The New York Times*, April 2, 2018. https://www.nytimes.com/2018/04/02/us/politics/border-patrol-trump-bra ndon-judd-fox.html.

Romero, Simon. 2019. "All Over U.S., Local Officials Cancel Deals to Detain Immigrants." *The New York Times*, June 28, 2019. https://www.nytimes.com/2018 /06/28/us/migrant-shelters-ice-contracts-counties.html.

Romo, Vanessa, 2018. "Hungary Passes 'Stop Soros' Laws, Bands Aid to Undocumented Immigrants." *NPR,* June 20, 2018. https://www.npr.org/2018/06/20/622045753/ hungary-passes-stop-soros-laws-bans-aid-to-undocumented-immigrants.

Roose, Kevin. 2019. "A Mass Murder of, and for, the Internet." *The New York Times*, March 15, 2019. https://www.nytimes.com/2019/03/15/technology/face book-youtube-christchurch-shooting.html.

Ross, Megan, Hepp Brooks and Kianna Gardern 2018. "White Extremist Groups are Growing-and Changing." *Center for Public Integrity*, September 5, 2018. https://pu blicintegrity.org/politics/white-extremist-groups-are-growing-and-changing.

Rumbaut, Ruben. 2008. "The Coming of the Second Generation: Immigration and Ethnic Mobility in Society." *The ANNALS of the American Society of Political Science* 620 (96): 96–236.

Rush, Nayla. 2019. "U.S. Resettled More Refugees than Any Other Nation in 2017and 2018." *Center for Immigration Studies*, March 14, 2019. https://cis.org/ Rush/US-Resettled-More-Refugees-Any-Other-Nation-2017-and-2018.

Ryan, Charlotte and William Gamson. 2006. "The Art of Framing Political Debates." *Contexts* 5 (1): 13–18.

Sachetti, Maria. 2017. "Immigration Judges Say Proposed Quotas from Justice Dept. Threaten Independence." *The Washington Post,* October 12, 2017. https://www

.washingtonpost.com/local/immigration/immigration-judges-say-proposed-quotas
-from-justice-dept-threaten-independence/2017/10/12/3ed86992-aee1-11e7-be94
-fabb0f1e9ffb_story.html.

Salzborn, Samuel. 2018. "The Antisemitic Turn of the 'Alternative for Germany'
Party." *Open Democracy*, December 9, 2018. https://www.opendemocracy.net/en/
can-europe-make-it/antisemitic-turn-of-alternative-for-germany-party/.

Sandhu, Serina. 2018. "Why Italy Wouldn't Accept a Boat Carrying 600 Migrants-
But Spain Will." *News I.* June 11, 2018. https://inews.co.uk/news/world/italy-mig
rants-boat-163564.

Santora, Marc. 2018. "George Soros-Founded University Is Forces Out of Hungary."
The New York Times, December 3, 2018. https://www.nytimes.com/2018/12/03/
world/europe/soros-hungary-central-european-university.html.

Santora, Marc. 2019. "Poland Bashes Immigrants, but Quietly Takes Christian Ones."
The New York Times, March 26, 2019. https://www.nytimes.com/2019/03/26/
world/europe/immigration-poland-ukraine-christian.html.

Santora, Marc and Anna Schaverien. 2019. "Anti-Brexit Protesters Descend on
London as Parliament Debates." *The New York Times*, October 19, 2019. https://ww
w.nytimes.com/2019/10/19/world/europe/brexit-peoples-vote-march.html.

Santora, Marc and Helene Bienvenu. 2018. "Secure in Hungary Orban Readies for
Battle with Brussels." *The New York Times*, May 11, 2018. https://www.nytimes.
com/2018/05/11/world/europe/hungary-victor-orban-immigration-europe.html.

Sassen, Saskia. 1988. "New York City's Informal Economy." *UCLA Institute for
Social Science Research* 4 (9). https://www.researchgate.net/publication/4803387
_New_York_City%27s_Informal_Economy.

Schake, Kori. 2018. "The Trump Doctrine Is Winning and the World Is Losing." *The
New York Times*, June 15, 2018. https://www.nytimes.com/2018/06/15/opinion/su
nday/trump-china-america-first.html.

Scharpf, Fritz. 2010. "The Asymmetry of European Integration, Or Why the EU
Cannot be a 'Social Market Economy.'" *Socio-Economic Review* 8 (2): 211–250.

Scheppele, Kim Lane. 2015. "Orban's Police State." *Politico*, October 15, 2015.
https://www.politico.eu/article/orbans-police-state-hungary-serbia-border-migrat
ion-refugees.

Scherer, Steve and Massimiliano Di Giorgio. 2014. "Italy to End Sea Rescue Mission
That Saved 100,000 Migrants." *Reuters*, 31 October 2014. https://www.reuters.
com/article/usitaly-migrants-eu/italy-to-end-sea-rescue-mission-that-saved-100,0
00-migrants.

Schreuer, Milan. 2018. "Government in Belgium Loses Majority Over U.N. Migration
Pact," *The New York Times*, December 9, 2018. https://www.nytimes.com/2018/12
/09/world/europe/belgium-government-un-migration.html.

Schueths, April M. 2014. "'It's Almost Like White Supremacy': Interracial Mixed-
Status Couples Facing Racist Nativism." *Ethnic and Racial Studies* 37 (13):
2438–2456. DOI: 10.1080/01419870.2013.835058.

Schwirtz, Michael. 2018. "At United Nations, Fears of a 'New World Disorder' as
Trump Returns." *The New York Times*, September 24, 2018. https://www.nytimes.
com/2018/09/24/world/united-nations-united-states-trump-isolationism.html.

Scuria, Leonardo. 2017. "Brexit Beyond Borders: Beginning of the EU Collapse and
Return to Nationalism." *Journal of International Affairs* 7(2): 109–123.

Selod, Sahar. 2014. "Citizenship Denied: The Racialization of Muslim Americans Post 9/11." *Critical Sociology* 41 (1): 1–19.

Semple, Kirk. 2018a. "Trump Threatens to Punish Honduras Over Immigration Caravan." *The New York Times*, October 16, 2018. https://www.nytimes.com/2018/10/16/world/americas/trump-immigrant-caravan.html.

Semple, Kirk. 2018b. "Mexico Once Saw Migration as a US. Problem. Now It Needs Answer of its Own." *The New York Times*, December 5. https://www.nytimes.com/2018/12/05/world/americas/mexico-migrants.html.

Semple, Kirk. 2019. "The U.S. and Guatemala Reached an Asylum Deal: Here's What it Means." *The New York Times*, January 7, 2019. https://www.nytimes.com/2019/07/28/world/americas/guatemala-safe-third-asylum.html.

Semple, Kirk and Paula Villegas. 2019. "'Catastrophic' Delays at U.S. – Mexico Border Follow Redeployment of Agents." *The New York Times*, April 5, 2019. https://www.nytimes.com/2019/04/05/world/americas/us-mexico-border-delays.html.

Serhan, Yasmeen. 2018. "Angela Merkel, Escape Artist." *The Atlantic*, July, 2018. https://www.theatlantic.com/international/archive/2018/07/angela-merkel-government-crisis-csu/564272.

Serwer, Adam. 2018. "Trump's Caravan Hysteria Led to This." *The Atlantic*, October 28. https://www.theatlantic.com/ideas/archive/2018/10/caravan-lie-sparked-massacre-american-jews/574213/.

Shaheen, Faiz. 2019. "It's not 'White Working Class.' The Real Home of Bigotry is Elsewhere." *The Guardian,* March 7. https://www.theguardian.com/commentisfree/2019/mar/07/white-working-class-bigotry-midde-income-earners-prejudice.

Shear, Michael. 2019. "Anti-Immigration Groups See Trump's Calls for More Legal Immigrants as a Betrayal." *The New York Times*, March 8, 2019. https://www.nytimes.com/2019/03/08/us/politics/trump-anti-immigration-groups-betrayal.html.

Shear, Michael and Thomas Gibbons-Neff. 2018. "Trump Sending 5200 Troops to the Border in an Election-Season Response to Migrants." *The New York Times*, October 29, 2018. https://www.nytimes.com/2018/10/29/us/politics/border-security-troops-trump.html.

Shoichet, Catherine and Paul Murphy. 2019. "The Militia Group Detained Migrants at the Border: Their Leader Got Arrested." *CNN*, April 27, 2019. https://www.cnn.com/2019/04/22/us/united-constitutional-patriots-what-we-know/index.html.

Sidner, Sarah. 2018. "White Nationalist Robert Rundo Arrested in Los Angeles." *CNN*, October 25, 2018. https://www.cnn.com/2018/10/24/us/rise-above-above-movement-robert-rundo-arrest/index.html.

Sifuentes, Edward. 2008. "Education: Proposition 227: 10 Years Later." *The San Diego-Union Tribune,* November 8, 2008. https://www.sandiegouniontribune.com/sdut-education-proposition-227-10-years-later-2008nov08-story.html.

Silva, Mathema. 2016. "They are Refugees: An Increasing Number of People are Fleeing Violence in the Northern Triangle." *Center for American Progress*, February 20, 2016. https://www.americanprogress.org/issues/immigration/reports/2018/06/01/451474/still-refugees-people-continue-flee-violence-latin-american-countries.

Silver, Beverly. 2003. *Forces of Labor: Workers' Protest and Globalization Since 1870*. Cambridge: Cambridge University Press.

Silver, Laura. 2018. "Immigration Concerns Fall in Western Europe, but Most See the Need for Newcomers to Integrate into Society." *Fact Tank*. https://www.pew research.org/fact-tank/2018/10/22/immigration-concerns-fall-in-western-europe -but-most-see-need-for-newcomers-to-integrate-into-society.

Snow, David A and Doug McAdam. 2000. "Identity Work Processes in the Context of Social Movements." In *Self, Identity and Social Movements*, edited by Sheldon Stryker, Timothy J. Owens, and Robert White, 41–67. Minneapolis, MN: University of Minnesota Press.

Snow, David A and Robert Benford. 1992. "Master Frames and Cycles of Protest." In *Frontiers in Social Movement Theory*, edited by Aldon Morris and Carol McClurg Mueller, 133–156. New Haven, CT: Yale University Press.

Snow, David A, Burke Rochford, Steven K. Worden, Robert D. Benford. 1986. "Frame Alignment Processes, Micromobilization, and Movement Participation." *American Sociological Review* 51: 464–481.

Song, Sarah. 2019. *Immigration and Democracy*. New York: Oxford University Press.

Southern Poverty Law Center. 2016. "The Trump Effect: The Impact of the 2016 Election had on Our Nation's Schools." https://www.splcenter.org/20161128/ trump-effect-impact-2016-presidential-election-our-nations-schools.

Southern Poverty Law Center Intelligence Report. 2019. "The Year in Hate and Extremism: Rage Against Chang." *Spring*, 2019. https://www.splcenter.org/sites/ default/files/intelligence_report_166.pdf.

Spagat, Elliot and Nomaan Merchant. 2018. "Immigration Agents Descend on 7-Eleven Stores in 17 States." *The Associated Press*, January 10, 2018. https://ap news.com/cb0ef682ea534ff0b5d31e7c054a079e/Immigration-agents-descend-on -dozens-of-7-Eleven-stores.

Specia, Megan. 2018a. "U.N. Agrees in Migration Pact, but U.S. Is Conspicuously Absent." *The New York Times*, July 13, 2018. https://www.nytimes.com/2018/07 /13/world/europe/united-nations-migration-agreement.html.

Specia, Megan. 2018b. "The Five Conflicts Driving the Bulk of the World's Refugee Crisis." *The New York Times*, June 19, 2018. https://www.nytimes.com/2018/06 /19/world/five-conflicts-driving-refugees.html.

Spoher, Thomas. 2019. "Frank Talk at the Munich Security Conference." *Heritage Foundation*, February 17, 2019. https://www.heritage.org/defense/commentary/f rank-talk-the-munich-security-conference.

Srikrishan, Maya. 2019. "Challenges to Operation Streamline are Moving Forward." *Voice of San Diego*, December 10, 2019. https://www.voiceofsandiego.org/topics/ news/challenges-to-operation-streamline-are-moving-forward.

Stack, Liam. 2019. "Facebook Announces New Policy to Ban White Nationalist Content." *The New York Times*, March 27, 2019. https://www.nytimes.com/2019/0 3/27/business/facebook-white-nationalist-supremacist.html.

Stanglin, Doug. 2017. "Businesses Across U.S. Close, Students Skip School on 'Day Without Immigrants." *USA Today*, February 16, 2017. https://www.usatoday.com/ story/news/nation/2017/02/16/a-day-without-immigrants-strike/97965460.

Stelloh, Tim. 2019. "Members of Group Giving Food, Water to Migrants Convicted of Misdemeanors." *ABC News*, January 20, 2019. https://www.nbcnews.com/news/us -news/members-group-giving-food-water-migrants-convicted-misdemeanors-n960816.

Stevis-Gridneff, Matina. 2020. "Vigilantes in Greece Say 'No More' to Migrants." *New York Times*, March 7, 2020. https://www.nytimes.com/2020/03/07/world/euro pe/greece-turkey-migrants.html.

Stiglitz, Joseph. 2019. *People Power and Profits*. New York, NY: W.W. Norton & Company.

Stone, Oliver and Peter Kuznich. 2012. *The Untold History of the United States*. New York: Gallery Books.

Strickland, Patrick. 2018a. "Europe's Antifascist Prepare to Fight against the Far Right." *Truthout,* February 24, 2018. https://truthout.org/articles/europes-antifas cists-prepare-to-fight-against-the-far-right.

Strickland, Patrick. 2018b. Greece Police: Racist Hate Crimes Nearly Tripled in 2017." *Aljazeera*, March 15, 2018. https://www.aljazeera.com/news/2018/03/g reek-police-racist-hate-crimes-tripled-2017-180315105439865.html.

Styrna, Pawe. 2020. "Agriculture and Immigration." *FAIR*. https://www.fairus.org/is sue/legal-immigration/agriculture-immigration.

Tarrow, Sidney. 1988. "The Oldest New Movement." In *From Structure to Action: Comparing Social Movements Across Cultures*, edited by Bert Klandermans, Hanspeter Kriesi and Sidney Tarrow, 281-3-304. International Social Movement Research I. Greenwich, CT: JAI.

Tavernise, Sabrina. 2019. "They Have Worked on Conflicts Overseas. Now These Americans See 'Red Flags' at Home." *The New York Times*, February 4. https://ww w.nytimes.com/2019/02/04/us/conflicting-experts-peacebuilders.html.

Taylor, Alan. 2017. "A Weekend of Protests Against Trump's Immigration Ban." *The Atlantic*. January 20, 2017. https://www.theatlantic.com/photo/2017/01/a-weekend -of-protest-against-trumps-immigration-ban/514953.

Taylor, Elizabeth. 2020. "Greece Accused of Human Rights Violations Against Refugees But What is Happening on the Ground?" *Exit News,* May 3, 2020. https ://exit.al/en/2020/03/05/greece-accused-of-human-rights-violations-in-lesbos-but -what-is-happening-on-the-ground.

Taylor, Verta and Nella Van Dyke. 2004. "Get Up, Stand Up: Tactical Repertoires of Social Movements." In *The Blackwell Companion to Social Movements Reader*, edited by David Snow, Sarah Sole and Henrik Kriesi, 262–293. Oxford, UK: Blackwell Publishers.

Teitelbaum, Benjamin. 2018. "In Sweden, Populist Nationalists Won on Policy, but Lost on Politics. *The Atlantic*, September 2018. https://www.theatlantic.com /ideas/archive/2018/09/in-sweden-populist-nationalists-won-on-policy-but-lost-on -politics/569968/.

Tesler, Michael and David O. Sears. 2010. *Obama's Race: The 2008 Election and the Dream of a Post-Racial American*. Chicago, IL: The University of Chicago Press.

The Economist. 2017. "What to Do When Victor Orban Erodes Democracy." June 22, 2017. https://www.economist.com/leaders/2017/06/22/what-to-do-when-viktor -orban-erodes-democracy.

The Economist. 2018. "The Open Future Festival of Steve Bannon." The Economist .com, September 4, 2018. https://www.economist.com/open-future/2018/09/04/the -open-future-festival-and-steve-bannon.

Thorton, Bruce. 2015. "The European Experiment Has Failed." *Hoover Institute*, March 5, 2015. https://www.hoover.org/research/eu-experiment-has-failed.

Tilly, Charles. 1978. *From Mobilization to Revolution*. Reading, Mass: Addison-Wesley Press.

Tilly, Charles. 2006. "Why and How History Matters." in *The Handbook of Contextualized Politics*, edited by Robert Goodwin, 417–437, Vol. 5. Oxford University Press.

Tilly, Charles. 2007. *Democracy*. Cambridge: Cambridge University Press.

Titus, Elizabeth. 2014. "Coulter Hits GOP on Immigration." *Politico*, August 2, 2014. https://www.politico.com/story/2014/03/ann-coulter-cpac-republicans-immigration-104448.

Tondo, Lorenzo. 2019. "Italian Authorities order Seizure of Migrant Rescue Ship." *The Guardian*, March 20, 2019. https://www.theguardian.com/world/2019/mar/20/italian-authorities-order-seizure-migrant-rescue-ship-mare-jonio.

Torreblanca, Jose and Mark Leonard. 2013. "The Continent-Wide Rise of Euroscepticism." *European Council on Foreign Relations*. https://www.ecfr.eu/page/-/ECFR79_EUROSCEPTICISM_BRIEF_AW.pdf.

Townsend, Mark. 2019. "UK Admits Only 20 Unaccompanied Child Refugees in Two Years." *The Guardian,* September 3, 2018. https://www.theguardian.com/world/2018/nov/03/uk-admits-only-20-unaccompanied-child-refugees-in-two-years.

Transactional Records Access Clearing House. 2016. "Continued Rise in Asylum Rates: Impact of Representation and Nationality." December 1, 2016. https://trac.syr.edu/immigration/reports/448/.

Transactional Records Access Clearing House. n.d. "Representations for Unaccompanied Children in Immigration Country." https://trac.syr.edu/immigration/reports/371/.

Tufeikci, Zennep. 2012. "New Media and the People-powered Uprisings." *MIT Technology.* https://cdn.technologyreview.com/s/425280/new-media-and-the-people-powered-uprising.

Turkewitz, Jule. 2019. "White Supremacist Plotted to Bomb Colorado Synagogue, F.B.I. Says." *The New York Times*, November 4, 2019. https://www.nytimes.com/2019/11/04/us/pueblo-colorado-synagogue-richard-holzer.html.

United Nations Human Rights Committee. 2018. https://www.ohchr.org/en/hrbodies/ccpr/pages/ccprindex.aspx.

United Nations Human Rights Committee. 2019. https://www.ohchr.org/en/hrbodies/ccpr/pages/ccprindex.aspx.

United States Department of Justice. 2016. https://www.justice.gov/eoir.

United States Government Publishing Senate Report 114-155. https://www.congress.gov/congressional-report/114th-congress/senate-report/155/1.

United We Dream Network. "Changing Lives One Work Permit at a Time." 2017. https://unitedwedream.org/wp-content/uploads/2017/07/uwd_ownthedreamreport_032015_v8_web.pdf.

Valverde, Miriam. 2018. "Donald Trump's Executive Order Ending His Administration's Separation of Immigrant Families." *PolitiFact*, June 25, 2018. https://www.politifact.com/article/2018/jun/25/donald-trumps-executive-order-ending-his-administr.

Van Dyke, Nella and Sarah Soule. 2002. "Structural Social Change and the Mobilization Effect of Threat: Explaining Levels of Patriot and Militia Organizing in the United States." *Social Problems* 49 (4): 497–520.

Van Wormer, Catherine and Rosemary Link. 2016. *Social Welfare Police for a Sustainable Future: The United States in a Global Context*. Los Angeles, CA: Sage.

Vertouec S. and S. Wessend. 2005. "Migration and Culture, Religion and Linguistic Diversity in Europe: An Overview of Issues and Trends." *Centre on Margination Policy and Society*. University of Oxford Working Paper 05–18. https://www.com pas.ox.ac.uk/wp-content/uploads/WP-2005-018-Vertovec-Wessendorf_Religious _Linguistic_Diversity.pdf.

Villegas, Paulina and Alan Yuhas. 2019. "Mexico Calls on U.S. to investigate Use of Tear Gas at Border." *The New York Times*, January 3, 2019. https://www.nytimes. com/2019/01/03/world/americas/mexico-border-tear-gas-investigation.html.

VOA News. 2017. "Hundred Arrest in Recent U.S. Immigration Enforcement Raids." *VOA News*, February 12, 2017. https://www.voanews.com/usa/over-680-migrants -arrested-us-immigration-raids.

Walker, Shaun. 2019. "Victor Obran Trumpets His 'Procreation Not Immigration' Policy." *The Guardian*, September 6, 2019. https://www.theguardian.com/world /2019/sep/06/viktor-orban-trumpets-far-right-procreation-anti-immigration-policy.

Waterson, Jim, James Ball, Ikran Dahir, Aisha Gani, Alex Spence and Talal Ansari. 2017. "Trump Retweeted Anti-Muslim Videos posted By Far-Right Group Britain First." *BuzzFeed News*, November 29, 2017. https://www.buzzfeed.com/jimwa terson/donald-trump-retweets-vidoes-posted-by-far-right-group.

Watkins, Ali and Nick Corasaniti. 2019. "New Jersey Grapples with Far-Right Extremism After Arrests." *The New York Times*, November 29, 2019. https://ww w.nytimes.com/2019/11/29/nyregion/michael-zaremski-joseph-rubino-essex-nj-w hite-supremacist.html.

Weiser, Benjamin. 2019. "Mail Bomb Suspect Accused of Targeting Clinton, Obama and Other Democrats to Plead Guilty." *The New York Times*, March 15, 2019. https ://www.nytimes.com/2019/03/15/nyregion/mail-bomber-cesar-sayoc.html.

Williams, Mathew, Peter Burnap, Amir Javed, Han Zio and Sefa Ozalp. 2019. "Hate in the Machine: Anti-Black and Anti-Muslim Social Media Posts as Predictors of Offline Racially and Religiously Aggravated Crime." *British Journal of Criminology* 6 (1): 93-117.

Willis, Oliver, 2019. "New Report Finds Violent Crimes by White Supremacists Hid Decade-High Under Trump." *American Independent*, July 31, 2019. https://america nindependent.com/violent-crime-white-supremacists-decade-high-under-trump.

Wilson, Christopher and Duncan Wood. 2016. "Understanding U.S.-Mexico Economic Ties." *Forbes*, September 26, 2016. https://www.forbes.com/sites/ themexicoinstitute/2016/09/26/mexico-institute-launches-project-examining-u-s -mexico-economic-ties/#5f159b2f7768

Wilson, Jason. 2018. "Who Are the Proud Boys, 'Western Chauvinists Involved in Political Violence?" *The Guardian*, July 14, 2018. https://www.theguardian.com/ world/2018/jul/14/proud-boys-far-right-portland-oregon

Wintour, Patrick. 2016. "Germany's Refugee Response Not Guilt Ridden Says Wolfgang Shauble." *The Guardian*, March 3, 2016. https://www.theguardian.com/ world/2016/mar/04/germanys-refugee-response-not-guilt-driven-says-wolfgang-sc hauble.

Wooden, Cindy. 2018. "Pulled from the Sea, Migrant's Rescue Puts Spotlight on Italian Policy." *America Magazine*, July 1, 2018. https://www.americamagazine .org/politics-society/2018/07/19/pulled-sea-migrants-rescue-puts-spotlight-italian- policy.

Woods, Heather and Leslie Hahner. 2019. *Make America Meme Again: The Rhetoric of the AltRight.* New York: Peter Lang.

World Report. 2019. https://www.hrw.org/sites/default/files/world_report_download /hrw_world_report_2019.pdf.

Wynne, Kelly. 2018. "Berlin Protest Against Racism, Right-Wing Populism Draws Over 200,000 People." *Newsweek*, October 13, 2018. https://www.newsweek.com/ over-200000-protesters-march-berlin-immigration-rights-and-equality-1168434.

Yan, Holly and David Williams. 2017. "Nationwide 'Day Without Immigrants' Shuts Down Businesses." *CNN*, February 16, 2017. https://www.cnn.com/2017/02/16/us/ day-without-immigrants-vignettes/index.html.

Yardley, Jim and Azam Ahmed. 2016. "Pope Francis Wades into U.S. Immigration Morass with Border Trip." *The New York Times,* February 17, 2016. https://www .nytimes.com/2016/02/18/world/americas/pope-francis-ciudad-juarez.html.

Yee, Vivian and Miriam Jordan. 2018. "Migrant Children in Search of Justice: A 2 Year-Old's Day in Immigration Court." *The New York Times*, October 8, 2018. https://www.nytimes.com/2018/10/08/us/migrant-children-family-separation-co urt.html.

Yeginsu, Ceylan and Iliana Magra. 2018. "London's 'Trump Baby' Balloon Flies as Protests Take Off Across U.K." *The New York Times*, July 13, 2018. https://www .nytimes.com/2018/07/13/world/europe/uk-trump-protest-may.html.

Yoon-Hendricks, Alexandra and Zoe Greenberg. 2018. "Protests Across U.S. Call for End to Migrant Family Separations." *The New York Times*, June 30, 2018. https:/ /www.nytimes.com/2018/06/30/us/politics/trump-protests-family-separation.html.

Yuhas, Alan. 2019. "U.S. Agents Fire Tear Gas Across Mexican Border." *The New York Times*, January 1, 2019. https://www.nytimes.com/2019/01/01/world/amer icas/migrants-border-tear-gas.html.

Zaveri, Mihir. 2018. "Jeff Sessions Faces Complaints from Fellow United Methodists Over Border Separations." *The New York Times*, June 20, 2018. https://www.nyt imes.com/2018/06/20/us/jeff-sessions-church-child-abuse.html.

Zeihan, Peter. 2016. *The Accidental Superpower: The Next Generation of American Preeminence and the Coming Global Disorder.* New York: Hachette Publishers.

Zhao, Christina. 2018. "Laura Ingraham Calls Child Detention Centers 'Essentially Summer Camps,' Slams 'Faux Liberal Outrage.'" *News Week,* June 9, 2018. https ://www.newsweek.com/laura-ingraham-calls-child-detention-centers-essentially -summer-camps-slams-982913.

Zraick, Karen and Julia Jacobs. 2019. "Charlottesville Attacker Pleads Guilty to Federal Hate Crime." *The New York Times*, March 27, 2019. https://www.nytimes. com/2019/03/27/us/james-alex-fields-charlottesville.html.

Index

public charge policy, 46, 66, 133
public opinion, framing of narratives to influence, 22
Public Religion Research Institute and the Atlantic, poll, 81
Pueblo Sin Fronteras, 39
push and pull factors, xii, 4, 20, 29, 119

Quillin, Bryce, 20, 56, 63
quota system, 1924, 130

race-driven extremism, 86
racial animosity, 93–94
racialization, 8, 80–81, 104–5
racism, 7, 17, 57, 69, 108
racist nativism, 20, 30, 52, 88, 98–99, 111, 130; conception of, 8–9; identification of, 105; theories, 85
Raid Rapid Response Networks, 116
rallies, 107–9
RAND Corporation, 51
Rathjen, Tobias, 104
Reagan, Ronald (President), 19
refugees. *See* immigrants/migrants
Remain in Mexico policy, 40–41
resource mobilization theory, 81
restaurant business, and Mexican workers, 118
The Right Stuff, 91
Rise Above Movement, 100
Roof, Dylan, 101
Roosevelt, Theodore (President), 17
Rumbaut, Reuben, 50, 65
Rundo, Robert, 100
Ryan, Charlotte, 52, 81, 92

Safe Release policy, ICE, 121
Salvadoran asylum seekers, 27–28, 40–41
Salvadorans migrations, 19
Salvini, Matteo, 52–55, 68, 73, 123, 124, 133
Samos island of Greece, 70
Sanchez, Pedro, 58
Sanchez, Pedro (Prime Minister), 58

San Diego County, 31
Sandinista government, 19
Sardines protest movement in Italy, 124
Sassen, Saskia, 56, 66, 118
savage, and senile peoples, 16
Save our State legislation, 108
Sayoc, Cesar, 91
Scarbough, Joe, 90
Schengen area, 51
Schengen zone, 50, 132
Schueths, April, 52, 85
Schindler's List (movie), 123
Selod, Sahar, 17, 20, 36, 58, 92
Senate Committee on Homeland Security and Government Affairs report, 2015, 16
the Sensenbrenner bill in Arizona (S.B. 1070), 109; faith-based groups role, 120; May Day demonstrations, 111; protest against, demonstrations, 110–11
sense of togetherness, 109
7-Eleven stores, 115–16
Sessions, Jeff (Attorney General), 37, 38, 40, 42, 43, 120
Show me your Papers law, 110
Silver, Beverly, 56, 66, 118
smugglers, 31, 35, 39, 129
Snow, David A, 4, 22, 52, 81, 85, 92, 109, 112, 114, 115
social media: role in political and social mobilization, 76–77; for spreading racist and hateful ideas, 93–95; as a tool of white supremacists, 86–92
social movements theories, xi, xiii, 3–4, 52, 54, 60, 75, 92, 125, 132
Söder, Marcus, 64
Soros, George, 61, 89, 91
Soule, Sarah, 3, 20, 49, 55, 77, 102
"Sound Strike" coalition, 117
Southern Poverty Law Center (SPLC), 30, 37, 86, 87, 91, 94, 100, 136
Spain: anti-immigrant sentiments, 58–59, 134; substandard conditions in,

About the Author

Victoria Carty is associate professor of Sociology at Chapman University. She has written dozens of journal articles and is the author of *Social Movements and New Technology* and *Wired and Mobilizing: Social Movements, New Technology, and Electoral Politics*, and coeditor of *Mobilizing Public Sociology: Scholars, Activists and Latin@ Migrants Converse on Common Ground* and *Scholars and Southern California Immigrants in Dialogue: New Conversations in Dialogue*.

www.ingramcontent.com/pod-product-compliance
Lightning Source LLC
Chambersburg PA
CBHW022315280326
41932CB00010B/1104